FIGHTING HIGHLANDERS!

The History of the Argyll & Sutherland Highlanders

The Yeomanry Regiments (1985)
Yeoman Service (1985)
The Scottish Regiments (1988)

FIGHTING HIGHLANDERS!

The History of the

Argyll & Sutherland Highlanders

P. J. R. MILEHAM

ARMS AND
ARMOUR

Arms and Armour Press
A Cassell Imprint
Villiers House, 41-47 Strand, London WC2N 5JE.

Distributed in the USA by Sterling Publishing Co. Inc.,
387 Park Avenue South, New York, NY 10016-8810.

Distributed in Australia by Capricorn Link (Australia) Pty. Ltd,
P.O. Box 665, Lane Cove, New South Wales 2066.

British Library Cataloguing-in-Publication Data:
a catalogue record for this book is available from the British Library

ISBN 1-85409-141-7

Jacket illustrations: Front, 'The Thin Red Line',
Robert Gibb's famous painting of the 93rd Sutherland Highlanders
facing Russian cavalry at the Battle of Balaclava, 1854.
Back, top, watercolour by Richard Simkin of various orders of
dress of the Argyll and Sutherland Highlanders.
Back, bottom, Hill 282, Korea, 23 September 1950. Major Kenneth
Muir, VC, and Major Gordon-Ingram fire the 2-inch mortar during
the desperate battle to hold the hill. Painting by Peter Archer.

Designed and edited by DAG Publications Ltd.
in QuarkXPress via TBL, Warley. Designed by David Gibbons;
edited by Michael Boxall; layout by Anthony A. Evans; halftone
camerawork by M&E Reproductions, North Fambridge, Essex;
printed and bound in Great Britain by
Hartnolls Ltd, Bodmin, Cornwall.

CONTENTS

LIST OF MAPS

FOREWORD

by

Major General D. P. Thomson, CBE, MC
Colonel, The Argyll and Sutherland Highlanders

By the standards of many British infantry units, the Argyll and Sutherland Highlanders, even though they celebrate their bicentenary in 1994, are still a young regiment. These last two hundred years, however, have encompassed many of the most important military campaigns in the history of our country and time and again 'The Argylls', as the world now tends to call them, have figured prominently in the thick of action.

Patrick Mileham's narrative, supported by a large number of excellent illustrations, traces the story of the regiment from its birth to the present day. Of course he has had to be very selective in his choice of material, particularly so in dealing with the two World Wars, when the Argylls fielded battalions in a variety of roles and in a number of different theatres of operations. At the same time, as far as the period since 1953 is concerned, the author has had a difficult problem, created by a lack of detailed records, except in regard to certain very specific events. The result is a book that is as comprehensive as its length allows.

It must always be remembered, however, that while history highlights great events such as the 'Thin Red Line' at Balaklava; the 2nd Battalion in Malaya or the 1st Battalion in Aden in 1967, the real strength of the regiment lies in the inspiration that its comradeship has provided to individuals and small groups of men fighting and dying in forgotten campaigns in far-flung parts of the world. Most appropriately, the Argylls' two mottos are: 'Sans Peur' – 'Without Fear' – and 'Ne Obliviscaris' – 'Do Not Forget'.

Patrick Mileham is a young Author whose own military experience has helped him to weave his way most successfully through the annals of the Argyll and Sutherland Highlanders. I commend this history to anyone with an interest in the British regimental system, and particularly to those for whom the Highland regiments represent the best that the system can produce.

AUTHOR'S INTRODUCTION

'This is a wonderful story,' wrote Field Marshal Montgomery in his own hand on the flyleaf of a copy of one of the battalion histories. 'It shows what the British soldier can do when properly led, and how he responds to a challenge — giving of his best when asked to face up to hard conditions. I know better than most to what heights the soldiers of Britain can aspire. Their greatness is a measure of the greatness of our national character, and I have seen the quality of our race proved again and again on the battlefield. No better example can be found than the story of the 93rd Highlanders unfolded in this book.' The story was that of the 2nd Battalion of the Argyll and Sutherland Highlanders during the Malayan Campaign.

The Regiment has been well served by authors in the past in recording the service of the 91st and 93rd Highlanders during the 19th century, and the numerous battalions of the amalgamated Regiment in the 20th. There are, however, gaps in the history, particularly during the Great War, and the fact that there has never been a full-length history of the Regiment means that a considerable library of volumes is required reading to give an adequate synoptic view of the Regiment's history.

The core of this book is a description of the changing and unchanging character of an identifiable body of fighting men showing a remarkable spirit of cohesiveness and continuity —the best aspects of the British regimental system, much in debate at the present time.

Published on the eve of the bicentenary, this volume is designed to fulfil three purposes: it provides in one volume the overall record of the Regiment's service and it brings up to date the story of the past forty years. Furthermore, the 'Argylls' have attained an exceptional prominence in recent years, and this needs to be set in its historical context.

Active service, domestic life and personalities form the fabric of this work, together with details of the changes in the organization and roles. The size of the book, however, dictates the need for selection from those recollections of eye-witnesses that were recorded. Military history can be written on a number of levels, and by tradition such a book as this does not dwell unduly on detectable shortcomings. Although I have been made aware of internal controversies, I have deliberately avoided judgments and comparisons with regard to particular battalions' performance and allowed facts to speak for themselves. That having been said, I have become particularly conscious of the lack of an adequate range of superlatives in the English language to describe the extremes of courage displayed and suffering endured by members of the Regiment on countless occasions over the past two hundred years. This is particularly true of periods of intensive combat during the two World Wars.

To reflect a particular tradition, common among regiments amalgamated in 1881, I have continued to call the Regular Army battalions by their numbers — the 91st and 93rd — until the Second World War. The officers and men of the time rejoiced in the distinctiveness of the two battalions. Modern-day members of the Regiment recognize the strength of the regimental family, comprising regular, territorial and cadet force members: they all wear the 'Thin Red Line' running through the red and white dicing in their Glengarry bonnets and spell their proudest battle honour with a `K'. I do not believe you will find a more fiercely distinctive military group anywhere else in the British Army.

Rumour has it that no Whitehall warriors or politicians dared to disband or amalgamate the Regiment during the current wave of reductions and reorganizations, after the experience of 1968-72. Perhaps in peace as well as war the essence of regimental spirit lies in self-fulfilling prophecy !

ACKNOWLEDGEMENTS

I am immensely grateful to General Sir Patrick Palmer, KCB, and Major General David Thomson, CBE, MC, the former and present Colonels of the Regiment, for so readily accepting my suggestion to write the history of the Argyll and Sutherland Highlanders. Their encouragement and support over the past three years has been most generous.

A number of officers of the Regiment have assisted with the task of reading through the chapters and checking facts and their interpretation; namely Major General J. D. C. Graham, CB, CBE, CStJ, Brigadier B. A. Pearson, DSO, BA, BL, Brigadier A. D. R. G. Wilson, CBE, Lieutenant Colonel G. P. Wood, MC, DL, Lieutenant Colonel A. D. Malcolm, OBE, TD, Lieutenant Colonel H. L. Clark, Major A. J. A. Stewart, and Major D. G. Wood, OBE, MC. I thank all of them for their patience and the graceful way in which they pointed out ways of improving the text.

At Regimental Headquarters, Stirling Castle, I received much assistance from the Regimental Secretary, Lieutenant Colonel Alastair Scott Elliot, and all members of the staff when I worked there on numerous occasions, for which I am most grateful.

Mention must be made of the painstaking editing by Michael Boxall and the design by David Gibbons, and I greatly appreciated the skill and enthusiasm of Mrs. Anna Gale and Mrs. Claranne Marshfield in typing from my manuscript. I also gratefully acknowledge the permssion of the Regiment and the Imperial War Museum to use illustrations from their collections.

I dedicate this book to my wife Alexandra and daughters Felicity, Sally and Arabella. The support they always give me is heartwarming.

Patrick Mileham
Gartmore, Stirlingshire

11

CHAPTER 1

THE CAPE AND PENINSULA

The 91st (Argyllshire) Highlanders, 1794–1815

STIRLING

'Bulwark of the North, Grey Stirling'; the grim fortress standing between Lowlands and Highlands, dominating the valley of the Forth, overlooking the old stone bridge over the River Forth and the frontier of blue-grey mountains; which has witnessed battles and skirmishes more numerous than in any other concentrated area of the British Isles; the battlegrounds of William Wallace, of Robert the Bruce, of Argyll and Mar; Stirling, the one-time Royal capital of Scotland, of Alexander I, of James II, who personally stabbed to death the Earl of Douglas in a room in the castle; of William the Lion, and of James III, who built there his parliament house; Stirling, the court of Mary Queen of Scots, the place of her coronation and that of her son James VI, the infant who was to unite the Crowns of Scotland and England; the stronghold captured during the Civil War by General Monck, but which held out against Bonnie Prince Charlie's Jacobites; the strategic Hanoverian garrison used for the final pacification of the Highlands. What a romantic and martial setting Stirling Castle presents to people of even scant imagination!

It was at Stirling Castle in 1794 that the history of one of our most famous British regiments began.

The French Revolutionary wars had broken out the year before, and had threatened with the military power of the levée en masse In the early 18th century whig clans, loyal to the protestant monarchy, had provided men for the Highland 'watch' companies, and they were the origins of the senior Highland regiment, The Black Watch, raised in 1739.

One difficulty faced by politicians of any period is to judge correctly how deeply lies the political loyalty of military officers. During this period, once the loyalty of Highland gentlemen could be assured, the men they brought with them could be trusted to be of the greatest fighting quality. So quite soon after the Jacobite rebellion of 1745 the government had capitalized on the supply of willing military manpower, and a number of regular regiments was raised in the Highlands. Military service offered the opportunity for honourable employment, pay, and the lawful wearing of Highland dress, which had been proscribed by act of parliament in 1746.

'I sought for merit wherever it could be found,' claimed William Pitt, Earl of Chatham, in 1766. 'It is my boast that I was the first minister who looked for it, and found it in the mountains of the north. I called it forth, and drew into your service a hardy and intrepid race of men: men who when left by your jealousy, became prey to the artifices of your enemies, and had gone nigh to have overturned the state in the war before last [War of the Austrian Succession]. These men in the last war [Seven Years

War], were brought to combat on your side; they served with fidelity, as they fought with valour, and conquered for you in every quarter of the world.'

Although the clan system was fast disappearing, with all the formalities and complexities of land tenure, personal service and military obligation, the traditional loyalties of the Highlanders found a new and perhaps simplified expression within the Highland regiments.

Warriors had assembled at Stirling over many centuries, and among other regiments near to our period, the 75th (Highland) Regiment of Foot (later to become the Stirlingshire Regiment and 1st Battalion, the Gordon Highlanders), had formed there in 1787 before embarking for the third Mysore War and the famous siege of Seringapatam.

Now, with the new French armies threatening Europe with revolutionary zeal, the government determined again to expand the size of the British Army by raising new regiments for regular and volunteer part-time service, as well as keeping the Militia on active duty. Quite apart from the threat from overseas, there was a requirement for a large garrison in Ireland. Thus on 26 May 1794 a new regiment, one of three from the Highlands, formed at Stirling Castle for inspection by Major General Lord Adam Gordon, in command of the forces in Scotland.

John, fifth Duke of Argyll had been authorized by a letter of 10 February to recruit this regiment 'within 3 months' for service overseas. No noble family in Scotland had been more loyal and energetic in supporting the Crown than the Duke's — indeed his own father the fourth Duke had led the Campbells at Culloden, and a cousin the second Duke had commanded the Hanoverian army at Sheriffmuir. But as the Duke was in his seventies, he deputed the task of raising the regiment — first numbered the 98th — to Duncan Campbell of Lochnell, a chieftain of one of the many sects of the great Clan Campbell, and third in importance after Argyll and Breadalbane. Lochnell had to find the complement of 1,064 men between the ages of 18 and 35 and of a minimum height of 5 feet 5 inches, to serve in the then normal size battalion of ten companies — eight battalion companies and one each of grenadiers and light infantry. Each company was to consist of one captain, three lieutenants, four sergeants, five corporals, two drummers and 95 privates. The grenadier company had on establishment the traditional fifers, and additionally several pipers were to be recruited for the regiment.

Levy money of five guineas was specified for the recruiting expenses of each man, and Argyll was instructed to recommend the names of three field officers for royal approval.

'His Majesty leaves to your Grace the nomination of all other officers, being such as are well affected to his majesty, and most likely in their interests and connections to assist in raising the corps without delay, who if they meet with his Majesty's approbation may be assured they will have commissions as soon as the regiment is completed.'

Sixteen years was the minimum age allowed for the lieutenants. Officers of course had to purchase their commissions and promotions in the ordinary way, the nomination and cash outlay being an investment and guarantee of loyalty to the monarch, as well as some measure of their likely keenness for active military duty.

There had been little difficulty in finding the officers and twenty-three of them bore the name of Campbell, but raising the rank and file presented considerable difficulty. The officers were expected to bring recruits with them and take a thoroughly active part in recruiting around the countryside, but in the previous fifty years some twenty-six regiments had been raised in Scotland on the regular establishment and chiefly for overseas service — a major drain of manpower of military age from a small country. Argyllshire had already provided the 74th Regiment to fight in the War of American Independence, before being disbanded in 1783. As an instance of demand and supply the Edinburgh *Morning Chronicle* of 29 May 1794 reported that:

'Yesterday, the Grassmarket was crowded with recruiting parties. A smart young countryman, being determined to enlist, collected the recruiting parties together, and fairly set himself up for public auction ... The bidders were many; and he was at last knocked down at twenty guineas.'

It was not recorded which regiment bought the canny Scot.

By the end of May, however, 741 sergeants, drummers and rank and file had been recruited for the new Regiment. About a third of them were Highlanders and the remainder came from the Lowlands, together with some from Ireland; many had seen previous military service.

Resplendent in their new uniforms, the Regiment paraded for the General, and such a body of men must have presented a magnificent and thrilling sight. The uniform was full Highland dress, kilt and plaid of green and black government tartan, red waistcoats for grenadiers, white for the rest, red jackets with yellow facings, with black stocks and white lace, red and white hose with scarlet garters and rosettes, shoes with yellow oval buckles and sporrans or purses — of wild-cat skin for the officers. The head-dress was the 'hummle' bonnet with a hackle, 'cocked and ornamented with ostrich feathers and with a diced border of red, white and green'. The officers and sergeants already carried the basket-hilted broadsword, and the officers also carried pistols. The flintlock muskets for the men, however, did not arrive until early June and other accoutrements had not reached the Regiment before it left Scotland. Shortages in the Quartermaster-General's department persist, as long as the British Army reduces in peacetime and has to expand unexpectedly for war.

The General apparently was pleased with what he saw. He noted 'the attention and good appearance of the whole', and accepted the Regiment for service.

In mid-June the Regiment, under the command of Lochnell, left from Leith harbour for the sea journey to Southampton, where a number of regiments were already garrisoned and under training, before sailing to various British possessions overseas. On 9 July the King approved the 98th (Argyllshire) Regiment of Foot, joining the Regular Establishment.

Originally destined for service in Guernsey, the Argylls remained in Hampshire and Wiltshire until May 1795, being supplied with a few local recruits — who it was reported 'were very shy of appearing in the kilt' which was hardly surprising — and further drafts from Scotland. When the Regiment embarked at Spithead on 5 May, 32 officers, 35 sergeants, 22 drummers and 759 rank and file were mustered.

THE CAPE, 1795

For the British the war on land had started inauspiciously. The French invasion of the Austrian Netherlands in 1794 had drawn a substantial British force overseas to assist the Austrians. Throughout 1794 and into 1795 the campaigning proved disastrous for the British troops commanded by Frederick, Duke of York: ill-provided and without a clear strategic purpose, the campaign ended with a retreat across north Germany to Bremen and substantial losses. As the popular ditty has it, 'He marched them up to the top of the hill, and he marched them down again.' To be fair the Grand Old Duke, actually only twenty-five years of age at the time, learnt from his experience and became a notable Army reformer later in the war.

The French Revolutionary Army successfully occupied Holland, formerly bound by treaty with Britain; this enabled the Dutch republicans to seize power, and declare a military alliance with the French. The new alliance caused consternation in London for several reasons. Commercially any hostility from the Low Countries had over the centuries been detrimental to British interests, and geopolitically it was dangerous as the British monarch was also King of Hanover, with substantial continental land holdings. Then, as a formidable sea power, Holland had numerous garrisons and territories in Africa and the East, of which the most important were the Cape of Good Hope and Ceylon, both on the sea route to the British possessions in India.

Launching a second force on to the European continent was not immediately feasible, so the British government cast its collective eye over the terrestrial globe to see where troops could be usefully employed in defending British interests. It was for this reason that an expeditionary force, which included the 98th Highlanders, was sent in the early summer of 1795 to seize Cape Town from the Dutch colonists, who had sided with the new republican government back in Holland. The orders given to the commander, Major General Sir Alured Clarke, were that once this first objective had been achieved, he was to proceed to India to reinforce the regular British garrison and army of the Honourable East India Company. Clarke, a veteran of the American War of Independence, was to achieve distinction three years later as Commander-in-Chief and Governor-General of India, finishing his service as a field marshal.

British soldiers in the 18th and 19th centuries frequently had to endure the very real hazards of long sea voyages and the hardship of shipboard life in fragile sailing craft. Over the years scores of transports were lost at sea and thousands of soldiers drowned, escaping the notice of popular history except in occasional instances such as the loss of the *Birkenhead*. Even landing where there was no harbour could be a treacherous operation. Fortunately the Argylls travelled on this occasion without mishap. After nearly three months at sea, and calling en route at San Salvador in Brazil, the expedition reached Simon's Bay a few miles south of Cape Town. The officers and men were nevertheless mightily pleased to see landfall, with the magnificent spectacle of Table Mountain and the wild and colourful scenery around. Such a sight warmed the hearts of the true Highlanders in the Regiment, reminding them of home. Surgeon Alan McLachlan in a letter wrote:

'A description of the country ... I refer you to the view of the Moidart Hills and Arisaig from your own door. If possible the hills here are more barren; then there are very extensive plains, mostly sand, which are by no means inviting; no wood; a vast variety of game, and wild beasts of every description to be met with here; abundance of grapes and almost all kinds of fruit to be met within Europe.'

The Argylls, however, did not land immediately. Being untried troops they were held in reserve.

Led by Major General James Craig, part of the force, which included the 2nd Battalion 78th Highlanders, the Ross-shire Buffs (later The Seaforth Highlanders), disembarked and fought a brisk action against the Dutch settlers at Muysenberg, on a narrow strip of land between the mountains and the sea ten miles from Cape Town. By 14 September the second part of the force, which did include the 98th, had disembarked and were ready to march on Wynberg, an outpost of Cape Town.

In this their first engagement 98th Regiment's battalion companies formed the centre of the British line, with Colonel Campbell of Lochnell personally in command, while the grenadier and light companies were detached and concentrated with the same companies of the other regiments. It was a brisk and businesslike affair. Faced with a strong and well-disciplined force, the Dutch on this occasion offered practically no resistance to the British advance, and in the brief fight only four of the 98th were wounded and none killed. In his dispatch Sir Alured Clarke reported:

'The enemy could see all our motions, and the country through which we had to pass for several miles being very favourable to the sort of warfare that it was their business to pursue (many of them being on horseback and armed with guns that kill at a great distance), I had reason to believe that we might be greatly harassed and suffer much on our route. Our loss, however, from the precautions taken and the shyness of the enemy, fortunately proved less than might have been expected.'

A hundred years later the descendants of these Dutchmen presented a much more formidable enemy to the descendants of the original Argylls. Two days after Wynberg, the Dutch agreed armistice terms and surrendered Cape Castle.

Junior regiments were usually accorded ostensibly the least important jobs, so when Sir Alured Clarke re-embarked with part of his force and set sail for India for further glory, the 98th remained as garrison troops in and around Cape Town. Their task was to guard the port and prevent enemy troops landing from the sea, as well as maintain peace among the somewhat aggrieved Dutch settlers. There they remained for six long years, a monotonous time indeed. Detachments had to guard outlying posts, displays of force had to be sent periodically to the numerous settlements, and drills in camp to be repeated endlessly to maintain a high state of readiness — together with the performance of all the endless routine tasks required of an army of occupation.

In 1798 there were fears that the Regiment might be disbanded; but instead it was re-numbered and re-named the '91st (Argyllshire Highlanders) Regiment of Foot'. In the same year Lochnell gave up command of the Regiment and returned home. For practical purposes Highland dress and the kilt had been replaced for the time being with the same uniform worn by British troops in India, of red jacket, white trousers, black gaiters and a black felt hat which resembled the civilian 'Homburg' of later date.

The period spent in South Africa, however, did not prove entirely uneventful. In 1796 there was a warning that an expedition had left Holland intent on the recapture of the Cape, and the Dutch fleet duly arrived on 3 August at Saldanha Bay, north of Cape Town. A detachment of the 91st was quickly dispatched, followed by a larger force which included the grenadier and light companies, while the remainder of the 91st under Lieutenant Colonel Wortley guarded the Cape peninsula. The Dutch admiral, however, did not disembark his troops, and his fleet was cut off from the sea by the British fleet under Admiral Elphinstone, later Lord Keith, leaving the Dutch no alternative but to surrender. The triumph of such a victory without bloodshed undoubtedly overcame any disappointment among the soldiers who had been denied a fight!

Other events which required the Regiment's attention included a brief insurrection by disaffected burghers at Graaf Reinet, some 500 miles from Cape Town, an incident in Cape Town itself when the naval and military storehouses were deliberately destroyed by fire, and a mutiny on board ships of the Royal Navy.

Then, in 1800 two companies of the Regiment took part in operations against Kaffir tribesmen who had committed atrocities against the settlers. Dark-green camouflaged clothing was worn on this occasion by the soldiers to give some protection from observation, but the Kaffirs:

'...were a formidable enemy. They are inured to war and plunder, and most of them are such famous marksmen with the darts, that they make sure of their aim at 60 or 80 paces distance. When you fire upon them they will throw themselves flat on their faces and avoid the ball. Added to this, as they reside in woods, in the most inaccessible parts in which they take refuge in being hard pressed by their enemies, an offensive warfare against them is inconceivable arduous.'

Garrison duties continued. New drafts joined and the seven-year men were discharged. When in 1802 the Treaty of Amiens was signed, one of the provisions was the restoration of Dutch power to the Cape. The new commanding officer of the 91st was particularly keen to discharge from the Regiment the older and less zealous officers and soldiers. This caused much friction, but there had been reports of indiscipline and drunkenness — ever the result of lack of excitement and activity among men of character — which indicated the need for such remedial measures. The Regiment, numbering 32 officers, 45 sergeants, 28 drummers and 400 soldiers, returned to Great Britain in early 1803, while the remainder transferred to other regiments which were destined for service in India.

ENGLAND – GERMANY – IRELAND

All was not well, however, with recruiting at home going from bad to worse. Dozens of regular and volunteer regiments were competing for the dwindling military manpower in Scotland, and it now is estimated that from 1795 to 1806 70,000 men enlisted and were embodied for full-time military service from a total population of less than 2 million. The Regiment undoubtedly had drawn strength from the Highland traditions, but it had not been a true 'clan regiment'. It was therefore with considerable difficulty that the officers of the 91st attempted to bring the Regiment back to strength. Some soldiers came from the new 2nd Battalion of the Regiment, formed in 1804 to draw soldiers from Argyll, Bute and Perth, while others came from all over the south of Scotland, England and Ireland — many of them directly transferring from the Militia. Highland dress was resumed in the same year, but the feile beag — or little kilt — took the place of the belted plaid.

While the Argyllshire Highlanders had been overseas the Royal Navy had scored notable victories, Napoleon's troops had been thrown out of Egypt, the Indian possessions held and the Irish rebellion crushed. There was, however, no real role for British troops in Europe before or after the brief Peace of Amiens of 1802 — 'A peace which all men are glad of, but no man can be proud of,' in the words of the playwright Sheridan, and questions were raised about the need to maintain so many British troops under arms. When the peace collapsed, there was a renewed fear of invasion from France. By 1805 Napoleon had some 150,000 troops earmarked for this task, and the maintaining of embodied troops proved to have been fully justified.

Service in England, however, was uneventful and tedious, consisting of drill, musketry and endless field-days. 'There is nothing going on here but drill from morning to night in this blasted place,' complained a captain in the Regiment. 'I do think any place would be better for a man to be in as a soldier.' The whole of the south of England resembled an armed camp, of regular regiments, embodied Militia, Fencibles and Volunteers, numbering nearly half a million men. Soldiers of the Regiment were sometimes allowed to help with the harvest, and some of the officers discovered the sport of fox-hunting.

In December 1805 1st Battalion of the 91st accompanied Lord Cathcart's expedition to Germany where it was felt more British troops should be held in readiness to assist Prussia, in case Napoleon should march northwards intent on giving battle. After a few weeks in the area of Hamburg, however, the expedition was recalled without any fighting. The same captain who found service in England dull complained, 'You may believe I am not sorry at leaving Germany, as there was nothing to do there. The part of the country I saw is miserable.'

The remainder of 1806 was spent in various camps in Kent, and Major General Hill reported:

'This regiment for its numbers is very effective, and due attention seems to have been paid by all ranks of its officers. Its discipline and interior economy are very good ... Men good and serviceable, regular and well-behaved, not young or very stout, but hardy.'

The term 'stout' was often used to denote robustness, and was not used pejoratively.

Service followed in various stations in Ireland, including Femoy, Mallow, Cashel, Enniscorthy and Dublin. As mentioned before, there had been a serious rebellion in the country in 1798, but duties in Ireland had already been the lot of most regiments both of infantry and cavalry for 200 years and more, and were to remain so to the present day. On this occasion, however, the period of duty for the 91st was short, a mere eighteen months; the Regiment's services were then required elsewhere for a real war.

THE PENINSULA, 1808-9

In November 1807 Napoleon decided to add the Iberian Peninsula to his conquests, and a strong army under Marshal Junot marched unmolested through Spain, ostensibly to punish Portugal for its assistance to the Royal Navy. Lisbon was seized but not before the Portuguese royal family had escaped, and in May 1808 the Spanish royal family was tricked into internment. Despite initial successes, the Spanish Army could not prevent French occupation, and an appeal was sent to London: clearly it was felt in Iberia that the time had now come for Europe to be saved by British exertion, rather than mere example.

Forming part of Brigadier General Catlin Crauford's brigade — he had commanded the Regiment in Cape Town — 1st Battalion, 91st Argyllshire Highlanders sailed for Portugal in July 1808 to join Lieutenant General Sir Arthur Wellesley's troops who had already landed. Wellesley, the victor of Assaye, at that time the senior British general, had been given as his mission the recapture of Lisbon, and the first encounter with the French took place at Rolica on 17 August, during which the Highlanders were held in reserve. The French withdrew and Wellesley advanced towards Vimeiro, 25 miles north of Lisbon, where Junot attacked the British on 21 August. Again the 91st were in reserve, but at one stage in the battle came under fire. The result was a crushing defeat for the French: their withdrawal was sanctioned by a somewhat shameful treaty — the Convention of Cintra — ordered by General Sir Hew Dalrymple, the Commander-in-Chief who had been placed over Wellesley's head.

Writing on his arrival in Portugal, Captain Donald Gregorson of the Regiment stated:

'We shall have a good deal to do before we conquer this country. The French are very brave, but they have no chance with our army.'

Later from Salamanca he wrote:

'This country is well worth fighting for. Our troops are in good spirits and eager to attack the French, and when we do meet I shall have no doubt of the result, if we are at all nearly equal in numbers.'

Alas it was not to be. The British Army had first to face a very great test and then campaign over the next seven years against much larger enemy forces, before the French were finally ejected from the Peninsula.

The news of Junot's defeat had infuriated Napoleon, and he himself set off to Spain at the head of 150,000 troops, while Sir John Moore, the new British Commander-in-Chief, had a force of only 35,000. The 91st, now commanded by William Douglas — who was to remain in command of the battalion for the next ten years —formed part of the Reserve Division under Major General Paget, and in November they marched from Lisbon to Salamanca, some 100 miles north-west of Madrid. In mid-December, however, Napoleon's army entered Madrid, and Moore decided to draw the French northwards to take the pressure off what remained of the Spanish Army in the south.

A successful battle at Sahagun on 20 December destroyed Soult's cavalry force, but Moore quickly realized the increasing seriousness of his position, when it was reported that Napoleon was marching on a line with the intention of out-flanking him. This would mean that the vital route to the safe port of Corunna would be cut and result in the destruction of the British forces. Moore therefore cancelled a night attack planned to destroy Soult's infantry, and ordered an immediate withdrawal northwards. In the words of Ensign Ormerod of the 91st:

'When our troops arrived at and around Grajal de Campos, we were marched from thence at about 9 o'clock at night [23 December] to make an attack on Soult, at least it was said so, and harangues and bloody preparations were made for the occasion: after marching in columns at the rate of a mile an hour, up to our knees in snow and pierced through and through with extreme cold winds for about 2 leagues [6 miles], we were ordered to the right about, and returned home at 1 o'clock in the morning, wet through with snow, which gave us severe colds and sore throats. At 4 o'clock we rose, and the baggage having been sent off before, we left Grajal de Campos, well knowing that a retreat was Sir John Moore's aim from the baggage being in front. [We] marched through deep water and boggy ground, our shoes and stockings often falling off ... roads almost impassable.'

So began the retreat, and while some troops displayed great discipline, the control and cohesion of a number of regiments was lost. The disorder and indiscipline did not spread to the 91st Highlanders, whose minds anyway were fully concentrated by proximity to the pursuing enemy, their place being in the rear of the army. Over the next fortnight they fought several actions and:

'All the way ... we experienced the most extreme difficulties; without shoes or food, obliged to march, men dropping down through hunger and fatigue — men, women and children in one heap — the Spanish artillery... clothes lying in the road, our horses not being able to draw them up such steep hills and time being precious. When we were passing the mountains two of our men fell down over a precipice. Every ten paces were horses killed ... the reserve obliged to cut off packs being so closely pressed.'

Many of the stragglers from leading formations were drunk and on the rampage and had to be cajoled along by the Reserve Division. After a terrible march the Division reached within four miles of Corunna on 11 January, but were obliged to wait for several days before embarkation could begin.

During the battle, launched by Soult on the afternoon of 16 January, the 91st Highlanders were hotly engaged fending off a major attack by dismounted dragoons and infantry, but miraculously their casualties were very light. That night they embarked, having lost 164 men during the previous weeks of most arduous campaigning.

Much has been written and said about the faithfulness and gallantry of some soldiers and craven fear and panic betrayed by others, but undoubtedly, while being a very dark event in British military history, there was more order than chaos and the small British Army held together long enough for a successful embarkation of the majority. The 91st by all accounts had fought and behaved in a most exemplary fashion.

From February to July 1909 the 91st Highlanders recuperated and re-trained in the south of England. News came through that some of their members, who had reached Lisbon, had been formed into a company and were involved in successful fighting on the River Douro during May 1809 and at Talavera in July.

Despite Lochnell's injunction that 'every parish must be visited, every pretty girl danced with and kissed: in short, every exertion must be made', recruiting in Scotland was even worse than before. Shattering news reached the Regiment in April, together with the 72nd, 73rd, 74th, 75th and 94th Highlanders: as a result of the scarcity of Highland recruits, the decision was made to remove these regiments from the Highland Establishment of the army. (In this context, of the men enlisted into the two battalions from 1800 to 1818, 1,569 were Scots, 350 Irish, 339 English and 219 foreign — mainly Swedish and German, enlisted by the second battalion.) The name officially became the '91st Regiment', and this decision meant that they had to abandon the distinction of wearing Highland dress. Although tartan trews and bonnets were worn for a further year, they were then replaced by grey trousers and black caps, indistinguishable from the dress of other line regiments.

As can be imagined, it was an extremely unpopular decision. The character of a regiment cannot quickly be changed, any more than the nationality of the majority of its members. Thinking ahead, they proved determined to hold on strongly to their Highland traditions, and after much lobbying the county name was restored in 1820. Orders in Gaelic could be heard on parade until 1839 and pipers were employed until 1850. The Regiment formally became 'Highlanders' again in 1864, but they had to wait until 1881 before readopting the kilt.

Notwithstanding this blow to regimental pride, the report on the Regiment in May confirmed that: 'The general appearance and make of the men is very good, and well calculated for the most active service': but it pointed out that while the 'men of the regiment are not deficient in their field movements ... the company officers require a further degree of instruction'. Improvements were soon noted, but real 'field movement' was not required of the 91st for three more years, since their next active duty brought them much hardship but no engagement against the enemy.

The 91st spent the second half of 1809 as part of the 40,000- strong Walcheren expeditionary force. Under command of the Earl of Chatham, the intention was that the Austrians should send an army to mount a joint assault with the British troops against Antwerp. They never arrived, Antwerp was quickly reinforced by the French, and the British force remained to garrison the low-lying and unhealthy islands of the Scheldt estuary. Although unmolested by the French, the British troops suffered severely; 4,000 died of disease, thousands more were sick and the force could hardly have defended itself had the French decided to attack. In September 1809 from 608 rank and file, the 91st could muster only 246 for duty. As a consequence of wounds, disease and debility after the disasters of the retreat to Corunna and the Walcheren expedition, 218 men of the Regiment died.

The 1st Battalion, 91st remained in England for three years until September 1812 when it was warned again for service in the Iberian Peninsula. After this period in England, the Regiment was altogether in finer shape than it had been at any time in its existence, and this was chiefly due to the tireless energy of Lieutenant Colonel Douglas and particularly his insistence on the younger officers carrying out their duties with much greater enthusiasm and dedication than was the usual custom. 'A very fine body of men, mostly young, though equal to any service. They are healthy and clean. This battalion is in a high state of discipline, and fit to be employed in any service,' was the report on the 91st for the year.

Landing at Corunna, now free of French troops, in October, the 91st marched south through the mountains, harried spasmodically by French cavalry, before concentrating with Wellesley, now Marquess of Wellington and Commander-in-Chief.

Much had happened in the Peninsula during the intervening three years. Wellington had totally reorganized his army, and now commanded Portuguese and Spanish troops as well as British. Although the allies could face the French on equal terms, to eject them from Spain was proving to be a lengthy and painstaking task.

From the immensely strong base in Lisbon, guarded by the fortified lines of Torres Vedras, Wellington's troops had set out to defeat Marshals Victor at Talavera (1809), Massena at Bussaco (1810), and Soult at Albuera (1811). The two great fortresses in western Spain — Ciudad Roderigo and Badajoz — had fallen to Wellington in early 1812, and in the most decisive victory of the campaign in Spain so far, he had destroyed the French under Marmont at Salamanca, in a battle where three French divisions were broken in a mere forty minutes. Madrid was entered by the British and Spanish armies, and the advance continued as far east as Burgos, before Wellington decided that a new French force under Joseph Bonaparte (the brother on whom Napoleon had bestowed the Crown of Spain) was too great a threat at the present time, and ordered a withdrawal to the Portuguese frontier. It was at this point that the 91st joined the campaign.

The final part of Wellington's campaign began in the spring of 1813, and it was to last for nearly a year. The 91st, still commanded by William Douglas, found themselves brigaded with the 42nd and 79th Highlanders under Brigadier General Denis Pack; the brigade was known as the Highland Brigade. In May 1913 they marched with 6th Division (commanded by Major General Sir Henry Clinton), on the left wing of the army (under Lieutenant General Sir Thomas Graham), through the mountains to Burgos in northern Spain and on towards the River Ebro near the Pyrenees.

On 21 June the Division was in reserve during the battle of Vitoria, but during the next week it advanced 50 miles through the mountains eastwards towards Pamplona. The assault on the Pyrenees, the natural mountain frontier between Spain and France, had begun. These picturesquely beautiful mountains posed enormous difficulties for military movement let alone penetration, particularly during the winter months, and it was to be a great test for all the troops taking part. For the 91st it was certainly the greatest challenge since Corunna, and of much longer duration. Tactically the key to the Pyrenees was the holding of the mountain passes through which could move the main bodies of troops. The main passes had first to be wrested from the French.

On 28 July the 91st took part in their first major engagement of the campaign. After marching through the passes of Roncevalles and Maya, Soult was discovered holding a forward position in the village of Sorauren. Wellington reported in his dispatch that:

'The 6th Division had scarcely taken their position [in the valley of the River Lanz, in rear of the left of 4th Division] when they were attacked by a very large force of the enemy ... Their front was, however, so well defended by the fire of their own light troops [light companies] from the height on the left ... that the enemy was soon driven back with immense loss from fire on their front, both flanks and rear'.

Twelve of the 91st were killed and 101 wounded during the fighting. Soult withdrew his main body but left a strong force in Sorauren village, '...one of the strongest and most difficult of access', wrote the Duke, that he 'had ever seen occupied by troops'.

'At daybreak the action recommenced on our right, by an attack from the enemy's left wing. The action continued very hot until noon, when the light companies of the Highland Brigade under the direction of Major McNeill, 91st Regiment, stormed and carried the village of Sorauren, when the enemy fled in all directions, leaving a vast number of prisoners in our hands. The Division continued in pursuit.'

The battles for the Pyrenees continued over several weeks and at the end of August the mighty fortress of San Sebastian was captured. In the meantime the 91st had been sent forward to guard the Bastan valley and pass of Maya. On 7 October their division was ordered to march towards Urdax as a feint, while Wellington crossed the frontier marked by the River Bidassoa, and at the end of the month accepted the surrender of Pamplona.

In November the weather became bad and the heavy rain turned to snow. Conditions in the mountains were appalling, but this did not prevent the troops carrying out their tasks with great energy and courage. The 91st were ordered to advance with their division towards the River Nivelle, the first river in France, and after a march through the night of 9/10 November, 6th Division forced its way across.

'I had the pleasure', wrote Wellington, 'of seeing the 6th Division ... after having crossed the Nivelle, having driven in the enemy's picquets on both banks, and having covered the passage of the Portuguese Division on its right, make a most handsome attack upon the right of the enemy's position ... and carry all the entrenchments and the redoubt upon that flank. [Both Divisions] co-operated on the attack at the second redoubt which was immediately carried ... We have driven the enemy from positions which they had been fortifying with great labour and care for three months.'

It was a most successful battle, and one conducted with a minimum of casualties — only four men killed and six wounded from the 91st Regiment.

The foul weather continued unabated for some weeks, and movement across the plains proved impossible. On 9 December the weather improved sufficiently for Wellington's plans for crossing the River Nivelle to be put into action. The 6th Division crossed on a pontoon bridge and the light companies captured outposts together with the village of Villafranca, while the 2nd Division crossed farther up-stream and forced the enemy to abandon the main positions and retreat to the fortress of Bayonne. Held in reserve for the next few days, the 91st then witnessed the fighting in the villages close to Bayonne.

It is always a commander's twin responsibility to win battles and conserve his force; often the effort is put into the former to the detriment of the latter, and then all can be lost. Wellington's greatness as a commander was based on his success in getting the balance of these responsibilities correct more often than his enemies, the result of his genius both intellectual and intuitive.

The atrocious weather continued, and Wellington decided that it was wiser to allow or rather force his troops to rest and reconstitute themselves for the time being. 'I should be guilty', said the Duke, 'of a useless waste of men if I were to attempt any operation during the violent falls of rain which we have here.' So the men were billeted where possible in buildings, although the living conditions were appalling and the food particularly meagre, so it was hardly surprising that most of the battalions including the 91st suffered many sick. They were without greatcoats, their uniforms quite worn out, the replacement clothing held up in Portugal, and as a participant observed: 'It is impossible to describe the painful state that some shoeless men were in, crippling along the way, their feet cut or torn by sharp stones or brambles.' And, '...the want heretofore of any regular supply of vegetables, with other little comforts in their messing', made life a misery. The regimental surgeon was accused of being negligent and Colonel Douglas, together with other commanding officers, was blamed by the brigade commander.

Wellington paused for several weeks to allow the recuperation and resupply of his troops. The Iron Duke was hard on his officers, but led by example. With the methods he had taught all his commanders of accepting and delegating responsibility for all matters, he ensured that they and the junior officers were chastened to put things right. The Regiment pulled itself together and quickly recovered from previous exertions despite the appalling conditions. 'We were getting hardier and stronger every day in person ... more confidence we feel in our strength and all in health and no sickness,' wrote a member of the Highland Brigade.

In February Wellington's army was ready to continue the advance. They crossed the river and marched into Bayonne, which Soult had abandoned, and followed the retreating French towards Orthes and Toulouse, 150 miles distant. By 26 February the 91st, still in 6th Division, were on the left bank of the River Adour opposite Orthes.

The following morning four of Wellington's divisions crossed by pontoon and 6th Division were formed on the right, facing the enemy's left centre.

'The enemy, fancying themselves secure on their fortified heights on one front ... did not molest us in crossing or in our formations afterwards. About 9 am all being in readiness, the Divisions moved down the main road towards Orthes, when coming abreast of the enemy's position each Division broke off the road, attacked, and carried the position to its front. About noon the enemy fled in all directions, the British pursuing them, loudly cheering...'

The light companies of the 42nd and 91st together with 42nd's grenadier company drove off a spirited cavalry attack early in the battle, and the remainder of the

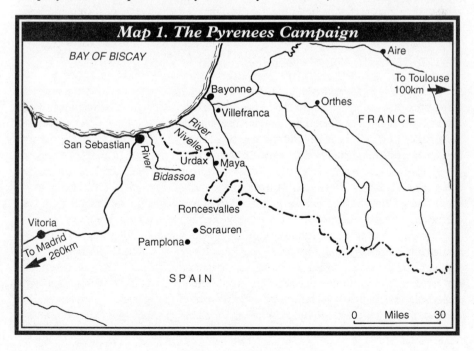

Map 1. The Pyrenees Campaign

two battalions assaulted the enemy's hill-top position as described. Four days after the battle of Orthes, 91st Regiment fought a brisk action near Aire.

The key to the whole of the defence of southern France was the fortified town of Toulouse, built on either side of the River Garonne and held in great strength by Marshal Soult. The weather had hardly improved during March as Wellington's army approached the city and they discovered that there were no bridges outside the city's defended area. In early April a bridge was built some fifteen miles downstream and 4th and 6th Divisions crossed. By 10 April a second bridge had been thrown across the river and only then was Wellington was ready to attack Toulouse.

The British and Allied troops were formed up north of the city behind a long hill — the Plateau of Calvinet — dominated by a high feature known as Mont Rave. The 42nd and 79th Highlanders and 91st Regiment quickly attacked the hill. 'Nothing,' said General Sir George Napier, 'could damp the courage of this column: the enemy's guns poured a torrent of fire upon it: still it moved onward while column upon column of the enemy appeared, covering the hill and forming lines in front and on the flanks of all our brave fellows who were near the top.'

But a withdrawal had to be ordered, since on the British right Spanish troops had failed to achieve their mission. Wellington personally rode up to rally them before the hill could be carried by a fresh attack. Napier continued:

'Under a tremendous fire of all arms of the enemy, they once more marched onwards, determined to do or die (for they were nearly all Scotch) and having gained the summit of the position, they charged with the bayonet, and in spite of every effort of the enemy, drove all before them, and entered every redoubt, and fought with such courage as I never saw before.'

Again the Spanish troops failed to gain ground, so it was necessary for the Highland Brigade to fight along the ridge, and take the enemy strong points in a farm, two redoubts and some lines of trenches, which they did with the bayonet.

Then, while the Brigade manned lines of defence, 6,000 enemy troops came up and:

'Having gained the proper point, they immediately rushed forward in such numbers as to overpower the 42nd, who were compelled to retire to the farmhouse; but being promptly supported by the 91st, they attacked the enemy, and drove them down the hill with great loss. The Highlanders also suffered very severely. Determined to carry the redoubts, a fresh body of the enemy advanced up the hill...' and the fighting continued back and forth for some time. In the middle of the battle Colonel Douglas of the 91st had to take over command of the Brigade, when Sir Denis Pack was wounded. Later in the battle the 91st were called upon to rush to the aid of 79th Highlanders, when the redoubt they were holding was almost overwhelmed. The Brigade remained on the ridge holding the ground as other troops fought for Toulouse itself.

Of all Wellington's Peninsular victories, Toulouse was the most evenly balanced and won by the narrowest of margins. The French were of course defending their own soil and Wellington described the battle as 'a very serious affair'. The Spanish troops had suffered a large number of casualties, as had 3rd, 4th and 6th Divisions. The 91st's losses were not as heavy as the other two battalions of the Brigade, but seven officers were wounded, nineteen NCOs and soldiers were killed and 93 wounded from a total of 557 who went into action.

The following day Toulouse was evacuated by the enemy, and it was discovered that Napoleon Bonaparte had already abdicated in favour of Louis XVIII on 6 April — the news having taken some days to reach the victorious Allies. Such was the nature of war and communications.

Although 91st Regiment had arrived only in time for the latter part of the Peninsular War, they had played their part efficiently, and had done all that was asked of them and more. Often seniority on the regimental roll determined a regiment's position on the battlefield, and junior regiments were frequently held in reserve or in support irrespective of military efficiency. Nevertheless the 91st were Peninsular veterans and proud of the honour. Of his Peninsular veterans Wellington was to say, 'There are no men in Europe that can fight like them ... they and I know one another exactly. We have a mutual confidence and are never disappointed.'

The 91st left France in June 1814 and took up duties in Ireland for the next nine months.

NORTH-WEST EUROPE

A second battalion of 91st Regiment had been in service since 1804, its purpose being to provide drafts for 1st Battalion; much of the time it was supervised energetically by Campbell of Lochnell, but its quality and strength varied greatly from year to year. Many regiments had adopted the system, formalized many years later, of forming a regimental infrastructure from which to sustain the active service battalion; but there was no regimental depot as such, and troops were billeted wherever accommodation could be arranged.

In July 1813 the Battalion sailed for Stralsund in Prussian Pomerania with a British brigade, whose purpose was to garrison parts of the Baltic coast. It was a short-lived expedition and the Battalion marched during the winter together with 4th Battalion, the Royal Scots to join Sir Thomas Graham's force besieging Antwerp. Part of the Battalion took part in a well-planned attack on the fortress of Bergen-Op-Zoom during March 1814, but the French proved to be in greater strength than was expected and could not be dislodged. At one stage in the fighting, the Colours were in imminent danger of capture, but were saved. On its return to Britain 2nd Battalion remained in being until disbandment in December 1815.

Meanwhile in April 1815 1st Battalion was sent to join the Duke of Wellington's army in Belgium after Napoleon's return to power. During the Battle of Waterloo on 18 June the 91st were held in reserve to the British right, in case the French should have attempted to outflank Wellington's Allied army. But for those members of the Regiment keen for a fight — and who denies such keenness — it was infuriating that there was no opportunity to take part in the famous battle, and 'Waterloo' could not be claimed as a regimental battle honour.

Their opportunity came, however, during the advance on Paris when their brigade was asked to capture the fortified town of Cambrai, still resolutely held by troops loyal to Napoleon. The light company was involved in the first assault party, and the main body of the 91st then successfully stormed over the town wall, and quickly occupied it. There the battalion remained for a few days, before continuing the march to Paris and the victory celebrations.

The 91st were stationed in the capital as occupation troops for the next three and a half years, during which time their long-serving commanding officer, Sir William Douglas, knighted at the age of 35 for gallantry, died. Their first twenty years of service had proved that the Regiment was indeed made up of 'hardy and intrepid' soldiers, well led and utterly dependable.

CHAPTER 2

THE LAST CLAN REGIMENT

The 93rd Sutherland Highlanders, 1799–1853

SOBRIETY AND OBEDIENCE

There is no doubt that the most distinctive regiments of the British Army were those that legitimately could be called 'clan regiments'.

The Highland clan system, where it existed, was based on the legal powers of the chief and his deputies, a complicated but not particularly consistent system of land-tenure and the obligation for personal service by the clansmen — including military service. In earlier times the chief possessed what were virtually sovereign rights over those who lived on his lands, which extended to those not necessarily his tenants but who relied on his protection. The so called 'clan regiments' of the 17th and early 18th centuries were comprised of the clansmen of military age, which meant almost any age from beardless teenagers to hardy men exceeding three score years and ten. They were only part-time soldiers, having occupations of every description in normal times. When called upon they were brave and impetuous, intensely loyal and proud, but they tended to fight as inspired individuals, lacking the drills and discipline which marked regular regiments. A number of 'clan regiments' fought on one side or other during the Jacobite rebellions of 1715 and 1745, but Culloden proved that such a military system, adequate for occasional tribal warfare in the Highlands, could not stand against regular troops in a set-piece battle.

Many of the descendants of these clansmen subsequently joined regiments in parish groups or families, to serve the Hanoverian Crown either for home defence in the Militia or Fencibles, or in Regular regiments for overseas service. As such they remained very often under the direct auspices or command of the chief's close family — some of whom it should not be forgotten had been deeply involved in the Jacobite cause. But then the term 'clan regiment' took on a different meaning. With direct or nearly direct antecedents in the Highland Military system, comprised of men bred with such fighting instincts, and given the formal structure and discipline of regular troops, the regiments became the most highly efficient units of military force in the British Army, fighting with distinction in the War of Austrian Succession, the Seven Years War, the War of American Independence and the wars and campaigns in India. These wars, however, had taken a toll on the military manpower of the Highlands as stated in Chapter 1.

Many of the so called 'Highland Regiments' were not by this definition clan regiments. Formed from a more remote locality, however, the new 93rd Highland Regiment and the second of the two regiments which later formed the Argyll and Sutherland Highlanders, was a true clan regiment and maintained their direct heritage longer than all the other Highland regiments.

In the northern county of Sutherland, where 'soldiering and droving were held to be the only worthy vocations for a man', the two chief families were the Sutherlands and the MacKays. The Earls of Sutherland and the MacKay Barons of Reay had supported the Hanoverians assiduously and held a benevolent yet firm control over the 22,000 souls who inhabited the county. According to Doctor Pococke, a visitor of the time, 'they are in general exceedingly hospitable, charitable, civil, polite and sensible'.

During the Seven Years War, the Sutherland Fencibles were raised in 1759 by Lord Sutherland, and the Hon Hugh MacKay, Lord Reay's son, was Lieutenant Colonel. Fencible regiments consisted of full-time 'volunteers' on the regular establishment (unlike the Militia, which was a form of compulsory service), but their service was confined to Britain. The Regiment served in Inverness, Aberdeen, Old Meldrum, Dundee and Edinburgh Castle before disbandment. There was of course no invasion during the four years of its existence, but it had a fine record for faithful service and exemplary behaviour — 'an honourable distinction that in a regiment of 1,050 men no restriction had been required and no man had been punished [i.e., flogged]', according to the historian of the Highland Regiments, General Stewart of Garth.

Responding to new dangers in 1779, another Fencible regiment was called into service at the behest of the young Countess of Sutherland, the heiress to the family title and lands, then aged fourteen years. William Wemyss of Wemyss, her cousin, aged nineteen and an ensign in the Coldstream Guards, was given the temporary rank of Colonel to raise and command it, the Countess expressing her regret that she was '...only sorry that I cannot command it myself'! The Regiment was recruited rapidly and embodied at Fort George in June. During the four years' of its existence the Sutherland Fencibles served in numerous parts of Scotland, including the Shetland Islands, but again there was no French invasion. Garth this time described them as an:

'Excellent, orderly regiment of well-behaved serviceable men, fit for any duty ... Always distinguished for sobriety, probity, and the most scrupulous and orderly attention to duty. Desertions for crimes requiring the check of courts-martial were totally unknown in the regiment.'

He also commented warmly on their domestic and home-loving sentiments, for 'they were always remitting money and sending home little presents for their friends'. Sir Walter Scott also noted in his journal that many of them were of great height, calling them the 'regiment of Sutherland giants'. They wore full Highland dress and the government pattern tartan.

In 1793 a third Fencible regiment was raised in Sutherland with Wemyss again in command, the men this time agreeing to serve for six years. Two years later another corps was raised in the county, known as the Reay or MacKay Fencibles. Both these Fencible regiments volunteered for service in Ireland, and the Reay Fencibles were involved in the battle of Tara Hill in County Meath against the rebels, accepting the surrender of the French expeditionary force after the battle of Castlebar near Killala Bay.

Regimental succession in the British Army is usually rigidly regulated, but some regiments have claimed dubious continuation of service at times where service was not really continuous, and got away with it in the fight for precedence. There is no doubt, however, that the Sutherland Highlanders' claims for antecedents was very strong.

The Sutherland Fencibles had been disbanded for the third time in April 1799, and paid up to the 22nd day of the month. Their Colonel, Major General Wemyss, however, shortly afterwards received a letter dated 16 April from the War Office. It read:

'Sir, I have the honour to acquaint you that His Majesty has been pleased to approve of a Regiment of Infantry of the line being formed under your command as Colonel, to be composed of such men and belonging to the Sutherland Fencibles as are willing to engage in your new Regiment, and to be completed of Recruits from that County and to be ready for inspection by a General Officer within three months of the date of this letter. The Establishment of the Regiment will be fixed at six hundred Rank and File, or at one thousand Rank and File, if it can be completed to that number by Sutherland men within the time above-mentioned.'

As was natural in a true clan regiment, an old-fashioned method of recruitment was invoked, which was not far removed from conscription. A census was taken of every parish and a quota was decided by the chief's representatives. Then:

'With a large snuff-box in his hand and an attendant with a bottle of whisky, [he] went along the ranks, and to every young man whom he wished to enter the corps, he offered snuff — the signal was perfectly understood — the young man stepped out, took his snuff and dram, and the clerk recorded his name and attestation. They were then collected and the King's Bounty Money paid to them.'

The majority of the men for the new regiment were recruited in this fashion. 'The young men themselves never seemed to have questioned the right assumed by their Chief over their Military services', even if their families were not pleased by the loss of their sons. Evidently the county could not sustain a regiment of the higher strength, but it was 'completed' by the recruitment of 653 men in August, 259 of whom had served in the Sutherland Fencibles. When the order to embody the Regiment at Inverness was given in August 1800, every man reported by the time required.

'Captains, Ensigns and staff appear proper to be recommended ... [the NCOs] smart young men, chiefly from the late Sutherland Fencible Regiment ... the Grenadiers are tolerable, the Light Company very good. The Front rank of the battalion of pretty good size — in the Rear rank there are some growing lads at present rather low and slight ... rejected 10. Men in general are not of large stature but are stout [sturdy] and fit for service.'

He did not mention the gentle giant 'big Sam', an old soldier whose reputation was widely known in the army, who measured six feet ten inches in height, and always stood at the right on parade, leading the columns on the march.

The vast majority of men were from Sutherland and many of the officers were drawn from the gentry of the county. Some of them had previous regular military service or were actually serving in other regiments at the time. Known at first as Major General Wemyss's Regiment, it was variously styled at the time '93rd Sutherland Highlanders', '93rd Regiment' and other variations. The 'Sutherland' title was not officially recorded until 1861.

The Regiment remained in Inverness for a month. They were without arms or clothing at first, but by Christmas 1800 some uniforms began to arrive, and continued to do so over many months, a delay which was not unusual at the time. By all accounts the uniforms were not well tailored. Jackets were red with yellow collar and cuffs, and with yellow facings for the officers. Various company differences of epaulettes and shoulder-straps were worn. The 'little kilt' of government tartan was issued together with hair sporrans, sashes for officers and sergeants, the hummle bonnet, black stocks, diced hose and buckled shoes. Muskets were not available for issue before the Regiment left Scotland, but again this was not unusual.

By all accounts the Regiment's stay at Inverness was uneventful, and the men behaved in an exemplary fashion. It was not considered necessary to mount guards, or place any men under arrest, which was most unusual and astonished the townspeople and military observers; apparently the men's 'religious and moral education formed the best guarantee of their conduct as soldiers'. Notwithstanding the 93rd's loyalty, obedience and high morale, their training in drills, field work and skill at arms was severely hampered because of the shortages of uniforms, arms and equipment, together with the fact that initially there were not enough officers to assist the commanding officer. Many of the officers were in the process of transferring from other regular regiments, and travelling from far afield.

The somewhat leisurely fashion in which 93rd Highlanders were raised reflected the state of the war at the time. Most of the action on land was taking place around the Mediterranean and those soldiers not required overseas were used for home defence. Indeed, as the 91st also had discovered, Britain was one large garrison, prepared to turn back the invader but with a government unsure how Napoleon could be successfully defeated on the continent, or even whether such action were possible.

The 93rd, many of them still in their home clothes, sailed during September 1800 in transports from Scotland to Guernsey, whose inhabitants welcomed them with the same enthusiasm as they had greeted previous Highlanders; the French had already attempted to invade the Channel Islands. Lieutenant Colonel Alexander Halkett, a man from Fife, was in command and the Regiment comprised eight companies until March 1801, when new drafts arrived to form two more.

News was heard in October that peace negotiations were being conducted and there was great rejoicing in the island with illuminations, volleys fired by the troops and a grand dinner party given by the officers. The Treaty of Amiens was signed in March 1802 and in September a warrant was signed for the disbandment of 93rd Highlanders, the pen on this occasion seeming to be mightier than the sword. Thus after two years' service, it appeared that the Regiment was to pass into oblivion like many others before, and without firing a shot in anger.

The inhabitants of Guernsey were sorry to see the Highlanders depart in six transports, bound for Scotland. Five reached Leith safely, but in a 'tremendous gale' off North Shields, the sixth transport, carrying some 70 members of the Regiment, was almost swamped. Surprised and grateful for their safety when the storm died down, they made land, whereupon in a display of the dual nature of the Scots, the Highlanders to a man bowed down before their Maker and collected a sum of money, which was duly presented to the Kirk at North Shields during evening service on the following Sunday. On the Monday they marched away with thankfulness in their hearts to join the remainder of the Regiment.

Napoleon's ambitions were only temporarily suspended during the period of fragile peace and a number of regiments due for disbandment, including the 90th (later

2nd Battalion, Scottish Rifles), 91st Highlanders, 92nd Highlanders (later 2nd Battalion, Gordon Highlanders) and 93rd Regiment had their orders for disbandment cancelled. Although the 93rd had already started to discharge some of their members, a counter order was given for them 'to be recruited to strength as fast as possible'. This was assisted by transferring across men from the Reay Fencibles, whose disbandment did go ahead. The Regiment was then quartered in Aberdeen and two other towns during the winter, before being ordered to move to Ireland.

The large number of troops garrisoned in Ireland so soon after the rebellion were kept extremely active in every part of the troubled country, conducting what, even in the 19th century, could be called mobile operations. The 93rd were constantly on the march, maintaining a presence and preventing the Irish from carrying out open guerrilla warfare. By all accounts the Regiment got on well with the population with 'its humane and soldier-like conduct, exemplary behaviour and conciliatory spirit'. The Highlanders could of course speak with and be understood by the Irish, being of common ancestry and language. An official account mentioned that the Regiment was 'a picture of military discipline and moral rectitude', while another assessed 'that although the junior regiment in His Majesty's service, they exhibit an honourable example, worthy the imitation of all'. Notwithstanding such praise, a tale is told of an incident when some members were:

'enjoying themselves in a public-house when in came an Irish bully to pick a quarrel with the kilted lads. They would not be drawn. The Irishman was a formidable fellow and ... Iain Beag [of the 93rd], a man of small stature but great activity told the Irishman he would have a go at him ... Ducking his head he made a rush at the giant, hit him with his head like a ram in the stomach, and laid him senseless on the floor. His companions now stood up, drew their bayonets and cleared the house.'

Such was the mettle of men of the 93rd. War was imminent again in 1804 but the Regiment had a further year to serve in Ireland. In May 1805 the Regiment was actually embarked on transports, waiting in Cork harbour with orders for Jamaica, when an urgent signal ordered them to disembark and deploy to Mallow to meet an expected French invasion. There were 150,000 French troops awaiting, encamped at Boulogne ready to 'force the wet ditch of the Channel', but it was a false alarm and 93rd Highlanders had to wait for a further three months before joining Sir David Baird's force bound for Cape Town.

THE CAPE, 1805

Baird, a redoubtable old Scottish soldier, had fought in numerous campaigns over the years. His portrait can be seen in the National Gallery of Scotland, depicting him in the act of discovering the body of his erstwhile gaoler of three years, Tippoo Sahib, ruler of Mysore, after the final capture of Seringapatam. Baird was a fine commander and had already served in the Cape during the previous occupation.

Cape Town, as described in Chapter 1, had been captured in 1795 by a force which included 91st Argyllshire Regiment; but at the Treaty of Amiens it had been returned to the Dutch. Now it was to be retaken in the same fashion as before, and the expedition was to be conducted with the greatest secrecy and surprise.

The 93rd Highlanders were part of the Highland Brigade, comprising 71st Highlanders (Baird's own regiment and later 1st Battalion, Highland Light Infantry), 72nd Highlanders (later 1st Battalion, The Seaforth Highlanders) and 93rd Highlanders, together with various drafts of other regiments. Disembarking the troops proved difficult because of strong winds and racing surf, but eventually they landed some fifteen miles from Cape Town at the northern end of Table Bay. Sadly, thirty-seven members of the light companies of the Regiment were drowned when one of the boats, according to Major Graham of Fintry:

'...could not be rowed clear of a rock, which she no sooner touched than she instantly turned bottom up ... our noble fellows ... were so loaded with ammunition, accoutrements, etc., they went down directly ... poor fellows! Not an hour before they were dancing reels to the bagpipes.'

During a skirmish with the Dutch on landing, another soldier was killed and two wounded. The Dutch Commander, General Janssens, had hurriedly managed to mobilize more than 2,000 troops, made up of Dutch, French, Germans, Japanese, natives and other assorted races — some of whom were mercenaries — and slaves. On 8 January Baird deployed his two brigades for a march on Cape Town, with the Highland Brigade on the left — the correct place for the junior Brigade in the days when strict precedence was jealously guarded. Emerging from the Blueberg hills, the British saw the Dutch army and immediately opened up with artillery fire. The Highlanders fired a volley at long range and then charged with the bayonet.

'It is impossible', wrote Major Graham, 'to give an idea of the badness of the ground over which our line had to advance, very deep sand and completely covered with a sort of brushwood, which is something like a gooseberry bush with thorn prickles on it, some as high as the chin ... the heat was intense ... [we moved] with a rapidity and regularity which was truly wonderful. The fire from the enemy's infantry only served to increase the rate of pace. When very near the enemy, the Highland Brigade opened a roaring fire to be sure, but they never halted. At length, seeing that Mynheer began to look round to see if the road behind him was clear, the order was given to charge, and to be sure, how the fellows did run!'

Janssens troops were chased more than three miles by the Brigade, before it was ordered to halt. Outnumbered three to one, the burghers and their troops must have recalled the equally swift Dutch defeat at Wynberg in 1795, but on this occasion they had put up a greater resistance, at least at first.

'The Scotch Brigade', wrote an eye-witness, Sir Robert Wilson, 'has certainly acquired great honour, not more for their courage than for their steady discipline; so good was their spirit that no wounded man that could serve left the ranks.'

And Sir David Baird in his dispatch said that 'Nothing could surpass or resist the determined bravery of the troops [of the Highland Brigade] headed by their gallant leader Brigadier-General Fergusson.'

Within twenty-four hours Cape Town and the nearby townships were occupied, the 93rd taking up residence in Cape Town Castle, while the Dutch troops headed off thirty miles to the east and the safety of the hills. A few days later they finally surrendered.

The Sutherland Highlanders quickly settled down to the life of occupying troops. Understandably the burghers were just as resentful as they had been during the time that 91st Argylls had spent in the colony, but there was little trouble from them or the tribesmen in the hills. As before, the soldiers spent some of the time in Cape Town and the remainder on detachment duty in various stations around the colony.

The nine years that the Regiment remained in South Africa proved to be a very tedious period, but the men seemed well content, for many of them remained when the Regiment returned to Britain. The records are full of praise for the members of the 93rd, who served their Maker and their monarch with equal diligence, and remembered their families so far away.

'General system of discipline', said the reports, 'and arrangements thoroughly good and efficient in all its branches. Every regulation attended to strictly and all orders duly complied with ... Severe punishments in the regiment were unnecessary, and so rare was the commission of crime that twelve or fifteen months together have been known to elapse without a single court martial being assembled for the trial of any soldier of the 93rd, whose presence besides — as an emphatic compliment to their steadiness — was generally dispensed with when the troops of the garrison were commanded to witness the infliction of corporal punishment.'

The soldiers' religious observance was the subject of much comment. 'In this regiment almost every man possessed his Bible ... and of about 750 men, 500 regularly received the Sacrament, having founded their own Kirk organization, and found the pay for their own Minister.' There was a regimental library and a fund for widows and orphans. 'Their frugality enabled them and their general sense of duty inclined them, to save out of their pay, considerable sums of money for the relief of their poor relations at home, sometimes as much as £50 and for the support of the Gospel.' It should be remembered that this was the time when many families at home were facing eviction in the Highland clearances. The regimental wives and children in Cape Town were treated with the greatest of respect and very well cared for, which was not the case in many regiments at the time.

The 93rd retained for very many years this distinction as honest sons of highly respectable folk, notwithstanding a humble station in life. This reputation for discipline and particularly sobriety, was somewhat rare in the army and, as the Duke of Wellington remarked, most soldiers joined for drink and were from sections of society that formed the 'scum of the earth'.

In April 1814 93rd Highlanders embarked at Cape Town and sailed for Plymouth, where they arrived without mishap. Of course they had missed, or been spared, the fighting in the Peninsular War, but at the time there was a major campaign being mounted by British troops in America, and it was in this that 93rd Highlanders were to fight. They had scarcely set foot on shore when they were warned for foreign service again, to help speed up the conclusion of the campaign. They were inspected and found fit for service.

THE NEW ORLEANS CAMPAIGN

The war against the United States, which had started in 1812, was the result of two factors, the American ambition to absorb Britain's Canadian possessions, and the activities of the Royal Navy, chiefly in blockading the US sea coast against French shipping. Fortunately for Britain the occupation of Canada by US troops was not achieved, and the British Army's successes on US territory, including the capture of the capital Washington, showed much greater generalship than had been displayed during the War of Independence three decades earlier.

At that time the United States' only possession on the Gulf of Mexico was the Louisiana Territory, sold by Napoleon in 1803 after a long occupation by the Spanish. (Spain still owned Florida, Texas and the whole of greater Mexico; and at this time, of course, was a firm ally of the British.) London, recognizing the possibilities of opening up a new campaign, decided to send an expedition to capture New Orleans and gain control of the Mississippi.

The force of 7,500, mainly veterans from the Peninsular War under the command of Wellington's brother-in-law, Major General Sir Edward 'Ned' Pakenham, reached Jamaica in November 1814. Ned had contributed to the brilliant victory at Salamanca. News of the expedition had reached the US Army, and Major General Andrew Jackson (later to be President of the United States) marched post-haste to New Orleans to prepare a defensive position a few miles from the city, whose population was mainly anti-American Creole and an anti-American.

Landing the troops was a difficult and dangerous task. It had been decided to take them up the Mississippi to Lake Borgne, a journey of some 75 miles but which would bring them to within twelve miles of the town, and this took a number of days in freezing December weather in open boats rowed by the sailors. When the 93rd disembarked fighting had already started. General Jackson had been extremely active in the meantime, throwing up a defensive line along the old Rodriguez Canal south of New Orleans, using cotton bales and earth-filled casks to augment the 20-foot thick breastworks. By Christmas Day the British troops had all landed, and for the next two weeks the two armies consolidated their positions while exchanging artillery fire. A probing attack by the British on 28 December failed, and the attempt to breach the American fortifications with a terrific artillery bombardment also was to no avail.

Pakenham decided to attack the American position on 8 January 1815, and at 4 a.m. his troops formed up in three brigades. The Light Company of the 93rd were in the left brigade under Lieutenant Colonel Creagh of the Regiment, the remainder of the 93rd being in the centre brigade under Major General Sir John Keane. Before the action began a number of Highlanders were observed to fall 'on their knees, and in solemn prayer committed their souls and bodies to God'.

'As we neared the enemy's lines', wrote Lieutenant C.H. Gordon, 'day began to dawn, yet we waited in vain for the signal rocket ... by this time the enemy could perceive us plainly advancing, and no sooner got within 150 yards of their works than a most destructive and murderous fire was opened on one column of round, of grape, musquetry, rifle and buckshot along the whole course and length of their line in front, as well as on our left flank.'

An American observer admitted to being, 'moved to tears as I saw man after man of magnificent Highlanders mown down. They moved forward in perfect order giving three cheers as they advanced.'

Meanwhile the Light Companies had achieved some success in capturing a redoubt, but unsupported and with severe casualties, they had to withdraw. Pakenham was killed early in the battle.

It was very soon evident that the attack was doomed to failure. 'Not daunted, however, we [the 93rd] continued our advance which in one minute would have carried us into their ditch, when we received a peremptory order to halt.' Keane was killed, the commanding officer, Lieutenant Colonel Dale, fell and the next senior officer, uncertain what to do, was under the impression he was not empowered to order a withdrawal.

'The officers and men being as it were mowed down by ranks, impatient to get at the enemy at all hazzards, yet compelled for want of orders to stand still — galled as they were by this murderous fire of an invisible enemy ... who kept discharging their muskets and rifles without lifting their faces above the ramparts.'

The 93rd stood 'like statues' without orders, their discipline causing amazement among the British eye-witnesses - '...nothing could exceed the steadiness and gallantry of His Majesty's 93rd Regiment. Lt Col Dale fell gallantly leading the Sutherland Highlanders to the attack ... the loss of an excellent man, and a brave soldier.' An American observer said later that it was: 'the most surprising instance of cool determined bravery ... standing in the midst of a most destructive fire, firm and unmovable as a brick wall'.

With such catastrophic casualties to his force mounting up in front of his eyes, General Lambert, the new British Commander, had no alternative but to order a withdrawal. When it came to the grisly task of counting the cost, the 93rd had suffered some 75 per cent casualties — 116 killed, 359 wounded and 81 missing — and the total British casualties were 2,492 against the Americans' 337. There was little Lambert could do but embark the remnant of his army on the transports and move down river to rejoin the fleet. It had proved to be a disastrous expedition, and with the same bitter irony of circumstance, experienced at Toulouse by the 91st a year earlier, it was discovered that a peace treaty had been signed between the United States and Britain some weeks before, in far off Ghent.

SERVICE, 1815-1853

The service of the 93rd Highlanders during the period from 1815 until the Crimea was similar to that of most regiments, what we would now call 'low intensity operations', serving on garrison duties in overseas possessions and at home.

These tours of duty, however, were not without incident. A second battalion, raised from the Depot of the Regiment at Inverness in June 1813, quelled a rebellion of the boys of Winchester College (school motto 'Manners Makyth Man') — 'forty of the 93rd ... advanced at the double against the boys, who thereupon fled in panic'. The Battalion then embarked for a year's service in Canada. On their return to Britain and before disbandment, the battalion was used in a show of force against striking miners in Durham; they, like the Wykehamists, quickly and meekly returned to work. Before the formation of police forces, in the vast majority of instances a military presence was usually sufficient to restore order, and bloodshed was rare.

This was not the case in Ireland during the period, where the 93rd spent the years 1815 to 1823. The 93rd were divided into numerous detachments — at one time no less than twenty-four simultaneously. At Tullow in 1817 the High Constable fearing a hostile crowd, ordered his escort of Highlanders to fire into the crowd, two Irishmen being shot dead and three wounded. At other times the 93rd returned to regimental duty in Dublin, where field days were held in Phoenix Park. Whatever the duties were, service in Ireland was always demanding, and much time was spent moving from one station to another.

'On the march, the men carried all their possessions, and while with the ammunition carts, bayonets were fixed all the way, making it very fatiguing. Some got blistered feet, but I have seen a man in great pain refuse to ride, or put his pack on the cart. It was considered unmanly and unsoldierlike to do so. Soap mixed with whisky, was a favourite remedy for blistered feet.'

But the Sutherland Highlanders, and the other regiments from northern Britain, were treated with greater respect and even affection by the Irish. This was because the Highlanders could understand the Irish, and their discipline and morale compared favourably with other regiments, being usually superior. The 93rd were well reported on by the Commander-in-Chiefs including their old commander, Sir David Baird, in 1820, who reported among other matters, that there had been no corporal punishment for two years. The Sutherland men retained their natural gentility and god-fearing earnestness. Lord Combermere really meant what he said when writing to Colonel Sir Charles Gordon, who had taken over command from Colonel Creagh, that 'No regiment in the service stands in greater estimation, or has been more conspicuous for its discipline and soldier-like conduct.' There was, however, one lapse.

In 1823, just before the Regiment's departure from Ireland, the townspeople of Mullingar in County Westmeath '...so provoked the Highlanders by defiance and insults' that some fifty or sixty soldiers leaving behind their firearms, set out from their barracks armed with sticks and missiles and attacked and beat up some of the locals. General Harris the area commander investigated the matter carefully and absolved the Highlanders from any blame, considering their action 'irregular' but thoroughly justified. This exoneration was confirmed by Horse Guards, although the 93rd's almost immediate departure for the Caribbean was put about by the disaffected Irish as being a punishment for the Mullingar incident. Word of the Regiment's lapse must have spread abroad because there is an apocryphal story of a Negro who was reputed by the *Glasgow Herald* to have commented: 'King George de Fourt was in such a rage and so great hurry to punish dem for their rebellious conduct dat he send his sogers off widout de breeches'!

The Regiment spent ten years in the Caribbean, which was becoming a more healthy station than previously it had been. Furthermore the garrison duties were light because the people of the islands were relatively well-disposed towards the troops and were peaceable. The high moral standing of the Regiment inevitably began to slip. 'The cause of default', commented Colonel MaGregor, 'is invariably rum-rum-rum — and, poor fellows, they have strong temptations to it, independently of its extreme cheapness.' Also the dilution of hitherto overwhelming 'Highland purity' was showing, including the somewhat insulting arrival of a draft of twenty-five former deserters from non-Scottish regiments. When the 93rd was ordered to return for home service, however, more than a hundred men had enjoyed service in the Caribbean so much, as to volunteer to transfer to other regiments stationed there.

After a brief stay in England, when 93rd Highlanders received their new Colours at Canterbury from the Duke of Wellington, they returned to Ireland for two years.

The insurrection of French Canadians in late 1837 was one of the most dangerous colonial incidents of the period. It immediately brought about an increase of regular troops from Britain to garrison the country, and 93rd Highlanders were sent there in January 1838. The situation required similar detachment duties as had been provided by the Regiment in Ireland, but the Highlanders were kept at company strength in their various posts throughout. When major trouble threatened again in the vicinity of Montreal, the whole Regiment was assembled, but as the situation changed they were broken up again to carry out separate tasks in the depths of the Canadian winter. Settling down later in Toronto, the 93rd soon discovered that a large number of Sutherland men and women had settled there, and the Regiment got on famously with them. The Regiment also took under its wing for training the recently embodied Militia regiment from Glengarry, a fine 'clan regiment', comprised of Gaelic-speaking Highlanders whose families had moved to Canada in the 1790s from the County of Inverness. It was an altogether happy time for the Regiment and marked by a resumption of its legendary good behaviour.

It was probably this reputation of being 'goody-goodies' which led to an incident, reminiscent of that at Mullingar, when the Reserve Battalion of the Rifle Brigade insulted the 93rd; the Highlanders turned out of barracks to take on the Green Jackets in a spirited inter-regimental fight. If the Highlanders' version is to be believed the 93rd won the battle; in any case, as before, they were exonerated from blame.

The Regiment returned to Britain in 1848 and despite recruiting difficulties, 'was the most exclusively national of any of the Highland Corps, about half the men ... speaking Gaelic'. They avoided service in Ireland for a while, and with a new Queen and relative tranquillity at home, the Regiment lived through the quietest period in its first half-century, only to be broken a few years later by events overseas where hitherto no British troops had ever served.

CHAPTER 3

GARRISONING THE EMPIRE

The 91st Argyllshire Regiment, 1815–1881

ISLAND SERVICE

To resume the narrative of 91st Regiment, it is necessary to turn back to the year 1818, the year in which they buried their beloved commander, Colonel Sir William Douglas, and left France not to return there for another 96 years. The next fifty years of the Argylls' history, however, makes dull reading compared with their Peninsular campaigning, as there was little active service of any significance.

Staging briefly in Kent, the Regiment embarked for three years' service in Ireland, a tedious task indeed then as now. After much badgering of the authorities by successive colonels, the Regiment was given permission to resume the county name, with the title 'The 91st Argyllshire Regiment'. This was especially pleasing for Lieutenant Colonel Donald McNeill of Oronsay, who was the sole surviving officer of those on the original roll of 1794. Repeated requests by McNeill and his successors, John MacDonald of Dalchnosie and Robert Anderson, to re-adopt the kilt were ignored.

From Ireland, the 91st sailed to the West Indies where, although there was now no danger from attack by the French, the presence of British troops was necessary to maintain peace in the Caribbean islands: colonists from other nations — Spanish, French and Dutch — could indeed be troublesome, as well as the native inhabitants, slaves and former slaves living on the islands. While spared casualties from military action, disease was endemic: in 1822 152 soldiers of the Regiment died of yellow fever, and during the nine years of service in Jamaica 20 officers, 30 sergeants and 576 rank and file perished. Of any military action other than garrison duties there is no record, but the Argylls received good reports on their efficiency.

After a year in England (1831-2), when the Regiment spent some time on detachment duty in various towns during the anxious period of the passage of the Reform Bill, they returned to Ireland and were stationed in County Westmeath with headquarters at Mullingar, the same town where nine years earlier the Sutherland Highlanders had impressed the Irish with a *pour mémoire* of Highland pride. But there was little time for anything except military duties in the troubled land, particularly when a wider section of the population than hitherto were now enfranchised.

In 1821 Napoleon Bonaparte had died, exiled and guarded by British troops on the Atlantic island of St Helena, one of the ports of call on the sea route to India. Fifteen years later it was still considered necessary to provide a garrison of battalion strength, supported by a battery of artillery. Whether or not there was real danger of a serious attempt by fanatical Frenchmen to seize the island and the grave of their hero, remains a matter of speculation, but the 91st provided three companies for six years on

St Helena from 1836 to 1842. In 1840, however, permission was at last granted to the French nation for the repatriation of Napoleon's embalmed body, and this occasioned the most noteworthy incident of the Regiment's tour of duty.

'An officers' guard of the 91st was mounted over the tomb. The night was wet and dark, and the work was carried on by the light of numerous lanterns fixed to the trees. A strong party of workmen was employed, and very few minutes sufficed to remove the iron railings and stone slabs, which exposed a square vault filled with clay and stones ... seven feet deep. It took nearly five hours to get through this ... and it was long past daybreak when the actual sarcophagus was reached ... The Abbé Coquereault read a short service and then the detachment of the 91st carried the coffin into a tent ... There were four coffins to be removed before the body was reached, one of tin, one of lead and two of mahogany.'

The Emperor's remains were in a state of complete preservation, and were quickly re-sealed in the coffin. Later in the day the Argylls and the local Militia escorted the coffin to the landing stage — the battery firing the minute gun — where the coffin was handed over to the French authorities, headed by the Prince de Joinville. A royal salute was then fired, an honour reserved for a crowned and anointed head — a distinction, which by military action and constitutional settlement, as well as by sheer force of character, Napoleon had earned for himself during his years of supreme power.

SOUTH AFRICA

Meanwhile three companies of the 91st had been detached for duty in South Africa in 1837. Since the periods of service in the colony by 91st and 93rd Highlanders recorded above, there had been a large influx of British settlers, and unrest had broken out between them and the Boers on numerous occasions. In 1835 the Boers had set off in large numbers from Cape Colony in what was known as the 'Great Trek' and, crossing the Orange River, founded a new colony, supposedly out of reach of British jurisdiction and interference. But in eastern Cape Province the Kaffirs had caused much trouble and the third Kaffir War was fought against them in 1834-5 by British troops, supported by both British and Dutch settlers. The three Argyll companies were based in the eastern part of Cape Colony, with their headquarters under Major Burne at Grahamstown, sending detachments to guard the line of the Great Fish River from marauding Kaffirs, and at the same time restraining the settlers from attacking the Kaffirs who had stolen large numbers of livestock.

The remainder of the Battalion joined them in 1842 and in the same year the regimental depot companies, stationed in County Kildare, were ordered to form a 'Reserve Battalion'. It appears that this device was used by a parsimonious government to increase the number of service companies of a regiment quickly, without increasing the establishment of officers necessitated by a 'second battalion' as well as more flank companies, another band and a new set of Colours. Initially the Reserve Battalion was expected to work as a wing of 1st Battalion, but it quickly became a separate entity. Originally there was no lieutenant colonel to command the reserve, but this was found unworkable and in due course one was appointed for the battalion, together with a separate officer establishment to match that of the 1st Battalion.

The formation of this 540-strong battalion was achieved chiefly by transfer of individuals to the existing depot companies from other regiments serving in Ireland. The largest draft — 146 men — came from 75th Stirlingshire Regiment, and 90th Perthshire Light Infantry provided another 40 (later respectively 1st Battalion, Gordon Highlanders and 2nd Battalion, the Cameronians (Scottish Rifles)). There were nearly 100 Lancastrians and more than 160 men from other English regiments, as well as 40 drafted from the Connaught Rangers and 83rd Dublin Regiment. A change from service in Ireland and a bounty payment was sufficient inducement for volunteers. But joining the parent battalion in South Africa proved to be a near disaster.

The arrival of the Reserve Battalion at Table Bay off Cape Town in August 1842 was marked by a furious gale which developed into a 'tremendous hurricane'. The transport *Abercrombie-Robinson* broke adrift from her anchors with the Battalion still embarked and was driven aground some way from the beach. The troops and other passengers were kept below decks for their own protection, and a number of attempts to send lines ashore failed. Two surf boats had been moved overland by rescue parties and Captain Bertie Gordon of the 91st, the senior officer present, ordered the women, children and sick to be landed first; then in strict order of precedence, detachments of 27th Inniskilling Regiment and Cape Mounted Rifles followed by companies of the 91st. Reduced to only one surf boat — the other was being used to rescue men from a convict ship nearby — the disembarkation continued.

'Nearly 700 ranks', stated Captain Gordon's report, 'completed their disembarkation after a night of great peril and through raging surf, without the occurrence of a single casualty ... Although it had been deemed prudent to abandon the men's knapsacks and the officers' baggage, the Reserve Battalion of the 91st went down the side of the shattered wreck fully armed and accoutred ... ready for instant service. It would be difficult to praise sufficiently the steady discipline of that young battalion, thus early tested during seventeen hours of danger ... That discipline failed not, when the apparent hopelessness of the situation might have led to scenes of confusion ... and so perfect was their confidence, their patience and their gallantry, that although another vessel was going to pieces within a quarter of a mile of us, and a crowd of soldiers, sailors and convicts were perishing before our eyes, not a murmur arose from their ranks. Every order ... was obeyed ... with the exactness of the parade-ground.'

This presaged the more famous shipwreck of the *Birkenhead* in 1852, in which the Regiment was also to suffer.

Despite their steadiness during the shipwreck the Battalion, under a new and unpopular martinet of a commander, Lieutenant Colonel Lindsay (formerly of 78th Highlanders, Ross-shire Buffs), did not at first behave creditably as was expected of the 91st, and there were a number of desertions very soon after the Battalion landed. For a new battalion this was a serious matter, particularly as the majority of members had come from other regiments for perhaps not the best of reasons. Captain Bertie Gordon and a mounted patrol set off to round them all up, which fortunately was achieved rapidly.

From 1842 to 1846 operations were conducted by companies of both battalions in the eastern Cape, sometimes against the natives and at other times against the turbulent Boers, who were causing trouble with both British settlers and the Kaffirs. In 1844 a field force which included members of the 91st Highlanders and 7th Dragoon

Guards crossed the Orange River and surprised a large band of Boers who had been harassing the Griqua tribe.

Both battalions were then involved in the fourth Kaffir War — the War of the Axe — which lasted for two years: it had been sparked off by the arrest of a Kaffir for stealing an axe, which resulted in an armed attack on the soldiers. The two major attacks were then launched at a large convoy of wagons near Trumpeter's Drift and Fort Peddie, where companies of 1st Battalion were stationed. At Fort Peddie, 8,000 Kaffirs were kept at bay by artillery fire, as an attack against them would have been suicidal. Bush warfare continued and the 91st sent companies to join two attempts to penetrate the formidable Amatola mountains, a depressing, fatiguing and, as it turned out, futile occupation. Compared with the light-footed and elusive Kaffirs, the soldiers were hampered in their progress by their uniforms, accoutrements and firearms, but:

'They could march from sunrise to sunset', wrote Surgeon Munro, 'and though without food and other refreshment during all that time, not a man fell out of the ranks, so great was their staying power and endurance; and they never got footsore or leg weary, for their feet were as hard as horn, and their muscles like whipcord. The only thing they appeared to dislike was a long halt during the march, for their old muscles got stiff, and would not relax again until they got quickly over a mile or two!'

But for the most part these operations had little effect on the enemy, and for 1st Battalion, 91st fighting was marked by only the occasional long-range shooting or sudden ambush to keep them on their toes — the Kaffirs melting into the countryside as swiftly as they had appeared. Munro complained of the 'terrible monotony and dreariness of such a life', but others, like Colour Sergeant Donald McKay and a private, found excitement while out foraging when they were surprised by three Kaffirs hiding in a plantation. One of them fired, 'the muzzle of the weapon almost touching the sergeant's body as he did so. McKay ... though wounded grappled with the Kaffir, and after a short struggle wrenched the gun from his hands, and clubbing it, struck his enemy a blow on the head which killed him. The other soldier made a desperate fight for life, during which he twice seized the blade of the assegai, only to have his fingers severed from his hands, in which defenceless condition the Kaffir stabbed him through the stomach and then through the heart, and [the soldier] fell dead ... McKay ... mounted and made his escape.'

McKay was obviously made of stern stuff; although a bullet had passed clean through his stomach, he made a complete recovery within two months.

The Reserve Battalion saw more action than the 1st. A force under Major Glencairn Campbell fought off a determined attack by some 2,000-3,000 Kaffirs while ascending the Amatola Flats, a plateau above the river of the same name, losing three of the 91st dead and three wounded. Shortly afterwards the baggage train was attacked and the oxen driven away, which hampered further progress. Three further days of fighting saw the force withdrawing to Block Drift, with further casualties: one of them was Private Ewell who had been captured alive, tied to a stake, then flogged and burnt to death.

The Kaffirs fortunately had few firearms and this enabled the detachments and companies to fight off further attacks. But owing to shortages of ammunition and provisions, so laboriously dragged by ox-cart from the coast, operations could only be very limited, apart from the occasional patrol. In September 1847 Macomo, a Kaffir chief, surrendered to Lieutenant Colonel Campbell, now commanding the Battalion, and asked for peace. His daughter, a considerable beauty named Amakaya, offered herself to the startled colonel to become the personal guarantor of her father's goodwill, 'she would leave her people and follow Colonel Campbell; his home would be hers; she would leave all and follow him.' Apparently Campbell would not dream of allowing her to do so, but a peace was nevertheless settled which lasted for a while. When 1st Battalion returned to England in 1848, the Reserve Battalion remained in Cape Colony.

In that same year the new Governor, Lieutenant General Sir Harry Smith (a Peninsular veteran who had married a Spanish lady under adventurous and romantic circumstances, and after whom the towns of Ladysmith and Harrismith were named), had extended British sovereignty over the Orange River settlements. This inevitably precipitated trouble from the Boers, and the Governor personally led a large force against them. A 2-company-strong detachment of the 91st distinguished itself at Boemplats in a bayonet charge, and in all marched more than 1,000 miles in less than two months across the veldt, a feat their successors were to emulate in the same country a little over half a century later.

In 1850 the eighth and most serious Kaffir War broke out and the 91st were sent to garrison Fort Hare under their new commander, Lieutenant Colonel Yarborough. In December a strong detachment led by the colonel, who claimed that all 'Kaffirland is my drill ground', set out with Major General Somerset to relieve Fort Cox and fought an action at Yellow Woods. Ten months later another detachment held off a strong attack at Waterkloof. Working alongside 74th Highlanders, they discovered that the natives were far better armed than before. In February 1852 the Reserve Battalion was again operating in the Amatola mountains with 74th Highlanders (later 2nd Battalion, Highland Light Infantry), near Waterkloof. On one occasion there was a spirited fight, described by Sergeant MacKay of the 74th:

'We had not gone far up this renowned Kloof before we were attacked in front and on both sides by immense bodies of Kaffirs. After nearly two hours hard combatting, with our savage foe, we were reluctantly compelled to retire. Down the steep incline the rushing hordes advanced ... The 91st met them gallantly pouring volley after volley at them though so little did the brave Argylls value their skins for, that although surrounded by thousands of Kaffirs, a party of this corps rushed up the hillside and captured a drive of horses — C/Sgt Laing ... was taken alive by the enemy ... I have heard he was crucified ... another man of the 91st was also taken alive and met with a barbarous death.'

Further stiff fighting continued in this area over the next few months.

The loss of the steamship *Birkenhead* in February 1852 is one of the legends of the British Army, and deserves mention here because one of the drafts on board comprised an officer, a sergeant and 60 soldiers for the Reserve Battalion of the 91st. It was almost a repetition of what had happened ten years before. Only a few miles from the spot where *Abercrombie-Robinson* had run aground, *Birkenhead* struck a reef off Simonstown, and within twenty minutes had sunk. Colonel Seton of the 74th, in command of the troops, ordered the women and children into the boats, while the men were lined up on deck as if on parade, as there was no space in the boats for all 631 on board. Even when the ship broke in two and began to sink: '...the men kept their places, though many of them were mere lads who had been in the service only a few months ... the ship broke again in two abaft the mainmast, when the hundreds who had bravely stuck to their posts were plunged with the sinking wreck into the sea. Until the vessel disappeared there was not a cry or murmur from the soldiers or sailors. Those who could swim struck out for the shore, but few ever reached it.'

Only seventeen of the 91st were saved.

After the end of the Kaffir War in 1853, the Reserve Battalion remained in the eastern Cape for a further two years, and on their departure from Fort Beaufort and Grahamstown, they received a touching address from the grateful population. Reverting to their old title of Depot Companies on their arrival in England, they ceased to be a battalion.

HOME DUTY AND INDIAN SERVICE

The 1st Battalion had quickly taken on a very different character in the period after their return to England in 1848. Many of the older soldiers retired and individuals left to join other regiments. The only remaining Argyllshire men were two Campbell officers, only one-fifth of the Regiment were Scots and the majority of those who filled the ranks of both officers and men were Irish. This, however, was no different from the position of many regiments at the time. The commanding officer, Colonel Lindsay, had allowed morale and discipline to deteriorate, and it was left to his successor, Lieutenant Colonel Glencairn Campbell, and his second-in-command, Major Bertie Gordon, to restore both efficiency and a proper character to the Regiment. This the two officers set out to do with enthusiasm. Despite their efforts to re-establish the Highland tradition by using the pipers on every occasion, a senseless order to disestablish them was given by an unsympathetic major general. Fortunately there was no mention of losing the county title; it was during this period that the army was learning to appreciate the territorial connections of the regiments. The pipers were duly reinstated when out of range of the general.

The 91st spent the years 1847 to 1853 in Ireland. This was a period of famine and terrible hardship in the country; some 800,000 people died of starvation and twice that number emigrated. The Regiment only met trouble in the last year when they were called out to avert a major outbreak in Monaghan, where 7,000 Irish assembled at the time of an election, appearing to be 'under orders'. The troops' presence was fortunately sufficient to keep the peace.

The Regiment's services were not required for the Crimean War, but from 1855 to 1857 the Argylls were sent to occupy parts of Greece, the Greeks for obvious reasons favouring the Russians rather than the Turks in that war. It was to the credit of the 91st and other British and French troops, that they got on well with their somewhat unwilling hosts and the time passed pleasantly enough. In 1858 the Regiment spent some months in the Ionian Islands which since 1814 had been a British possession before reunification with Greece; Corfu was an even more pleasant station than the mainland.

Spared the dangers and rigours of both the Crimean War and Indian Mutiny, ten years duty in India after the latter event was the lot of the Argylls. In September 1858 they were conveyed by sea to Alexandria in Egypt, and because of the Khedive's edict that British troops should not travel in uniform but as 'civilians', the sight of a battalion dressed in white duck trousers and forage caps mounted on donkeys for the journey to Suez, must have been truly comical. This was, of course, some years before the Suez Canal was built.

The Regiment landed in India and set off inland to Kamtee near Nagpur in the Central Provinces, claimed by Colonel Gordon to be 'the most barbarous, the most inaccessible and most neglected, and the most forgotten station in British India'. They were quickly involved in various forays and expeditions, hunting rebels still at large after the Mutiny.

Campbell soon left on promotion and Lieutenant Colonel Bertie Gordon succeeded him in command. This was a period of great stability for the Regiment and Gordon worked very hard to attain the highest state of efficiency possible. By and large British soldiers were happy to serve in India now that peace had been restored. Native servants were provided and, with the post-Crimea reforms to the army, life in the ranks became much more civilized. Gordon saw that much-needed improvements to the soldiers' quarters were carried out, two gymnasiums were built, a reading-room and coffee room were furnished complete with a dance floor, and the soldiers were encouraged to follow the gentle pursuit of horticulture in the gardens he set aside for them, as well as to indulge in 'manly sports and recreations'. During the hot weather the Regiment was marched out of camp before sunrise 'to high ground, where coffee was served and sports were enjoyed, so that every soldier is compelled to breath a different stratum of air once a week'. Furthermore he encouraged the education of the soldiers and instituted a system of competitive examination for promotion in the non-commissioned ranks, alongside the more traditional system of seniority by length of service. The commanding officer also brought together all the regimental documents that could be found and insisted on keeping proper records thereafter. Needless to say the Argylls soon received outstanding reports for their efficiency when the time of annual inspections came round.

Colonel Gordon also was determined to restore to the 91st its original 'nationality' and Highland dress. While on leave in 1863 he approached the Duke of Argyll, told him that the Regiment presently comprised 241 Scots, 501 English and 323 Irish, and gained the Duke's assurance that he would help to ensure that the Regiment concentrate on recruiting only Scotsmen. In 1864 the Regiment was at last redesignated the 91st Argyllshire Highlanders and this was greeted with great rejoicing. There was some confusion over the tartan to be adopted, the Duke insisting on the 'dark-green and blue tartan of the Campbells'. Colonel Gordon, not wishing the tartan to be like that of The Black Watch and Sutherland Highlanders, who wore the 'government' tartan, recommended a red stripe like that worn by the Cawdor branch of the Campbells. The Duke did not approve, the tartan being too like those of the Lamonts and Murrays of Atholl, so various authorities were consulted and a gentlemanly battle was waged — at one stage the Argylls nearly had both a red and a white stripe added.

Eventually the colours chosen were of green and blue, slightly brighter than those of The Black Watch, and with the red stripe. The complete uniform was announced in an Army Order as follows:

'Her Majesty has been graciously pleased to approve of the 91st Foot resuming the appellation of the 91st Argyllshire Highlanders, and being clothed and equipped as a non-kilted Highland corps. Tunic, as worn in all Highland regiments, trews, of the Campbell tartan. Chaco, blue cloth with diced band and black braid. Forage Cap, Kilmarnock, with diced band. The officers to wear plaids and claymores. The alteration of the dress is to take place from April 1st, 1865. The white waistcoat with sleeves, issued to Highland regiments, will not be worn by the 91st Foot.'

The Regiment had to wait a few more years before they became a kilted regiment, but it should be pointed out that trews as much as the kilt, denoted the status of Highland gentlemen in the early 18th century, and in the 1860s the 71st, 72nd, 73rd and 74th Highlanders all wore trews rather than the kilt.

Although the Regiment had by its exertion enormously improved conditions at Kamptee, when they moved to Jubbulpore in 1863 they found the barracks in even worse condition and they suffered from frequent epidemic illness while stationed there. In 1868 the Argylls left for England.

HOME SERVICE

Service at Dover and Aldershot from 1868 to 1871 was uneventful apart from domestic occurrences. New Colours were presented at a splendid ceremony at Dover by Mrs Bertie Gordon deputing for the Duke of Argyll, while the Archbishop of Canterbury consecrated them on behalf of the Almighty. Two years later the much loved Gordon gave up command of the Regiment, having served in it for half its period of existence and 'was a powerful factor in moulding the history of the regiment as well as its efficiency'.

Then, in 1871 the Duke's heir, Lord Lorne, married HRH Princess Louise, the Queen's fourth daughter. It is reputed that Her Majesty was quite relieved to gain a homegrown son-in-law, the earlier dynastic marriages not having proved particularly happy ones from a domestic point of view. Princess Louise was a lively and talented woman, and a very competent artist and sculptress. The Regiment provided a guard of honour, the band and pipers for the ceremony at Windsor, a handsome gold brooch, a replica of the officers' plaid brooch, was presented to the bride by the officers, and the soldiers subscribed towards a silver biscuit box in the shape of a regimental drum. The officers of the guard attended the luncheon party, and were entertained alternately by the pipes and drums of the 91st and the band of the Grenadier Guards. A year later the Queen 'granted the Regiment the privilege of always marching past with pipes', and:

'...the 91st Regiment, the Argyllshire Highlanders, being in future styled the 'Princess Louise's Argyllshire Highlanders' and of its being permitted to bear on its Regimental Colours the Boar's Head [the Campbell's crest] as a device, surmounted with the motto 'Ne Obliviscaris' ['Forget not'] with the Princess Louise's coronet and cipher in the three corners.'

While Lieutenant Colonel Sprot, the commanding officer, tentatively suggested that the wearing of the kilt should also be considered, the Commander-in-Chief and Secretary of State for War ruled that the extra one shilling per man could not be provided from the public purse for the restoration of the garment.

The Argylls spent the years 1874 to 1879 in Ireland, first in the North, then at the Curragh near Dublin. The chief incident in which the Regiment was called to the aid of the civil power was a protest march in Belfast in 1877. Fortunately there was little trouble on this occasion.

THE ZULU WAR

At Aldershot in early 1879 the 91st were mobilized for service in South Africa. The Zulu War had started after King Cetewayo had provoked the mounting of a punitive expedition under Lord Chelmsford to advance on the Zulu capital at Ulundi. The main part of the British force had been destroyed at Isandlhwana on 20 January, but the gallant defenders of Rorke's Drift had survived a massive attack. Then the Zulu stronghold of Eshowe was occupied by a new column under Colonel Pearson, and Colonel Evelyn Wood destroyed the main Zulu army of 24,000 men at Kambula on 29 March. It remained for Lord Chelmsford to re-form a column of two divisions and administer the *coup de grâce*.

Marching with the first division, the Argylls experienced foul weather without the benefit of tentage on their way to meet the enemy at Eshowe. They carried the minimum of baggage and 70 rounds of ammunition, with an immediate reserve of 30 rounds carried on pack mules to the rear of each company. After they had spent a night in the open at Gingindlovu, a large number of Zulus approached and made ready to attack, using their usual horn-shaped formation. The defending British troops, who had lain in a square formation during the night, made ready to fight. The Gatling and naval 9-pounder guns opened fire first as the Zulus encircled the square. The Argylls in the position farthest from the original line of Zulu advance, were then attacked for a space of twenty minutes, but their fire held the Zulus at bay until they drew off. The mounted troops then did great execution among the retreating natives.

Gingindlovu was the last major engagement of the war; Eshowe was relieved and Cetewayo was subsequently captured. Peace was quickly agreed and the 91st were ordered to return to Durban. Three companies were then sent to garrison the island of Mauritius, and one company sailed to St Helena for the same purpose. The remainder of the Regiment moved to Capetown, and the Argylls remained in detachments for many months, until after the amalgamation in 1881 with 93rd Sutherland Highlanders.

CHAPTER 4

FROM THE CRIMEA TO LUCKNOW

The 93rd Sutherland Highlanders, 1854–1881

THE CRIMEA

The 93rd Highlanders had seen little active service since the New Orleans campaign, but in mid-century they were precipitated into two major wars in quick succession.

The Crimean War, according to the criteria for mounting successful foreign wars — clear war aims, a force tailored to overcome the enemy's capabilities, effective command and control, and a well-organized logistical system in support — was an ill-organized affair indeed. Despite some military reforms, the British force that embarked to fight the Russians was closer in spirit, armaments, tactics and command to the memory of Waterloo four decades earlier, than it was to the first of the modern industrialized and mobile wars which broke out only six years later in the USA.

'What was novel', asserts Correlli Barnett about the Crimean War in his book *Britain and Her Army*, 'was not the experience of the troops or the working of the military system, but that for the first time the home public was really aware of these things and that for the first time such things had become unacceptable by the general standards of the epoch.'

As the war unfolded the nation began to take a real responsibility for the Army.

The Royal Navy was of course responsible strategically for keeping the eastern Mediterranean free of hostile warships, in support of the Straits Convention of 1841, which denied the right of Russian warships of the Black Sea Fleet to enter the Mediterranean. Tsar Nicholas I, however, out of a strong sense of Christian duty amongst other motives, had sought to promote the independence of the Turkish possessions of Bulgaria, Serbia and other Balkan provinces by placing them under the protection of Russia. Furthermore Russia claimed to be the protector of Eastern Orthodox Christians in all Turkish territory. To be fair to Russia, this is just what the French and British had demanded and achieved with regards to Greece and the Holy Places in Palestine. The new French Emperor Napoleon III disbelieved the strictly religious purpose of the Russians, and Britain saw it as a geostrategic threat to the routes to India, through the Levant and across the Suez isthmus. (The building of the Canal was begun in 1859.) The British were also watching the borders of the Russian Empire spreading ominously in the direction of India, and this more than any other aim induced the government to join the war preparations. For their part, none of the other European powers wished to see Turkish power replaced by Russian power over navigation on the Danube, or control of the Bosphorous.

Under provocation the Turks declared war on Russia in October 1853 and Omar Pasha's force defeated the advancing Russians in battle beside the Danube in Roumania. The Russian fleet of six ships of the line and three frigates, destroyed a

Turkish fleet of similar size at Sinope, the chief port on the northern coast of Turkey. This drew ships of the Royal Navy into the Black Sea, and when in March 1854 the Russians crossed the Danube into Bulgaria, the British and French declared war on Russia. In anticipation, a large expeditionary force of French and British troops had already begun embarking, and over the next few weeks arrived at Varna, the Bulgarian port just south of the Danube where it entered the Black sea.

British troops remained inactive while the Royal Navy set about bombarding Russian shore batteries. It was, however, a large army of Austrians approaching the Russians from the east that persuaded them to withdraw from Bulgaria, which they did by August. Thus the Allied war aims had actually been achieved without committing French and British troops to battle. But the impulse to pre-empt any further Russian ambitions and satisfy that expensive commodity 'military honour', led the Allies to decide on an invasion of the chief naval ports in the Crimea, the epiglottis-shaped area of Russia projecting into the Black Sea. While the utility of the campaign can be easily derided, historical facts are historical facts and for better or worse, the Ottoman Empire survived for another 60 and more years until the British and French caused its eventual demise.

The 93rd Sutherland Highlanders had been warned off for overseas service on 12 February 1854 and were rapidly made up to war establishment by drafting in soldiers from other Highland regiments. Before embarking at Plymouth they were addressed by Major General Sir Harry Smith, already known to the 91st in South Africa and also a New Orleans veteran:

'You were then as now a credit to your country ... soldiers have nothing to do with the cause of quarrels, their duty is to fight ... Go forth — fight her Battles — your strength and courage shall be a terror to your enemies — success shall follow your arms and victory your standards ... Colonel Ainslie, I wish you and these Highlanders every success.'

Captain John Ewart described his soldiers as they embarked on the steamship *Himalaya* on 27 March: '...a thousand very fine set of fellows, as splendid looking soldiers as could be found in the world, imbued with a magnificent spirit, and ready to go anywhere and do anything.' Such was proper regimental pride. Great ceremonial attended the departure of the troops and it must be admitted that the enthusiasm for this military adventure was universal among the population at home, even if there were political misgivings in government.

The 93rd numbered 34 officers, 107 non-commissioned officers, 21 drummers, 950 private soldiers; two-thirds of the rank and file were Highlanders, while almost all the remainder were from the Lowlands. A high proportion were Gaelic speaking and had no English; without doubt the Battalion had still remained more truly Highland in character than any other contemporary unit. Five pipers were added to the establishment formally that year, although they had always been retained unofficially.

Himalaya's voyage to the Mediterranean was pleasant enough compared with experience aboard some of the other sailing ships. The troops disembarked at Malta where the same festive enthusiasm greeted them, and they met up with French troops, now their allies. The 93rd then re-embarked and sailed to Gallipoli where they landed and set up local defence-works, suffering from the intense cold that their successors of 5th Battalion would face 61 years later in a similar expedition. Finally they reached camp near Varna on 15 June having called at Scutari on the way, and under Major General Sir Colin Campbell formed the Highland Brigade with the 42nd, The Black Watch and 79th Cameron Highlanders in 1st Division. The Division was commanded by HRH The Duke of Cambridge, who was to become Commander-in-Chief and doggedly hold on to that post for so many years.

The army languished in Bulgaria during the heat of the summer and suffered from much sickness; more than 400 men of the 93rd were affected, 54 dying, chiefly of cholera. It was therefore a relief when the Allied army embarked for the final leg of the journey to the Crimea.

There was no resistance to the landing, but the infantry had to wait two days for the arrival of the cavalry and artillery. On 19 September the Allied armies, comprising 27,000 British, 23,000 French and 8,000 Turkish troops, marched by divisions towards Sevastopol, twenty-seven miles to the south, with the British on the left and most exposed flank. That evening the divisions formed into line and camped just north of the River Alma. In the morning the Russians were reported to be advancing and the Army was ordered to form up ready for battle, with the Light Division in front and 1st Division behind. To the right of the Highland Brigade was the Guards Brigade.

On the morning of 20 September the Army advanced towards the Alma and in the same formation prepared for battle. Sir Colin gave instructions to his Brigade, telling them to resist orders for firing, to keep rank, and not '... go off carrying wounded men. If any soldier does such a thing his name shall be stuck up in his parish church.' The wounded were to await the bandsmen who had been given some first aid instruction. In the afternoon the leading troops of the Light Division were 'hotly engaged' and their advance was blocked by the defended earthworks in the Russian centre. The Highland Brigade moved up to a vineyard and were ordered to load and uncase the Colours — the final symbolic act before expected action. Orders were then received to pass through the Light Division and storm the enemy earthworks, defended by Russian riflemen and five field guns.

The Brigade waded through the Alma which was waist high and, led by Sir Colin, began to ascend the steep slope to the south of the river, in echelon rather than in line.

'One shell knocked over three or four of the Light Company,' reported Captain Ewart, an officer who rose to become Colonel of the Regiment. 'A Russian rifle regiment was one of these firing at us and poor Abercromby, who was a few paces to my right, was shot through the heart, one of my sergeants being about the same time shot through the body, and one of my corporals, a fine young lad, in the stomach. The whistling of the balls was something wonderful ... Had we paused we should have suffered heavy loss ... but we at last reached the summit ... we at once opened fire, the men firing by files as we advanced.'

Another observer reported that the arrival of the Highlanders 'storming over the crest ... seemed to be almost mad with warlike joy ... Its formation of course disturbed by the haste and vehemence of the onset.' Sir Colin did not, however, allow the shock action to be dissipated and kept the 93rd in formation, despite '...great difficulty in restraining them from following the enemy'.

Two Russian regiments seemed ready to charge the 93rd, but 79th Highlanders reached the top of the slope at that moment and the whole Brigade was ordered into line. The soldiers reacted with a loud cheer and the Russians began to retire, particularly when it was apparent that their own cavalry would not charge the British. A Russian general who was taken prisoner, stated that their infantry '...would not stand firm after they caught sight of the bare legs and waving plumes of the tall Highlanders emerging from the smoke'. It did not take long to clear the ridge and the Division advanced a mile and bivouacked for the night. The casualties were light — a phenomenon frequently noted when shock action is successfully used — one officer and five soldiers being killed, and three sergeants and 37 soldiers wounded.

A few words must be said about their remarkable commander. By special permission of the CinC, Sir Colin Campbell adopted the Highland feather bonnet in place of his cocked hat, a special hackle being made up for it, red for the 42nd and white for the 79th and 93rd. A brilliant fighting soldier and legend in his lifetime, Sir Colin was the son of a Glaswegian carpenter named Macliver, but when he received his commission in the 9th Foot under the sponsorship of his mother's brother, Colonel John Campbell, he assumed that name. He had a distinguished service throughout the Peninsular War, and in numerous overseas operations including China and India. He was not merely a soldiers' soldier, however, and with a strong personality and intelligence to match, he recognized the value of conserving the strength and cohesion of his troops and their best use on the battlefield, unlike some of the more aristocratic and amateur British commanders of the war.

BALACLAVA

A week later most of the British Force had taken up positions close to Sevastopol, the massive fortress town on the western coast of the Crimea, held in great strength by the Russians. The 93rd Sutherland Highlanders were sent to Kadekoi to the south of Sevastopol, guarding the landward approach to the harbour of Balaclava held by the British and the chief port for the re-supply of the Allied armies. In early October a Russian foray by cavalry, infantry and guns approached Balaclava, but withdrew. From his headquarters in the town, Sir Colin prepared the defences of the area as rapidly as possible, which proved necessary because the Russians advanced again on 25 October with 25,000 troops and 78 guns, intent on seizing the port. Lord Raglan, the CinC, had barely worked out any plans for the defence of Balaclava; his subordinates were left to make decisions on the spur of the moment throughout the battle.

Several Turkish-held redoubts on Causeway Ridge, running east to west two miles to the north of Balaclava, were quickly seized by the Russians under the eyes of the 93rd Highlanders a mile across the valley. The Highlanders were supported by a battery of guns and the two British cavalry brigades were drawn up ready to charge. To prevent unnecessary casualties from fire from the Causeway, Sir Colin Campbell, who took personal control of the regiment, ordered them to withdraw from the crest of the hill on which they were formed up, and lie down out of sight. There was then a lull while the Russians manoeuvred in the open ground between.

The main body of the Russian cavalry, unaware of the Highlanders behind the crest, began to advance at the trot towards the British cavalry; at that moment, when 400 of the Russian cavalry wheeled off to seize the hill and an artillery battery, Sir Colin Campbell ordered the 93rd to rise and advance from the dead ground.

'There is no retreat from here, men!' urged Sir Colin. 'You must die where you stand.' 'Ay, ay Sir Colin,' the Highlanders replied, 'and needs be we'll do that.' 'The silence was oppressive,' wrote William Russell, the famous war correspondent, who witnessed the battle:

'Between the cannon bursts, one could hear the champing of bits and clink of sabres in the valley below. The Russians drew breath for a moment, and then in one grand line charged towards Balaclava. The ground flew beneath their horses' feet; gathering speed at every stride, they dashed towards that thin red streak tipped with a line of steel.'

The steadiness of the troops under this threat was marvellous to watch.

Campbell had taken a calculated risk in keeping the Highlanders in line two deep, which maximized the effectiveness of their rifle fire: 'I did not think it worthwhile,' he explained afterwards, 'to form them even four deep.' Had the Russians got as close as the artist Robert Gibb depicted in his famous painting, only a Square could have saved the Highlanders. When the Russians came within range of the Minié rifles, the 93rd were ordered to give one, then another volley at 250 yards' range.

'We did not know you were lying down behind the hill', explained a Russian cavalry captain ... 'until you started from the ground and fired a volley at us ... We were unable to rein up or slacken speed ... before we received your second volley, by which almost every man and horse in our ranks was wounded.'

The accuracy of the concentrated fire had a devastating effect on the Russian cavalry whose nerve visibly evaporated and, as a body, wheeled to the left. This gave the Highlanders another opportunity for a volley into the cavalry's flank before it broke ranks and headed in disarray back towards the Causeway. It was with some difficulty that Sir Colin and Colonel William Ainslie managed to restrain the Highlanders from breaking ranks and rushing at the enemy with the bayonet.

The main body of the Russian cavalry was then subjected to the might of the British Heavy Cavalry Brigade, whose famous charge took place directly in front of the 93rd Highlanders, and which proved decisive. Balaclava was saved by these two actions, while the charge by the Light Brigade farther to the north — assuming the role of heavy cavalry in a supremely courageous but costly fashion — made little contribution to the victory.

While the main part of the Army besieged Sevastopol, the 93rd Highlanders with the rest of the Highland Brigade remained in the area guarding Balaclava from entrenched positions. In November Prince Menshikov, the Russian Commander, attempted again to break through to relieve Sevastopol, but in the furious and bloody Battle of Inkerman — a battle described by a French general as *'quel abattoir'* — the attempt was thwarted.

During the terrible Crimean winter of 1854–5, the British Army suffered severely from cold, disease and near-starvation. While some troops improved and manned the elaborate trench system, others spent much of their time carrying stores, particularly artillery shot and shell, from the port to an inland depot.

'To carry such heavy loads over a good road', wrote Surgeon William Munro, who served with the 93rd throughout the Crimea and Mutiny, 'would have been a severe labour in itself, but to flounder under them through deep tenacious mud into which at every step the men sank half-way up to the knee ... made the labour ten times more severe.'

Wet through, exhausted in body and spirit, '...they were obliged to sit or lie down ... on the damp ground within their tents and shiver from the cold until the next issue of grog'. Fuel was scarce, the salt rations almost uneatable, and the tents afforded no warmth and scant shelter from the rain and snow.

'Food, shelter and proper clothing', Munro went on, 'were all that he required to enable him to undergo any amount of labour and exposure, but these were not supplied in time to save many a life.'

Buildings were taken over for hospitals, but there was little comfort and hardly any medicines, and for too many of the soldiers the hospitals merely became places in which to die. When portable huts, hospital supplies, clothing and other comforts began to arrive towards the end of the winter, 969 cases of mainly intestinal and respiratory illness had already been treated in the regiment, but 88 died during the winter.

In late February 1855 Sir Colin Campbell intended to lead, in conjunction with the French, a large expedition in a probing attack on a Russian position at Tchorgoum. The French force, however, had been stood down because of the weather and Campbell could do nothing but withdraw, having at least given the Russians a fright. Belatedly, in 'a spirit of cordiality'! the French appeared to cover the withdrawal. In March matters improved for the Regiment. They were now living in huts and new '...coats, kilts, purses, hose and feathered bonnets arrived'. Drafts from home also arrived, chiefly Highlanders, and a fourth regiment, 71st Highland Light Infantry, joined the Highland Brigade.

Then in May 93rd Highlanders, with the remainder of the Highland Brigade, joined an Allied seaborne expedition some 16,000 strong to seize the port of Kerch. There the Russians had established a vast depot for the resupply of all their troops in the Crimean military region. Sailing past Sevastopol to deceive the Russians, the Allied sea transports then sailed back at night and headed the hundred miles eastwards towards Kerch.

There was some resistance from Russian warships and shore batteries, but the troops landed safely and advanced with little opposition towards the town. The Russians blew up the powder magazines before withdrawing and the Allies occupied the town quickly. Another depot at Yenikale, fourteen miles' distant, was seized and enormous quantities of ammunition, grain, building materials and other stores were captured. Although the Highlanders acted with their usual firm discipline, French and Turkish troops burnt down large parts of both towns. The mission achieved, the 93rd were ordered to return to Balaclava by sea in early June.

The Allied siege of Sevastopol was daily becoming more earnest during the summer of 1855. Elaborate earthworks had been thrown up close to the Russian fortifications and extensive sapping work had been carried out. Then on the night of 17/18 June there was a simultaneous attack on the two strongest points, the Malakov and the Redan, by the French and British respectively; the Highland Brigade were in reserve. The attack on the Redan failed, and over the next week 93rd Highlanders took their turn in holding some trench-works against Russian counter-attacks.

Sporadic alarms and sorties persisted during the months of July and August, during which time the Highland Division was formed, with Sir Colin Campbell succeeding to a proper Major General's command. Major Ewart took temporary command of the Regiment in the absence of Lieutenant Colonel Ainslie, and worked hard to improve the Regiment's camp, furnishing a reading-room and canteen 'in which beer, porter, cheese, butter, eggs, figs, biscuits, jam, pipes and tobacco were sold; a welcome contrast to the winter privations'.

In early September another attempt to capture Sevastopol was launched. The French attack on the Malakov was entirely successful, as they had sapped to within twenty-five yards of the walls and rushed in at the given signal. No such elaborate preparations had been made for the British attack on the Redan, which was a sharply angled stone-built fortification, and the majority of the troops in the assault force were newly arrived. Although many of them successfully crossed the 500 yards of open ground under heavy fire and reached trench works within 25 yards of the Redan, they could not be induced to go any further. There were well over 2,000 British casualties and the attack again failed.

The more seasoned troops of the Highland Division were quickly placed into the forward trenches, but any further assault that day was considered too dangerous. During the night, however, Lieutenant McBean, the adjutant of the 93rd, went forward to bring in some of the wounded, and discovered a distinct absence of Russians. A composite party from the Division went forward again with McBean and discovered that the Redan had been entirely evacuated. Sir Colin Campbell thought it prudent not to occupy the Redan immediately, and this was a fortunate decision because shortly afterwards there was an enormous explosion which destroyed most of the fortress. The following morning the British and French occupied the whole of the southern part of Sevastopol, discovering that the Russians despite blowing up the fortress, had left a large number of guns behind and had scuttled their fleet in the harbour.

From then on there was little further fighting and the life of the occupation troops improved. The Highland Division was augmented and formed into two brigades with the arrival of two battalions of Royal Scots and 72nd Highlanders; 71st HLI were part of the garrison force left at Kerch:

'Thus housed,' wrote Surgeon Munro, 'and with abundant store of all things necessary to health and comfort, and with piles of books (which had been sent out to us from home) to read, and no hard work to do, we cared not for floods of rain, nor for the bitter north winds with their driving clouds of snow and sleet ... our lives were being passed in ease and even luxury, when compared with the previous year.'

The experience of brigading Highland regiments, tried in the Peninsular War, had again proved a great success and for the next 90 years there was more often than not a Highland Brigade serving either at home or abroad. One feature of massing Highlanders together was the holding of Highland Games, and at one such event in March 1855 93rd Highlanders won the reels and Highland fling, and were runners-up in the hammer and tossing the caber. They then won their Brigade rifle match, beating The Black Watch into second place.

An armistice was entered into in March 1856 and the Crimean War ended in friendly parades and exchanges between all the assembled armies, the Russian Commander reviewing the British and French Armies in a grand parade. Sir Colin Campbell held a farewell parade for his soldiers.

'Old Highland Brigade! I have now to take leave of you ... here again to see you as a body, a long farewell! I am now old and shall not be called to serve any more ... you will tell the story of your immortal advance in that victorious echelon up the Heights of Alma, and of the old Brigadier who loved you so well. Our native land will never forget the name of the Highland Brigade, and in some future war that native land will call for another, and to equal this which it can never surpass.'

But Sir Colin's words were prophetic only in part, since his greatest military service was yet to come and 93rd Highlanders were soon again under his Command. With their final embarkation for England on 13 June came the permission to carry on their Regimental Colour the battle honours 'Alma', 'Balaklava' and 'Sevastopol'.

The remainder of 1856 and first half of 1857 were spent in the south of England being brought up to strength. In March 1857 their old divisional commander, the Duke of Cambridge, presented new Colours at Dover. Although warned for service in China in early 1857, it was not until June that the Regiment finally embarked. According to the records it numbered 48 officers, seven staff officers, 61 sergeants, 29 pipers and drummers and 980 rank and file; 31 officers were Scottish, seventeen English and seven Irish, while of the men only 25 were English and 51 Irish: 450 of the Scots soldiers could only speak Gaelic: exclusive of boys, the average height was 5 feet 8 inches, chest measurement 38 inches and age a little over 25. Such detail is important in a regiment reconstituting itself after a war, and preparing for further active service.

While all battalions and regiments claim to be a 'fine body of men' every day of the week, there is little doubt that 93rd Highlanders really were extraordinarily fit men, with an especially keen regard to their duty and obedience, together with the maturity which gave them a tremendous reserve of courage and endurance during active service. Their fighting reputation was by now almost legendary, giving them as individuals and collectively that added moral courage which is the real strength of the regimental system. Their cohesion in battle — a modern concept for an old phenomenon — was of course to be severely tested again, and sooner than expected.

THE INDIAN MUTINY

In these post-imperial days, when Britain's role in the world is both ill-defined and of ambiguous significance compared with its mid 19th-century political, economic and strategic importance, it is easy to denigrate the actions of our ancestors with all the arrogance of historical hindsight. In the 1850s, the conduct of Indian affairs was much more the preserve of private enterprise than it was deliberate public policy. The 23,000 troops of the British Army were, after all, in support of the army of the Honourable East India Company, which numbered about 14,000 Europeans and some 260,000 native troops. In the area where the Mutiny was concentrated there were only two resident British battalions.

'The whole lowering sulphurous mass of unease and distrust' in the army in Bengal, Oudh and the Punjab was the cause of the mutiny. Like the fatal bullet which killed Archduke Franz Ferdinand in 1914 (he had almost been killed accidentally some years earlier during a shooting party in England), the grease for the new cartridges issued to the Army in India was incidental. Once alerted to the offence which could be taken by the sepoys, orders were quickly given that 'Indian battalions would make their own arrangements for lubricating the new cartridges with vegetable oil and beeswax': furthermore, instructions were given that the cartridges were to be broken by hand and not with the teeth. But suspicion was running so high that the sepoys believed the British were deliberately trying to destroy their religion and caste system, and they were receptive to the multitude of rumours that spread across the northern provinces of India. It was extremely difficult for the Europeans to gauge whether there were real danger to the fabric of British rule, and assess the necessity of consequences of any pre-emptive military action. What was certain later was that there was no central plot to the Mutiny, little co-ordination between mutinous regiments and groups, and only local leaders: the revival of the Mogul dynasty could scarcely have been on the agenda of the mutineers as has been sometimes suggested, and there was no political agenda at all. The British, however, paid dearly for complacency and mistakes with eighteen months of hard fighting.

The serious wave of rumours had started in Dum Dum in January 1857. In March an infantry battalion was disbanded peaceably in Barrackpur, and 7th Irregular Cavalry and another battalion in early May. On 10 May the troops at Meerut mutinied and murdered the few British officers and civilians they could find. By nightfall on the following day violence had spread to Delhi and the city was soon in the hands of the mutineers, together with large quantities of ammunition. In May and June dozens of military stations were seized, but in the main the mutineers remained in their separate localities. The complexity of the situation was such as to make it very difficult for the few British troops to be used systematically and to best effect, and there was considerable confusion.

At Lucknow the Mutiny had at first been contained, but soon, the situation becoming more threatening, Europeans there were forced to barricade themselves in the Residency, the official seat of the chief political officer of the Company. In July at Cawnpore on the River Ganges, 40 miles away, all the European men, women and children were massacred without warning in a particularly gruesome manner. General Havelock rushed with a relief force to the town but was one day too late and found no survivors. In September Delhi was recaptured after a week of intense fighting, but three attempts had to be launched before Lucknow was finally recaptured months later in March 1858.

On arrival at Simon's Bay near Cape Town on 9 August destined for China, 93rd Highlanders were told the news of the Indian Mutiny. All troops that could be spared from every overseas garrison were required immediately to reinforce the British troops in Bengal, and so it was with a renewed sense of purpose that the Regiment faced their forthcoming duties. On 20 September the SS *Mauritius* arrived at Calcutta with two-thirds of the Regiment who were met by the newly promoted Commander-in-Chief, Lieutenant General Sir Colin Campbell, and an enthusiastic crowd of expatriates on the dockside.

Despite an acute shortage of transport, guns, ammunition and general stores, it was necessary to send the Regiment into action as soon as possible. Travelling in detachments by various means, 93rd Highlanders reached Benares, Cawnpore and various other stations, 300 miles inland from Calcutta by mid October. The detachments, under Lieutenant Colonels Leith-Hay (Commanding Officer) and

Gordon, and Major the Hon Adrian Hope, concentrated at Fatepore, half-way between Cawnpore and Benares. On visiting the scene of the massacre of the Europeans at Cawnpore three months earlier and seeing for themselves evidence of the terrible atrocities inflicted on the men, women and children, the Highlanders needed little further encouragement to fight for the restoration of *pax Britannica* in the troubled sub-continent.

The first engagement for the Regiment was against some mutineers at Khaga, 24 miles away. A hundred soldiers under Captain Cornwall, joined by detachments from the Royal Navy, Royal Engineers and two other infantry regiments supported by Bengal Artillery, attacked the fortified village and cleared it of mutineers. 'The

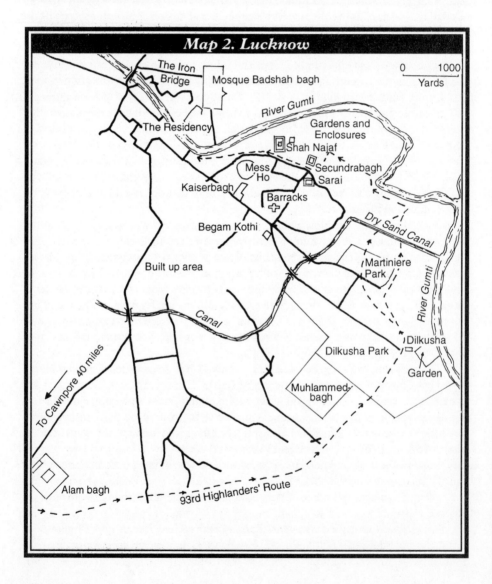

Map 2. Lucknow

accurate firing of the Highlanders', declared the force commander, 'deserves special commendation.'

With the possibility of further mutineers joining those now besieging Lucknow, the CinC decided that a relief force should be mounted as quickly as possible. The first attempt, by Sir Henry Havelock and Sir James Outram, had successfully relieved the garrison, but before they could withdraw all the European and loyal troops to safety, the mutineers had once again encircled the city.

The 93rd Highlanders were part of Brigadier General Hope-Grant's force and during the approach march two successful skirmishes were mounted by detachments under Lieutenant Colonels the Hon Adrian Hope and Ewart, both newly promoted. Then on the outskirts of Lucknow, Hope and four companies of the 93rd quickly relieved a small garrison at the outlying Alambagh palace and led them to safety. Sir Colin Campbell arrived on 11 November and it was obvious to him that the only way he could relieve the garrison was for his 4,200 troops to effect a temporary breach through the lines of the mutineers.

'Soldiers,' urged Sir Colin, addressing his troops in the somewhat pompous but nevertheless sincere tone of the times. 'We are about to advance to the relief of our countrymen and countrywomen besieged in the Residency by overwhelming numbers of rebels. It will be a duty of difficulty and danger, but I rely on you.'

His troops responded with unabashed cheering, and Campbell could hardly have failed to notice that the vast majority of the 93rd were wearing their Crimean ribbons. An incident, however, exposed the human weakness even of this fine regiment, when the following day a picquet disturbed some hornets which put a hundred Highlanders, some lancers and gunners to flight. They were stung about the head, face and hands, but fortunately not on their bare knees. Such is the tragi-comedy of war.

On 14 November Campbell's main force reached Lucknow, with the 93rd Highlanders in the 4th Infantry Brigade providing a separate rearguard of 200 under Ewart. Approaching from the south they met resistance in the Dilkusha Park and what remained of the Martinière College. British and loyal native troops now had to fight systematically through built-up areas and gardens, always a difficult task. Then, during the first evening's fighting, the 93rd attempted in a bold movement to swing westwards and cross a canal, but they were blocked by a large body of mutineers. There was sporadic fighting throughout 15 November.

The following morning the main force marched across the by now dry canal and westwards through the Secundrabagh gardens, with the purpose of storming the Secundrabagh palace. Many of the largest and most important dwellings in Lucknow were walled and capable of being defended. During the assault the 93rd Highlanders were divided into two detachments: five companies, including the grenadiers, commanded by Leith-Hay, formed up opposite the southern wall; and the other companies under Ewart, faced the eastern wall of the Secundrabagh. Guns were brought up to breach the walls and while this was in progress Leith-Hay seized the Serai (harem) enclosure and sent two companies with other troops to storm the barracks.

Then came the day's major task. For an hour and a half the two 18-pounder guns hammered the walls of the Secundrabagh and succeeded in making a small hole about three feet square in the south-eastern bastion. Sir Colin ordered a drummer to sound the 'Advance' whereupon the whole British line leaped to their feet and charged.

'It was not so much a cheer,' reported an eye-witness, 'but a concentrated yell of rage and ferocity that made the echoes ring again ... Pipe Major John McLeod with seven pipers struck up the old Highland Charge, the Haughs of Cromdell.'

Two companies of the 93rd rushed to the breach while the others headed for the gateway. One by one the Highlanders clambered through and into the room behind. Reputedly Captain Burroughs was the first to enter, but Ewart was not far behind with Lance Corporal Dunley and a 14-year-old Drummer, James Grant.

As the Highlanders debouched into the courtyard and passageways, fierce hand-to-hand fighting ensued. Burroughs led a party to seize the gateway and was only saved from a savage cut to the head with a native tulwar (sword) by his feather bonnet. There was a tremendous fight for the gates both inside and outside the walls. Ewart, having personally dispatched six mutineers, killed another two native officers and seized the Colour they were guarding.

The gates were eventually forced and the loyal 4th Punjab Rifles stormed in through the gateway and another breach in the wall nearby. The defenders, numbering some 1,800, were forced back. A terrible slaughter was meted out, but as the saying goes 'those who live by the sword must die by the sword', or in this action chiefly by the bayonet. Of the 93rd Highlanders, two officers and 20 rank and file were killed and seven officers and 68 other ranks were wounded, including the intrepid John Ewart.

But this was not the end of the day's work. A double-walled enclosure protecting a mosque known as the Shah Najaf was held in strength by the rebels, and Sir Colin Campbell, ever present on his grey horse, ordered the 93rd to prepare to assault it. Still commanded by Colonels Leith-Hay and Hope, the 93rd had re-formed under heavy rifle fire from the enemy and rushed to the walls of the Shah Najaf dragging one of the naval guns. Even at close range, the gun could not penetrate the wall to allow the troops entry, but after a while the bugles inside sounded the 'Advance' and the 'Double', which the British thought signalled an attack in the open. They accordingly prepared for this eventuality.

By now it was dark and suddenly all firing ceased. Then it was discovered that the mutineers had abandoned the Shah Najaf through a rear gate. Two more officers and thirteen other ranks were wounded in this engagement and three rank and file were killed.

Although the 93rd occupied the Shah Najaf overnight, it was discovered at daybreak that the mosque had been prepared for demolition by the enemy. Then Adjutant McBean, Sergeant Hutchinson and Drummer Ross scaled a minaret and showed the Colours to the defenders of the Residency some 400 yards away. Ross sounded the Regimental call on his bugle, and then a second time, followed by 'Cock o' the North' in defiance of orders to come down — the rebels were firing at him by that time. Those in the Residency dipped their flag three times in acknowledgement, and the pipes of the 78th Highlanders could also be heard: they had been active in the first relief and now were part of the garrison in the Residency. Later that day other parts of the town fell to the loyal troops and in the afternoon Havelock and Outram came forward from the Residency and met Sir Colin Campbell.

It was clear to all that Campbell's relief force could not for long remain in Lucknow, as ten times the number of mutineers held other parts of the town or were close by. Within the next four days a thousand sick and wounded, six hundred women and children, the Oudh royal family, treasure, money, stores and grain, together with some guns, were moved from the Residency. The relief force withdrew the way it had come at dead of night. Despite his wounds, Lieutenant Colonel Ewart commanded the companies of 93rd Highlanders acting as rearguard. Campbell asserted that the withdrawal 'was a model of discipline and exactness', and in the same order he recorded that '...the storming of the Secundrabagh and the Shah Najaf has never been surpassed in daring, and the success of it was most brilliant and complete.' He spoke with the authority of a Peninsular and Crimean veteran, and his words could hardly have been more sincere.

Six members of the Regiment were awarded the Victoria Cross: Captain Stewart for leading an attack on two enemy guns defending the Mess House; Staff Sergeant John Paton for reconnoitring the Shah Najaf and finding a breach; Lance Corporal John Dunley for being the first soldier to enter the Secundrabagh and protecting Captain Burroughs; Private David MacKay for capturing enemy Colours in the Secundrabagh; Colour Sergeant James Monro for saving Captain Welch in the Secundrabagh; Private Peter Grant for killing five rebels who were pursuing Lieutenant Colonel Ewart in the Secundrabagh; Ewart, Burroughs and Lieutenant Cooper were also recommended for but not awarded the VC.

After this second relief, General Havelock, a fine commander and one somewhat underestimated by historians, fell sick of dysentery and died. Sir James Outram, actually his senior in the Army though acting in his civilian capacity as Resident, decided to remain in the Alambagh at Lucknow with a garrison of 4,000 troops.

It was impossible for Campbell to defeat all the mutineers in the locality without more troops and weeks of fighting. What troops he had were more urgently needed elsewhere. The whole column moved off towards Cawnpore forty miles away and, as they approached, it was evident that the garrison there was under attack. Campbell left the infantry to guard the slow-moving part of his column and raced with his cavalry and guns to secure the pontoon bridge over the Ganges, his only access to the city. The bridge was intact but the Gwalior mutineers, some 2,000 strong under Tantia Topi, had continued to occupy part of the city together with Nana Sahib's force. Fortunately the civilians and sick could now be sent down river. For the first few days of December, the situation in and around Cawnpore was fluid while troops arrived, reconnaissance was conducted and Campbell drew up his plan. There were several skirmishes and bombardments and both Lieutenant Colonel Ewart and Captain Cornwall were wounded, Ewart losing his arm on this occasion.

It was finally decided to take on the rebel army in the open ground south of Cawnpore, and Campbell determined on a feint against the centre and right of the enemy, while attacking in the greatest strength possible against the left, which included the Gwalior contingent's camp. Sir Colin rode into battle at the head of the 93rd Highlanders, with companies of 42nd Royal Highlanders behind. Under heavy artillery fire the attack went in, the Highlanders leading in double column of sections and then in line, and drove the enemy, who had not drawn up in formation, around the eastern part of the city and across its southern face. Firing grapeshot, the enemy artillery caused a number of British casualties, and the Highlanders had to help drag up some guns to return the fire before the enemy camp could be finally overrun. This was achieved at the double by Nos 7 and 8 Companies, but except for a few wounded mutineers, they found the camp deserted.

In the afternoon the same companies were sent out in pursuit and they brought in more guns, ammunition, livestock and stores to augment those found in and around Cawnpore, all of which were of great use to the British and loyal troops. The remainder of the 93rd were used to sweep northwards to the west of the city and, although a detachment under General Mansfield could probably have cut off the mutineers fleeing from the city to the west, it was decided rightly or wrongly to shield the British troops against further casualties now that both groups of mutineers had been broken and were in flight. Several more men of the 93rd had been killed and wounded in this part of the battle. The capture of Cawnpore was the turning-point of the Mutiny. Forces commanded by the two best leaders of the mutineers had been decisively beaten, and with the arrival of more British troops it was now possible to defeat the mutineers in detail.

Two days after the battle, and disappointed at having been restrained by General Mansfield, the 93rd Highlanders with the bulk of their brigade were allowed to pursue the mutineers heading west towards a ferry site at Serai Ghat on the Ganges, some thirty miles away. The brigade outflanked the mutineers who, under fire, abandoned fifteen guns and scores of carts laden with stores and loot. On 1 January 1858 the brigade was in action again, this time to secure a bridge at Kala Nadi; and a few days later they broke up a rebel column of 5,000 at Shamshabad and captured eight more guns.

The Governor-General of India, Lord Canning, then issued instructions that Lucknow should be finally captured from the rebels, and the CinC assembled an army of sufficient size to achieve this mission. During January and February 1858 20,000 troops (fifteen British and two native battalions) and 54 guns were concentrated between Cawnpore and Lucknow. There were still more than 100,000 rebels with a hundred guns in the area of Lucknow.

On 1 March Campbell reached the Alambagh, three miles from Lucknow, and a day later he seized the Dilkusha palace for the second time. A bridge was thrown across the River Gumti and despite some rebel artillery fire and skirmishes, Lucknow was encircled during the next few days. A further 10,000 loyal native troops arrived with another 50 guns and, to boost the morale of both the Commander and the 93rd Highlanders, Sir Colin received at that moment a letter written personally by the Duke of Cambridge announcing that he had been given the colonelcy of the regiment.

Campbell, while a brilliant tactician, has been blamed for the length of time it took to capture Lucknow; but it was a vastly complicated mission. The mutineers had taken every opportunity to fortify many of the buildings and enclosures, and there were three miles of defences all around. Once inside the first line, breaching the second and third became easier.

The Maritinière College was captured on 9 March and on the 11th the Secundrabagh and Shah Najaf fell. The Queen's Palace, the Begum Kothi, was the next objective and, after thirty-six hours of artillery bombardment, the 93rd Highlanders were ordered to take it, two breaches having been made in the walls by

Sikh Sappers supported by native troops. The left wing with Lieutenant Colonel Gordon in command, comprised the Light and Nos 5, 6 and 8 Companies, and the right wing under Lieutenant Colonel Leith-Hay, the Grenadiers and the other companies — less No 7 which had been specially ordered to act a guard of honour to Jung Bahadur, the Nepalese commander, who had arrived with a further 15,000 troops. This dignitary having seen the regiment on parade in 1850, had offered to buy it on the spot.

At 4 p.m. the attack started to the sound of the pipes. Crossing an unexpected ditch, the Highlanders rushed through the breaches and, in hand-to-hand combat, set about those mutineers that had not fled. On the right, the Grenadier Company almost captured the Begum herself and cut off the retreat of eighty women of the harem. The gate was soon captured and flung open. On the left the Highlanders entered the gardens and swiftly cut off the escape of many of the mutineers; those that emerged through a prepared bolt-hole met the rifle fire of members of Nos 5 and 6 Companies who had doubled round the left side of the Begum Kothi. Some 900 rebels were trapped and killed in the fighting in the palace, and the action was completed by 6 p.m. Adjutant McBean had personally cut down eleven rebels and was awarded the VC 'for distinguished personal bravery'.

Campbell, at that moment meeting his distinguished Nepalese guest and hearing of the success of his Regiment said, 'I knew they would do it.' The protection of the captured women of the harem was then entrusted to the 93rd, as being the most reliable of all the troops for such a delicate task. But the Regiment played no part in the final actions in the city, the capture of the Kaisarbagh Palace which was unfortunately the scene of unnecessary slaughter, looting and wanton destruction. In the battle two of the Regiment's officers and thirteen soldiers had been killed and three officers and 63 soldiers were wounded or missing.

A week later, brigaded with 42nd and 79th Highlanders in a new Highland Brigade, the Regiment set off to the region of Rohilkand in pursuit of rebels. A somewhat futile engagement was fought at Rooyah on 15 March, when the enemy decamped in a sandstorm and the Brigade commander, the Hon Adrian Hope, was killed. The 93rd were particularly sad about the death of 'their' brigadier, who had fought with the Battalion as Major and then Lieutenant Colonel earlier in the campaign.

Continuing the march:

'We were oppressed by the intolerable heat,' wrote Surgeon Munro, 'scorched by the blazing sun ... wearied and exhausted by the want of rest and sleep, and disheartened by the daily loss of comrades who fell victim to heat apoplexy. The bronzed lines of health had faded from our faces ... The elasticity of step with which we had moved ... had changed to a weary, listless walk ... There was no jest or laughter in the ranks.'

At the end of April the force rejoined Sir Colin Campbell for the march on Bareilly, held by Khan Bahadur Khan with 20,000 troops and thirty guns. It looked as if there was to be a hard set piece battle to be fought over ground crossed by a steep-sided stream. At the start the enemy cavalry were forward of the stream, but under artillery fire they quickly withdrew. Then the regiments of the Highland Brigade advanced steadily, and the mutineers fell back under the weight of fire. There was some hand-to-hand fighting but the battleground was quickly cleared, the city entered and the cavalry set off in pursuit of escaping mutineers.

The 93rd Highlanders remained in Bareilly until October when they were engaged in hunting down mutinous gangs, the chief operation being the seizing of the fort at Mitauli. In early 1859, after the transfer of power from the Honourable East India Company to the Crown, the 93rd marched 400 miles to Sabatha near Simla in the foothills of the Himalayas as garrison troops.

1859-1881

The years following the Mutiny were noted for domestic matters for the 93rd Highlanders. Their Colonel, now Field Marshal Lord Clyde, took leave of his adopted regiment. Lieutenant Colonel Leith-Hay handed over command and Ewart left for the 78th Highlanders. In 1861 the county title was formally restored, although they had always been known as the Sutherland Highlanders, and the battle honour 'Lucknow' was granted in 1863, to be worn on the Colours with the 'Cape of Good Hope' and three Crimean battles.

The Regiment remained in India until 1871, serving in various stations, but there was little active service. After their exertions from 1854 to 1858 they deserved a rest — more than 700 of those serving in the Lucknow campaign wore the Crimean medal. But in 1862, while serving in the Peshawar valley on the north-west frontier with Afghanistan, they were ravaged by cholera, which carried off 93 men and weakened many more. At the end of that year they moved to Sialkot, 50 miles from Lahore, in the Punjab.

'Sialkot is situated 1,129 feet above sea level in the middle of an open plain', wrote Surgeon Munro, 'and there is probably no station in the plains where the climate is so equable, or so well suited to the European constitution ... Geese and wild duck of many varieties abound in the rivers and jheels and were brought in in great numbers by officers and men. Many of the soldiers were keen sportsmen, some having good double-barrelled guns of their own, and others keeping greyhounds and indulging in coursing. I always remarked that the sportsmen of the regiment were the most sober and healthy.'

Others, under official encouragement, became keen gardeners, and barracks all over India from this time took on a newly attractive aspect. With the soaring mountain wall of the Himalayas but a few miles off, few Highlanders could have been unmoved by the beauty of the place. Keeping the troops occupied in an endeavour to offset the habit of heavy drinking, always a problem in peacetime, taxed the time and efforts of the regimental officers; although hitherto noted for its sobriety, the Sutherland Highlanders as much as any battalion were afflicted by the scourge of heavy drinking during periods of inactivity.

In November 1863, however, there was a brief period of active duty when the Regiment was called upon to help deal with insurgents operating in the area of the Khyber Pass, 250 miles to the north-west. A force under Brigadier Sir Neville Chamberlain, which included the 71st Highland Light Infantry, had already suffered greatly in the fighting.

Right: Duncan Campbell of Lochnell, who raised the 98th, later 91st Highlanders in 1794 on behalf of John, Duke of Argyll.

Right: Colonel Sir William Douglas depicted as a major in 1804. He was a particularly successful commanding officer of the 91st during the Peninsular Campaign. Painted by Douglas Anderson, from a watercolour by Mrs Cox, the Colonel's niece. (Estate of Matthew E. Taylor)

Left: Major General William Wemyss of Wemyss served with the Sutherland Fencibles and raised the 93rd Highlanders on behalf of the young Countess of Sutherland in 1800.

Below: The landing of the Light Company of the 93rd Sutherland Highlanders at the Cape of Good Hope on 6 January 1806.

Right: Sergeant, private and officer, 93rd Sutherland Highlanders of 1810. The regiment was serving in Cape Colony at this period, as had the 91st some year earlier. (Watercolour by Richard Simkin)

Right: The Battle of New Orleans, 1814. The steadiness of the 93rd Highlanders under fire from the American troops was an example of unparalleled obedience and extreme bravery.

Right: A brilliant officer, Captain, later Major General, John Ewart who led companies and columns of the 93rd in the Crimea and during the Indian Mutiny. A photograph of 1852.

Above left: Drummer Stephen Duffus, 93rd Highlanders, photographed in 1852.

Above: Boy Laing, son of Sergeant Laing of Captain Ewart's Company of 1852.

Left: Pipe Major James Wilson, 93rd Sutherland Highlanders. Painted by D. Cunliffe in 1853.

Right: Officers of the Light, Grenadier and Battalion Companies, 93rd Sutherland Highlanders, 1853.

Below: Non-commissioned officers and bandsmen, 93rd Sutherland Highlanders, painted in a Highland setting by R. Poate in 1853. The lance corporal on the left is wearing a foul-weather cover over his feather bonnet.

Top left: Captain Bertie Gordon, later Colonel and Commanding Officer of the 91st, was not only an excellent field commander, but fought a relentless campaign over many years to restore the regiment's Highland character and uniform.

Centre left: Active service – crossing the Chumie River, Eastern Cape Colony. The 91st spent many years in garrisoning British possessions in South Africa during the 19th century. A contemporary print from a drawing by Major Ward.

Bottom left: The wreck of the troopship *Abercrombie-Robinson* in 1842. Drafts of the 91st Regiment were saved by feats of remarkable seamanship during a storm off Cape Town.

Above: 91st Argylls in South Africa. A photograph of operations against the Zulus in 1879.

Below: A group of officers at rest during the campaign in Zululand, 1879.

Above: The 91st Argylls defeat the attacks of the Zulus at Gingindlovu in 1879, which avenged the Zulu victory at Isandhlwana three months earlier. A contemporary engraving.

Below: The 93rd Highlanders at Scutari on their way to the Crimea. An early photograph by Robertson.

Above: Orlando Norie's watercolour of the 93rd's Thin Red Line at Balaklava 1854. The boldness of the battalion's extended frontage, allowing for highly effective fire from the new Minié rifles, completely broke the Russian cavalry charge from a distance.

Right: Colin Campbell, Lord Clyde. A soldier's soldier and leader by example, he became the Colonel of the 93rd after the Crimean and Mutiny battles in which he and the regiment were so closely involved.

Above: When naval gunners had breached the walls of the Secundrabagh, the 93rd Highlanders were able to approach and force an entry, November 1857.

Left: With colours uncased the 93rd Highlanders charge towards the Secundrabagh at Lucknow, November 1857. Painting by W. Skeoch Cumming.

Above left: The 93rd Highlanders storming the breach of the Secundrabagh at Lucknow in November 1857.

Above right: The 93rd Highlanders frequently faced hand-to-hand fighting in enclosed spaces during the Mutiny. The native tulwar was a formidable weapon; as was the British bayonet. From a contemporary engraving.

Below: John Ewart (without bonnet) leads the 93rd Highlanders through the breach of the Secundrabagh at Lucknow in November 1857. Watercolour by Orlando Norie.

Above left: Lieutenant and Adjutant William McBean won the VC at Lucknow in March 1858. A labourer from Inverness, he enlisted in 1835 and retired as a Major General at the end of a distinguished career in 1878.

Above right: The brilliant and brave surgeon of the 93rd Highlanders, William Munro saw action in fifteen battles with the Battalion. He was recommended for the award of the VC during the Mutiny, and retired as a Surgeon General.

Below: This engraving depicts the battle of Cawnpore in December 1857, where the 93rd Highlanders fought in open battle against the Mutineers.

Above: It stretches the imagination to guess the aim of this regimental event. 93rd Highlanders take part in the 'Sutherland Games' at Chobham Camp, Surrey, 1870s.

Below: The Pipers of the 91st at Pietermaritzburg, Natal in 1884.

Top: 93rd Highlanders carry out the drill movement of 'Independent Firing', 1890s. Such drills were adequate in defeating native warriors, but a few months of service in the Boer War taught commanders and soldiers quickly the value of fire, manoeuvre and seeking cover, tactics which preserved lives and won wars.

Above: In full-dress uniform, the Argyll and Sutherland Highlanders 'hold a road' during manoeuvres in the Home Counties, *c.* 1895.

Above: The 1st Stirlingshire Volunteers of 1872. The Rifle Volunteer movement, from which developed the Territorial Force, was a phenomenon of a new type of militarism which swept through the prosperous classes all over Britain from 1859.

Below: The Duchess of Montrose presents Colours to the Territorials at Dumbarton in 1909.

Above: The 93rd halt on the march through the Tochi valley in 1897.

Below: The 93rd were drenched during a rain storm, while on active service in the Tochi valley. Blankets and uniforms were spread out to dry in the sun. Sketch by Sergeant W. G. Stonor.

Travelling through the Sherandaia Pass, the baggage train of the 93rd was left unguarded and was attacked, many of the stores being lost. Further reinforcements arrived during December and a major attack on the rebel stronghold of Ambala was mounted. The capture and burning of the village was sufficient to convince the tribesmen — the only way they understood — of British determination to guard the frontier region, and the 93rd returned in due course to Sialkot.

Training, parades, interior economy, sport, gardening and a modicum of family life was the lot of the 93rd for the next three years. For those without wives there were of course always local women to offer comfort; regimental records, however, are coy on the subject. Then came the long march back to the Central Provinces in relatively easy stages, allowing the officers to conduct a grand shoot of deer at Agia, before reaching Jhansi. There the devoted Munro left the regiment, a greatly loved member who had been refused the award of the VC at Lucknow because 'the Cross was not given to Doctors'. He subsequently reached the rank of Surgeon General.

In 1870 the 93rd Sutherland Highlanders moved to Cawnpore and Jubbulpore, where they expected to entrain for Bombay but found that the railway was not completed! A further march to Nagpur was required and with great celebration the Regiment finally embarked on 15 February, bound for the Firth of Forth, for the final stage of their journey to join the Depot Companies at Aberdeen. There they found:

'...the railway station and the streets all the way to the barracks were crowded, every window appeared to be occupied, flags were flying and garlands stretched across the street. Slowly and with difficulty progress was made through the dense mass of people, cheering all the way and welcoming the return of the 93rd.'

While stationed at home the Sutherland Highlanders spent a pleasant enough time, strengthening their ties with their native land, devoting energy to creating a regimental infrastructure, receiving new Colours, enhancing the stock of regimental silver and other property, and facing the organizational changes of the Army. In 1872 the establishment was reduced to 33 officers, 49 sergeants, 40 corporals, eighteen drummers, five pipers and 480 private soldiers. Service followed at Aldershot, the Curragh near Dublin and then Gibraltar. The original son of the regiment, William McBean, VC, who served in command for five years until retiring in 1878, was granted the honorary rank of Major General. He had started life as a labourer from Inverness, and by sheer ability had risen all the way through the ranks of his regiment. It was in 1881 while the 93rd were in Gibraltar, that they learnt of their amalgamation with the 91st Argyllshire Highlanders.

CHAPTER 5

THE ARGYLL AND SUTHERLAND HIGHLANDERS, 1881–1914

AMALGAMATION AND DOMESTIC MATTERS 1881-1899

The suffering of the Army in the Crimea and the shock of the Indian Mutiny increased the growth of public awareness of the need of reform. The experience of the American civil war and the campaigns in central Europe also signalled to our island nation that warfare was rapidly changing in industrializing countries, both in terms of the increased fire power of weapons and the accelerating mobility of troops. Two decades of major improvements and modernization followed.

The British Army, however, was constituted for home defence, garrisoning the Empire and acting in aid of the civil power in Ireland. It was small compared with the armies of other European nations and did not attract expenditure on the scale of the Royal Navy, always the first line of defence of both Britain and the imperial possessions. The Army was designed for only limited war outside Europe and against inferior troops, be they tribesmen, local forces or troublesome colonial expatriates. The greatest danger was perceived as the overland expansion of the Russian Empire, which is why a large native Army was maintained in India, albeit stiffened by British Regiments.

The spirit that was professionalizing both traditional and new occupations in Britain, however, was also reaching the armed forces and the proprietorial nature of the regimental system was changing for the better.

There was a marked reduction in the numbers of officers on half pay or on indefinite leave, serving only when it suited them. The tradition of officers transferring to other regiments as opportunities arose for advancement was dying out. From the time of the abolition of the purchase of commissions in 1871, officers became more and more individually identified with 'their' regiment, in which they served for most of their service. More than ever they were joining a profession, the profession of regimental soldiering. Loyalty to the regiment became more important than loyalty to almost anything, including the Army as a whole. Through the regiment the officers and men expressed their duty to the monarch and the constitution with almost religious fervour. As such, the regimental system's heyday lasted from this period until the Second World War, although there were drastic modifications in both 1914 and 1939.

Army reform was chiefly the work of Edward Cardwell and Hugh Childers, successive Secretaries of State for War, and their tireless efforts brought the Army to a state of efficiency which served Britain's purposes well until the end of the century. The reforms were carried out in stages. In 1870 the War Office Act and Orders in Council brought the Army under the administrative control of the Secretary of State, reducing the power of the Commander-in-Chief. As early as 1856 a Royal

Commission had found that purchase of commissions was unprofessional and grossly inefficient, and Cardwell decided that it stood in the way of his other reforms and should be ended. Eventually the Queen was prevailed upon to sign a royal warrant abolishing it, thus avoiding Parliament where the Lords had already thrown out a bill.

The pace of building of depots and barracks also accelerated, a great improvement on the tented or wooden-hutted camps and the practice of billeting troops on the inhabitants of towns and villages. The Enlistment Act of 1870, which fixed the engagement of private soldiers at six years with the Colours and six with the Reserve, was a great improvement to the terms of service, while the provision of welfare services for the troops dramatically improved during this period.

The structure of the Army was then scrutinized by the Localization Committee, which in due course established the Brigade District and Depot system. Single-battalion regiments were linked in pairs, depots were established to administer up to four regular battalions (of which one was invariably stationed overseas) together with Militia regiments, and the initial training, drafting and administration of reserves became the responsibility of the depot commander (a lieutenant colonel) and his staff. The 91st Highlanders were thus 'linked' with another non-kilted regiment, the 72nd Highlanders (later 1st Battalion, The Seaforth Highlanders), under No 58 Brigade District Depot at Stirling, while 93rd Highlanders were linked with 92nd Highlanders (later 2nd Battalion, Gordon Highlanders), their Brigade District Depot being No 56 at Aberdeen. Although many infantry regiments already had local territorial roots, this system defined the recruiting areas: hitherto the Highland regiments once raised, had recruited anywhere in Scotland.

The reason for the amalgamation of the 91st with the 93rd Highlanders in 1881 is somewhat mysterious. The official regimental histories are silent on the matter, but one regiment was less averse to the amalgamation than the other: the 91st were very keen to adopt full Highland dress again and like a number of other regiments — the 72nd, 73rd and 75th — became kilted on amalgamation with already kilted regiments. In this way they all seized the opportunity and unequivocally re-joined the 'Highland Establishment' of the Army.

Another clue to the feelings of the two regiments about amalgamation was that initially the Regiment was called 'Princess Louise's Sutherland and Argyll Highlanders', but the less cumbersome and more strictly precedential county order was reversed in 1882. The Headquarters of the 'Regimental District' and Depot was in Stirling Castle, arguably the finest depot for its position and associations in all the three kingdoms.

Neither of the new battalions of the Regiment lost their separate identity, as did many of the new regiments — such as 92nd Gordon Highlanders whose traditions eclipsed those of the 75th Stirlingshire Regiment, or in modern times the Royal Scots Greys which submerged the spirit of the 3rd Carabiniers. The two battalions called themselves respectively the '91st' and '93rd' until after the Second World War, and maintained separate traditions with fierce pride, even though officers and men frequently transferred between the battalions.

The new regiment adopted the 93rd set of the government tartan, which was of a lighter shade than the Black Watch version. The Regiment's facings continued to be yellow for both battalions, and HRH Princess Louise herself designed the new badge, which remains to this day the Campbell boar's head device and the wild cat of the clan Sutherland, joined together by the Princess's own cipher. The regimental mottoes were confirmed as '*Sans Peur*' ('Without Fear') and '*Ne Obliviscaris*'('Forget Not').

The Cardwell and Childers reorganizations thus tied down 'regimental areas' on the Prussian system, which also helped in the calling up of reservists and enabled a local infrastructure to develop. The greatest change for 2nd Battalion, therefore, was the fact that all regimental recruiting was conducted within the recruiting area where 1st Battalion had already concentrated their efforts, namely Argyll, Dumbarton, Renfrew, Stirling and Clackmannan. This happy choice certainly was to save the Regiment from further amalgamation, such as occurred in the 1991 announcement of Defence cuts.

The reorganization of 1881, however, did not only affect the regular regiments. During the 18th and 19th centuries lords lieutenant were obliged to provide a quota of troops, usually by ballot, for the County Militia, unless an act of parliament were in force actually suspending them. (This was of course the reverse of the position for regular regiments; to this day the Army Act has to be endorsed each year to legalize the Army's continuation.) Control of the Militia remained with the lords lieutenant under the Home Office until 1871, when the War Office took over the responsibility.

In many counties the Militia predated the union of the kingdoms and Argyll was one of them. The Stirling Militia was in existence in 1639 and was embodied for active service in 1745-6. In 1799 it became part of the 5th Regiment of North British Militia (Fife), and four years later was designated the 'Stirling, Dumbarton, Clackmannan and Kinross Militia'. In the Crimean War, numerous Militia men were recruited for regular service, and the title 'Highland Borderers' was added in recognition. The Renfrew Militia was also involved in the 1745 rebellion and fought for the Hanoverian army at the battle of Falkirk, Bonnie Prince Charlie's victory in 1746. Later it became known as the 'West Lowland Fencibles' and served in Ireland during the rebellion in 1798. A year later it was incorporated into the 7th Regiment of North British Militia (Ayr and Renfrew) but re-adopted the title Renfrew Militia in 1801.

In the 1881 reforms the Militia battalions were formally brought into the regimental district organization and their names became those of the new regiments. Thus the 'Highland Borderers Light Infantry' became the '3rd Battalion Argyll and Sutherland Highlanders', and the Royal Renfrew Militia the '4th Battalion'. The depot commander at Stirling became responsible for their administration and training.

The present day Territorial Army infantry regiments trace their direct descent from the Rifle Volunteer Movement of 1859. In that year Napoleon III had defeated the Austrian army in North Italy, and there were fears that a surprise invasion of Britain was possible with the aid of steam-powered transports. In 1860 the various Rifle Volunteer Corps in Renfrew were formed into the 1st, 2nd and 3rd Administrative Battalions, Renfrew Rifle Volunteers. In the same year thirteen corps in Stirlingshire, twelve in Argyllshire, fourteen in Dumbarton, and others in Clackmannan and Kinross were also formed into administrative battalions. The speed of rationalization of the corps into manageable battalions, however, did not extend to their uniforms; they embraced a wide variety of grey, rifle-green and red jackets with trews, trousers or kilts of various tartans. In 1881 these battalions were incorporated into the Argyll and Sutherland Highlanders as the 1st (Renfrewshire), 2nd

(Renfrewshire), 3rd (Renfrewshire), 4th (Stirlingshire), 5th (Argyllshire) and 7th (Clackmannan and Kinross) Volunteer Battalions of the regiment. The 1st Dunbartonshire Volunteer Rifle Corps, although in the 91st Regimental District, remained separate and wore different cap and collar badges and belt buckles.

Thus was formed a regimental family and infrastructure which was to prove of immense practical use in times of national emergency in the future.

THE 2ND BATTALION, 1881–1914

The 2nd Battalion remained stationed in the United Kingdom for a number of years after amalgamation. The regimental records reveal a busy life of training, musketry, parades, guards of honour, sport and a host of domestic events. For instance in 1889 the Battalion won the Army football cup. Two years later they lined the route in London for the state visit of Wilhelm II, the new German Emperor and nephew of Princess Louise. He was to bring much trouble to Europe in a few years' time.

Later in the same year the 93rd embarked for northern India, where it was reported that 500 members joined the Army Temperance Association, forswearing the demon drink. They were stationed variously at Ambeyla, Dagshai, Mian Mir and Lahore. Again the records contain mainly domestic matters amongst the detail of garrison duties. In 1894 they took part in the Durbar at Lahore and in the Highland Brigade games the 93rd won '...the mile, quarter mile, 200 and 100 yards races, throwing the light hammer, and march, strathspey and reel in the piping competition'. Two years later they repeated their success at football, winning the Murree football cup, open to all regiments in northern India. Enteric fever carried off fourteen dead in 1892 and six years later, 41 died of disease, but by then they were serving in Central India, with its altogether much less hospitable climate. Exchanges of both officers and men between the two battalions was becoming more accepted, and the system was proving itself against all former prognostications.

During the years that the 93rd remained in India, there was only one period of active service. In 1897 Wazir tribesmen treacherously turned on an escort to the British Political Officer, killing and wounding a number of officers and men. An expedition was quickly mounted and the 93rd were mustered and moved by train to join the other troops. The weather on the North West Frontier was particularly hostile, with temperatures by day of 116° dropping only to 98° at night, so it was less unpleasant to march by night. Many of the soldiers suffered from heat stroke and when the heat eventually moderated, it poured with rain. The Brigade, made up of the 93rd Highlanders, three Indian battalions, a cavalry squadron, an artillery battery and a company of sappers and miners, marched along the Tochi valley, in due course reaching Datta Khel, the tribal centre. The temperature became much colder the higher they climbed into the mountains.

The expedition lasted from June 1897 to January 1898. Various patrols were sent out, their purpose being to dominate the countryside: occasionally they were shot at and naturally they returned fire vigorously. The Wazir leader, Sadda Khan, at last submitted in November at a specially arranged Durbar, at which a mountain goat was ceremoniously presented to the General, who passed it on to the 93rd. It was promptly named 'Sadda Khan' and treated equally ceremoniously.

In 1907, five years after the end of the Boer War, the Battalion sailed for South Africa and were stationed in the Orange River Colony. There they earned the praise of the GOC, General Townshend, which appears more sincere and spontaneous than many similar addresses:

'This battalion is particularly alert and quick on manoeuvre, when pitted against other corps; its marching powers are the highest I have seen for a long time, in fact I cannot remember having seen a finer battalion since the Nile expedition in 1885.'

In 1910 the 93rd returned to Scotland, first being quartered in barracks at Glasgow and then returning to the north in 1912 to garrison Fort George. While there the Battalion erected a cairn on the spot where the 93rd Highlanders first formed up in August 1800. For the Regiment it was the last notable event in a very quiet period, broken by an incident at Sarajevo a few weeks later.

1ST BATTALION — THE BOER WAR

Meanwhile the 91st had been serving in South Africa with a company on detachment at St Helena for the two years before amalgamation. Peacetime duties in and around Capetown continued until 1883 when they moved to Pietermaritzburg in Natal. A year later the Battalion was sent by detachments into Zulu territory where the natives were threatening trouble. 'The country round about', an accompanying newsman wrote, 'is simply perfect — forest, hill and stream combine their charms and leave nothing to be desired in the landscape.' But the troops '...did not live in clover ... enduring all the rigid discipline of a campaign without its excitement and possible honour'. A show of force by a column of some 3,000 British troops including the Argylls and native levies, and a symbolic submission by the rebel leaders within sight of King Cetewayo's grave (he had died a few months before, having been allowed to return from exile after the Zulu War) sufficed to bring the operation to a close.

In 1855 the 91st Highlanders left South Africa for a three-year tour of duty in Ceylon, now Sri Lanka. It passed without military incident and reports indicate that they spent a pleasant enough time on the island. All sorts of extramural activities were followed, including boating and commercial pearl-fishing: when the officers appeared to be making too much profit on the latter activity, it was forbidden by the authorities. It is recorded that their last act before sailing for Hong Kong in 1888 was to beat the Gordon Highlanders' football team by six goals to nil. Then as now Scottish regiments were 'football mad'.

Service in Hong Kong was also a pleasant experience and regimental sports flourished as never before; various officer teams took part in competitive rowing and were particularly successful. When the Duke and Duchess of Connaught visited the colony in 1890 the Battalion mounted a memorable torchlight tattoo. Parades were held for the jubilee of the colony and the visit of the Tsarevitch Nicholas, soon to succeed to the imperial throne as the last Tsar of all the Russias. On another occasion the Argylls worked hard to save life and property during a particularly devastating typhoon.

In 1892 the 91st returned to Scotland after thirteen years of foreign service. On the way home 400 men were transferred to the 93rd, having regular service still to complete before discharge — six years with the Colours usually meant six years overseas. In exchange the 93rd had left behind 228 NCOs and young recruits. The full meaning of amalgamation and the increased efficiency of the overseas battalion was now obvious.

Princess Louise met her 1st Battalion in Edinburgh on 15 October, the first time for many years, and she presented Colours with the new devices. Edinburgh remained the home of the Battalion for two years and the Centenary of the regiment was marked by three balls, respectively for the officers, the warrant and non-commissioned officers and for the men. More than 1,000 guests attended the officers' ball, led by the Duke and Duchess of Argyll, Princess Louise's parents-in-law. Two years at Aldershot followed, noted for the improvement in the state of training: royal reviews, field days, manoeuvres and competitions of all sorts kept them busy, interspersed with the continued success of football. In 1896 they returned to Scotland and in 1898 the 91st were stationed in Dublin under the command of Lieutenant Colonel Hannay, by repute a man determined to show the world that the 91st was the best battalion in the best army in the world. Then suddenly in August 1899, he received a confidential letter warning that the 91st might be required for service in South Africa.

The second Boer War was the result of deteriorating relations between the British in southern Africa and the self-governing Boer states of Transvaal and the Orange Free State, which were under the suzerainty of Great Britain according to the constitution drawn up by Britain. Constitutional changes which had been demanded for several years by the Boers were consistently refused, and an influx of British and other nationals into the Transvaal, in search of wealth in general and gold in particular, sparked off an invasion by Transvaal Boers against Natal in October 1899. After a reversal at Glencoe, the Boers laid siege to Ladysmith, Kimberley and Mafeking. Thus started a war, by at most 83,000 Boer irregulars, with only 40,000 in the field at the height of the fighting, who did not have a centralized command and control system, against a force eventually numbering 450,000 British Regulars, volunteers from Britain and the dominions, and native troops. The war was to cost the Boers some 4,000 lives, the British 22,000: at least half a million horses perished.

The 91st mobilized in late October, a fresh draft and more than 500 reservists arriving within a few days, but the Battalion was then quickly ordered to send 150 men to the Cameron Highlanders in Gibraltar. Sailing in the SS *Orcana*, the 91st numbered 29 officers and 1,078 rank and file, and arriving on 17 November at Capetown — familiar to many of the older soldiers — the Argylls entrained immediately. Their orders were to join the Highland Brigade, commanded by Major General Andrew Wauchope, the brigade being part of Lord Methuen's force in the west. Their task was to relieve Kimberley and Mafeking. Khaki jackets and kilt aprons were worn, and the officers were issued with rifles and bandoliers in place of their broadswords, which were of little use against the sharp-shooting Boers.

After stopping at various camps on the way, the 91st were given fresh orders; they were to join the 5th Brigade under Lord Methuen on the River Modder. Thus the Battalion came under fire from the Boers' guns for the first time at 6 a.m. on 28 November, as their Brigade deployed ready to move forward against Boer positions covering the railway bridge and settlements around the river. Methuen believed that there were only a small number of Boers, but it soon became obvious that there was not only quite a large force, but with good fields of fire for both rifle and field gun, the enemy could cause maximum delay to the British relief force.

The 91st were in reserve to start with, but as the Brigade advanced cautiously, so companies were called forward to fill the gaps between the companies of other battalions. Lieutenant Thorpe led a charge by 'E' Company to the river bank, but found no cover and the river proved too deep to cross. Lord Methuen then personally led a group of thirty men from 'E' and 'F' Companies along a ravine so as to be in a

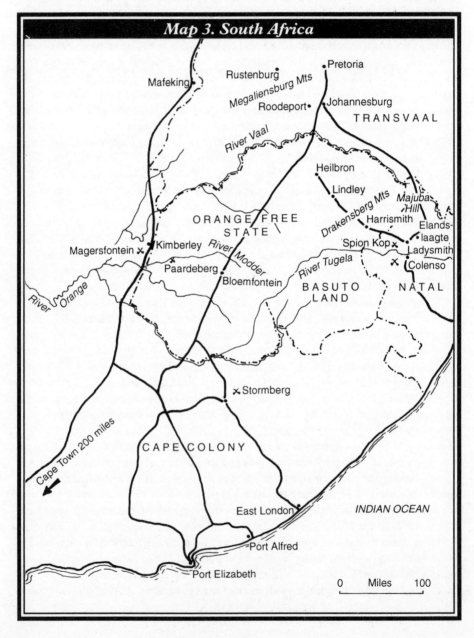

Map 3. South Africa

position to cover an attack against a farm house, mounted by the remainder of the companies together with some members of the King's Own Yorkshire Light Infantry. A company under Lieutenant Baker-Carr then reached the river and, joined by the 150 men of 'E' and 'F' Companies and other detachments, forced a crossing.

'We then made a dash for the river and formed a hand-in-hand chain across,' wrote Baker-Carr. 'The river was rather more than waist deep and a fair current. [Captain] Irvine and I were first over, and stopped at the far side to pull a few men up the bank and made for the houses. We went through these and then formed up all the men of the regiment we could collect. We then proceeded in open order along the right bank of the river through thick oak scrub and trees.'

But little progress was achieved by the battle of the River Modder.

If Lord Methuen and other British commanders had envisaged set-piece battles in this war, this 'battle' clearly required vastly different tactics from those which the Army had been used to. Every position reached by the British remained in range of the Boers' deadly fire, and even the men in reserve could find no cover. The Argylls' companies, lying in the open for much of the day, were pinned down by rifle and gun fire, the backs of their legs burnt by the scorching sun, and without food or water. By the end of the day two officers had been wounded, nineteen other ranks killed and 101 wounded, eleven of these subsequently dying of their wounds. The enemy quietly disappeared during the night, a tactic the British had to get used to, adding to the intense frustration of this war.

The Argylls camped by the River Modder, awaiting the arrival of the other battalions which were to make up the Highland Brigade, namely 1st Black Watch, 1st Highland Light Infantry and 2nd Seaforth Highlanders. Kimberley, besieged by the enemy some twenty-five miles to the north, was blocked at the half-way point by about 5,000 Boers at Magersfontein Hill.

On 10 December Methuen ordered an advance towards Magersfontein; The Black Watch were sent ahead to cover the move of the artillery, which comprised five batteries. The remainder of the Brigade took up a position two miles south of Magersfontein Hill, partially concealed, but with little chance for carrying out administrative tasks and subject to spasmodic rainfall during the day, while awaiting the orders for battle.

Perhaps those who planned the battle had in mind a repeat of the dawn attack on the Egyptians at Tel-el-Kebir in 1882, which was one of the fastest battles on record for the British Army. Another Highland Brigade had of course shared in the glory on that occasion. But for some unaccountable reason or just pure oversight, no reconnaissance of the enemy entrenchments was made at Magersfontein. Had this been carried out, Wauchope and Methuen would have soon discovered that the enemy trenches were along the foot of Magersfontein Hill, not on the slope or summit, and extended in an 'L' shape to cover the approach to the hill by enfilade fire, making a particularly effective 'killing zone'.

The Brigade was aroused at 11.30 p.m. and marched off an hour later. The Black Watch were in the lead, followed by the Seaforth and 91st Highlanders who were to file to the left of The Black Watch when the start-line was reached, forming up with two companies of each battalion in the front line. The HLI were in reserve. But the night march was chaotic: they were lashed by driving rain, there were more obstacles to overcome than had been allowed for, and the troops got mixed up in the dark. A change of orders put the Argylls to the right of The Black Watch, and the whole deployment was behind time, as well as being too far forward. The start-line ended up by being only 400 yards from the enemy.

It was still dark when the Boers opened fire and the two leading Argyll companies were caught while forming up on the start-line:

'Suddenly from the hillside in front of us', in the words of Colour Sergeant McInnes, 'a bright light flashed twice, followed by a couple of rifle shots. Immediately on the level in front of us, a concealed trench opened a terrific fire ... the flashes as though a million electric lights...'

An officer described the experience:

'The intensity of the fire seemed tremendous. I can distinctly remember standing absolutely thunder-struck at what seemed like a shower of bullets whistling past on all sides. It gave me the feeling that I could almost feel and see them...'

In the chaos there were a succession of contradictory orders, including 'Lie down!', 'Move to the right!', 'Fix bayonets and charge'. The bravest troops in the world could scarcely have stood the slaughter and there was a spontaneous withdrawal of the front line into the ranks of those behind. McInnes continues:

'I witnessed one of the bravest deeds I ever saw, for suddenly there broke forth the strain of 'The Campbells are Coming', and there was Jimmy MacKay, the corporal piper of the 91st, standing up fearlessly playing the regimental tune, facing the storm of bullets in a valiant attempt to stop the retirement becoming a rout. The pipers of various regiments broke out playing almost immediately after.'

Some of the front troops, however, had charged and penetrated an enemy position on the right, but they too had to pull back when a group of Boer horsemen raced up to relieve their friends. Thus 'A' Company remained in a forward position all day, while the rest of the Battalion, with the other Highland battalions, pulled back some 200 yards and tried to sort themselves out. The Argylls' commanding officer, Colonel Goff, had been killed and Major Wolrige-Gordon took command.

By now it was fully daylight and the artillery began to fire on the Boer positions; there was a spontaneous cheer from the hard-pressed Highland Brigade. During the day there were sporadic attempts, led by individual officers of the various regiments with mixed sections and companies, to rush the Boer positions. One such under 2nd Lieutenant Neilson succeeded in wiping out a detachment of the enemy in the angle of the 'L'-shaped defences. But for the most part the Highlanders lay in the open between 150 and 500 yards from the enemy, in the scorching sun, unable to form up or withdraw, without a resupply of food and water until the middle of the afternoon. Every individual was a target for the Boers and the casualties mounted steadily: the Highlanders had very few opportunity of firing back.

When the synergy of a number of fighting units has thus been destroyed, and otherwise brave and well-disciplined men are exposed in such a way, the restoration of order let alone the offensive is difficult to achieve. General Wauchope had been killed early in the battle. With the assistance of some cavalry and members of the Guards Brigade giving covering fire, Lieutenant Colonel Hughes-Hallett of the Seaforth Highlanders, now commanding the Brigade, eventually managed to give orders for a gradual withdrawal — much of it achieved by the Jocks crawling on their bellies.

There was little doubt that the artillery, which kept up a steady fire all day, contributed greatly to saving the Brigade from annihilation. The casualty rate varied between battalions; of the Argylls, three officers, 32 rank and file were killed or died of wounds shortly afterwards, and 77 all ranks were wounded. The feeling of failure was a terrible shock to the fierce pride of the Highlanders, and wounded deeply.

Returning to their camp by the River Modder, the Brigade spent several weeks reconstituting itself. With the defeat at Magersfontein in the west and similar disasters at Stormberg in the centre and Colenso in the east all in one week — 'Black Week' — operations came to a confused standstill. The mobilization of a large army of Regulars, Militia and Volunteers from all over the Empire was the immediate result. In due course the Battalion was joined by 1,500 reinforcements during the war: two volunteer companies joined in 1901 and the third in March 1902 while the remainder arrived in drafts made up of reservists, Militia reservists and reservists from 2nd Battalion, together with young recruits.

In February 1900 the Brigade was sent to Koodoosberg, some twenty-five miles west, under their new Brigadier Sir Hector MacDonald. They seized a drift (ford), and during the fighting to capture Koodoosberg Hill most of the 91st remained guarding the drift. The arrival of mounted troops resulted in the Boers' withdrawal, so the Brigade returned to the River Modder.

But there was no rest. Although Lord Roberts, now 68 years old, was CinC in South Africa, his newly arrived chief of staff and virtual field commander was the hyperactive captor of Khartoum, still in his forties: matters under Lord Kitchener quickly changed. Fresh troops had also started to arrive although they were of mixed quality. It was then that the Boer leaders, Cronje and De Wet, chanced their fortune by attempting to penetrate territory dominated by the British. The next battle proved to be the turning-point in the war. Four British brigades advanced and attacked 5,000 Boers at Paardeberg.

There was no magic about the success of the battle. Starting in the early hours of 18 February 1900, after an unopposed march of thirty miles to Paardeberg Drift, the Argylls' first task was to escort the guns and then to follow the south bank of the Modder. By this time the Brigade was exposed to fire from the Boers to the north of the river, but fortunately on this occasion it was possible for companies to cover one another by fire and manoeuvre. The 91st continued to move along the river line and kept up their rifle fire until the ammunition gave out. Other troops, having crossed the river, were pressing the Boer positions. They included the Mounted Infantry commanded by the Argylls' former CO, Colonel Hannay, but sadly he was killed during the battle. The attrition of the Boers' strength was working, and in due course they were surrounded. Cronje finally surrendered his force on 27 February, after bravely facing several days of artillery bombardment.

In early March the Highland Brigade advanced with their division towards Bloemfontein, capital of the Orange Free State, in the centre of the battle zone. Here the Boers were outflanked by cavalry, and on 15 March they abandoned the town to the British. There was a two-week pause during which the troops feverishly set about the task of reorganizing themselves. In the words of the divisional commander:

'As soon as the [communication] line was open, tents and stores were brought up and the ragged weary men got rest, shelter, food and band instruments ... Clothes and boots came less quickly, and, although the middle part of a Highlander is always presentable, his footgear is no more everlasting than that of other people!'

Many of the troops were smitten by bouts of enteric fever, and the respite did not last long. At the end of the month the Battalion was in action again at Bushman's Kop, and a few days later a draft of reserves arrived, with the 1st Volunteer Company from Scotland.

April saw much manoeuvring and fighting, and the Argylls were in action near Lindley between Bloemfontein and Heilbron. On 28 April another engagement was fought, at Roodepoort where the Boers counter-attacked and the Highland Brigade was hard pressed to resist the enemy. When they entered Heilbron, at the end of this phase, the 91st had marched 130 miles in eight days, five of which had seen them engaging the enemy.

While Lord Roberts continued his march on Pretoria, which surrendered on 4 May, the Argylls remained in Heilbron with the Highland Brigade. The Boers were still very active in the area, and the Highlanders spent a great deal of their time escorting the supply columns. In mid July the 91st were called to Pretoria to form a new brigade with Sir Ian Hamilton's mobile division, a more exciting task than escort duties.

For a fortnight the division marched north of Pretoria, seeking out General Botha's force. But the Boers proved more agile than Hamilton's force and contact was not made despite all their exertions. August was spent in pursuing De Wet's commando west of Pretoria: in 28 days the Argylls marched 325 miles, with only five days' rest in 43. This was followed by a further three weeks spent in chasing General Botha, again to the east of Pretoria. From now on the Boers had no firm bases and could only wage guerrilla warfare, using their long-range rifle fire and rapid movement as best they could.

From September 1900 until April 1901 the Argylls were based at Rustenburg, 50 miles west of Pretoria, with the task of guarding various passes in the Magaliesberg Mountains. The Boers' commandos were reducing in size all the time and were no longer able to take their own supply columns along with them. But they could and did attack the British ox-drawn convoys upon which the huge British force relied. In the new year the policy of clearing Boer farms and 'concentrating' the families in camps to prevent them sheltering their soldiers, involved some work for the battalion. It was an unpleasant task and one which brought opprobrium on the British in due course for inventing the concentration camp concept, although reparations were paid to the Boers at the end of hostilities.

The blockhouse system was Kitchener's chief device to restrict the Boers' free movement and hundreds of them, linked together and surrounded by wire, were built during 1901. But the Argylls were for a while spared from guarding them and instead were employed in the mobile columns, still operating to the east of Pretoria. Their job was to seek out the increasingly elusive Boers who, whenever they were encountered, put up strong resistance, and continued to attack the supply columns whenever they could. Half the Battalion operated with Colonel Beatson's Column and the remainder, under Major Woolrige-Gordon, joined Colonel Benson's column. There were some successes during the ensuing weeks; prisoners were taken and a large number of cattle confiscated. Hundreds of miles were covered, many of them by night, but it was a most exhausting business for both British and Boers.

'British leaders', according to *The Times History*, 'realized the best way of catching a commando at a disadvantage was to march to it by night and attack at dawn. The Boer detested this method ... pounced on while still in laager, he was liable to panic. Benson's force was a reliable weapon, and its Colonel a born guerrilla leader. He carried out a demoralizing system of warfare.'

Benson particularly praised the marching ability of the Argylls, since most of his column comprised mounted troops, and the Highlanders shared a remarkable adaptability to the somewhat unconventional style of fighting on the veldt.

From October 1901 to March 1902 the Battalion was split into numerous detachments to guard the blockhouses, and the time passed uneventfully. Finally during the last two months of the war some of the 91st joined General Walter Kitchener's column in the Western Transvaal. While peace negotiations were being conducted with the Boers' representatives, final drives against men still under arms were conducted, and the Argylls had the satisfaction of rounding up numerous enemy.

On the British side an overwhelming number of troops, firepower, mobility and effective restriction of their enemies' movement, finally overcame the resistance of the Boer, whose own courage and persistence could never be doubted. Their skill as soldiers had been severely underestimated in 1899 and the British learnt many valuable lessons. From a regimental angle, the records state that by the end of hostilities the 1st Argylls had marched nearly 3,500 miles and their death roll had risen to seven officers, ten senior NCOS, eleven corporals and 115 private soldiers.

The experiences of the war in South Africa led to many changes in the British Army. The realization that the Army had been ill-prepared tactically and strategically to fight against an intelligent enemy, conducting mobile operations with modern fire arms, was taken to heart. The Esher Committee was set up in London and reported in 1904 with some very helpful recommendations. The use of non-regular troops, Militia, volunteers, and reservists was acknowledged as contributing to the eventual success of the war; such categories could not be ignored in future wars on the same scale. Conscription on the European scale had strong support among some sections of society at the time, but it was even more strongly resisted. The higher command of the Army and a General Staff system of command and control for the brigade and divisional organization, was set up and in due course the rationalization of the reserve army and Territorial Force was carried out under the Scots lawyer Richard Haldane. This enabled much-needed changes in staff procedures, training and logistics to be implemented, and all these reforms stood the Army in very good stead in 1914, although the scale and duration of the war to come could scarcely have been envisaged on the evidence of the lessons learnt in South Africa.

The 1st Argylls remained in South Africa for the year after the war. The Battalion was reconstituted over the months, took part in the parade in Johannesburg to commemorate the coronation of the new King, and attended the unveiling of the Memorial to the Highland Brigade at Magersfontein. They left for the United Kingdom in 1903.

The years 1903 to 1909 were spent in Longmoor and Bordon camps, among those gloomy pine forests on the fringes of Aldershot, and then at Chatham. A fine memorial to the Regiment's dead was unveiled at Stirling and the 91st provided the Guard at Buckingham Palace in 1908, the first time a Highland Regiment had carried out this duty. A period was then spent on garrison duty in Malta before the Battalion moved to India, where it was stationed at the outbreak of the First World War.

CHAPTER 6

FRANCE AND FLANDERS, 1914–1916

BRITISH EXPEDITIONARY FORCE

The political constraints on German industrial and economic expansionism collapsed in the fateful month of August of 1914. In Britain many had foreseen it for years, but conscription had been steadfastly resisted and the British Army had remained small, compared with those on the continent. In Germany, the explosion into action was seen as both inevitable and natural, and was relished by a large section of the population. 'For a rising state', wrote General von Bernhardi (his book *The German Way of War* was published in Berlin in 1914), 'which has not yet attained the position due to it, which is in urgent need of colonial expansion, and can only accomplish it chiefly at the cost of others ... We must rely on our sword, renounce all weakly visions of peace, and eye the dangers surrounding us with resolution and unflinching courage.'

The hidden agenda was of course the German fear of democracy in general and socialism in particular, the power of which was becoming increasingly apparent, based on the socialist successes in the 1912 Reichstag elections.

War aims were only thought out vaguely by the combatants. The British instinctively wished to keep in check and, if necessary, help to destroy the Germans' military power on the high seas, lest they should start threatening British colonies. But Britain scarcely wanted a European war, and the sending of the British Expeditionary Force to Belgium was based on the doctrine that 'we must make war as we must, not as we should like' — in the words of the new Secretary of State for War, Lord Kitchener. Nobody envisaged the full duration of the war of attrition and the extent of sheer slaughter, resulting in the moral and military collapse of four protagonists before the end of hostilities.

Following the fortunes of individual regiments and their battalions during the four years of fighting on the Western Front is a very disjointed task, and it is easier to chronicle those battalions which fought in other theatres. As a regiment the Argyll and Sutherland Highlanders fought in four of the campaigns, during the course of which 91st and 93rd Regular Army battalions were joined in the field by their five Territorial battalions and four newly formed Service battalions. Other home service and training battalions of the regiment were also raised.

To base new armies on the existing regimental system was a decision made by Kitchener as soon as he had been appointed and had begun to plan the huge force that was necessary. He at least guessed that it was to be a long war. New 'Kitchener battalions' of the Regiment were raised from the recruiting area one at a time, numbered and known as 'K1', 'K2' and 'K3'. The spirit of these battalions is captured in the brilliant period-piece book *The First Hundred Thousand* and its sequel *Carrying On*: readers who have not the stomach for the following pages, might read Ian Hay's words, since they are a thinly disguised, perceptive and highly amusing account of the 10th Argylls. Most of the Regiment's battalions remained more or less intact, but the individuals in them changed many times in the four years — killed, wounded, posted to command or train others, or promoted to the Staff.

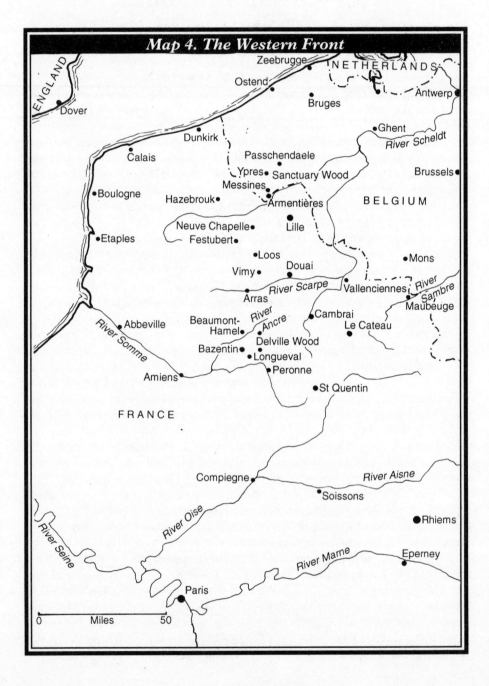

Map 4. The Western Front

The 93rd, stationed at Fort George, received their mobilization orders at 5.30 p.m. on 4 August. Contingency plans had already been made and there had been much prior activity. By calling up reserves the Battalion quickly reached its war establishment and entrained for Southampton on 9 August. Initially they were an unassigned reserve battalion, but after two weeks of mainly fatigue duties in support of the movement of supplies in France, the Battalion moved up to Valenciennes, twenty miles south-west of Mons, as part of 19 Brigade, joining 1st Middlesex, 2nd Royal Welch Fusiliers and 1st Cameronians. Their task was to safeguard the lines of communication to the forward British formations.

The German Army, however, was heavily engaging the front line of the British Expeditionary Force (initially one cavalry and six infantry divisions), which was defending some twenty-one miles of the Mons-Condé Canal on the Allies' left flank. The momentum of the German attack soon proved to be too great for the BEF which was heavily outnumbered. At midnight on 23 August the withdrawal began, but apart from one platoon, the 93rd Highlanders were not engaged during the first two days as they conformed to the withdrawal plan. This involved some rapid marching south-east to Le Câteau, while keeping a sharp lookout for German cavalry which were expected to achieve a breakthrough in one or more places at any time. It was the stand at Le Câteau that saved much of the British Army.

On 26 August 5th Division, now supported by 19 Brigade, was ordered by II Corps' commander, Lieutenant General Sir Horace Smith-Dorrien, to defend the area to the south-west of Le Câteau. Companies of the 93rd Highlanders were sent forward at various times to support other battalions or fill gaps, and they were all engaged by the enemy. Half of 'C' Company was destroyed in a forward position, but half of 'B' Company, with members of the Suffolk Regiment, bravely fought on as long as they could.

'The Suffolks and Argylls opened rapid fire to their front with terrific effect,' read the official account. 'Two officers of the Highlanders (Captains Maclean and Bruce) in particular bringing down man after man ... The Germans kept sounding the British "ceasefire" and gesticulating to persuade the men to surrender ... At length the enemy from the rear bore down all resistance ... [The British] had for nine hours been under incessant bombardment ... and they had fought to the very last'.

And a German officer described the engagement:

'I did not think it possible that flesh and blood could survive so great an onslaught. Our men attacked with the utmost determination, but again and again they were driven back by those incomparable soldiers.'

Those who were still alive were captured by the enemy. The other half-companies quickly combined with 'D' Company and slowed the German advance to the south of Le Câteau. The CO, Lieutenant Colonel Moulton-Barrett rallied 'A' and the remainder of 'D' Company together with other troops, and held a low ridge of ground to the south-west for two and a half hours.

After eleven hours of battle it was clear that the German advance had been so effectively delayed as to allow the other divisions of the BEF to make a break to the west. The accuracy of the British rifle fire had caused extremely heavy German casualties, and this led them to believe that the BEF was much larger than it actually was. But the enemy was meeting no conscript army: the 'Old Contemptibles' formed the best Army that Britain had ever put into the field and Smith-Dorrien was the architect of its salvation by the brilliant rearguard stand at Le Câteau. (He received little credit for it from his superiors and was later sacked by Sir John French.)

The 93rd had suffered grievously; some 160 were killed or wounded and 300 were missing — which included the unknown dead, dying, captured and a few still at large behind enemy lines. Because the remainder of the Battalion had not had the opportunity to re-form, the subsequent retreat from Mons was a matter of marching and surviving. They were a part of an army that was in full retreat but by no means defeated. For some unaccountable reason the German Army then wheeled south and south-eastwards, giving the Allies more time to hold the line and prepare for future engagements.

By the end of the month, and after many miles of marching and some action, 93rd Highlanders had managed to re-form, albeit as a very depleted battalion. During the Battles of the Marne and Aisne the 93rd were in reserve in their original 19 Brigade, but were called upon to man the line for a period and to help with various engineer tasks.

FIRST AND SECOND YPRES

In October the reinforced BEF moved a hundred miles to the north, where it was responsible for the left of the Allied line bordering the Channel. The 93rd took their turn in the newly constructed front on 2 October, and their first action was in support of the French a day later near Armentières. In this battle — First Ypres — most of the fighting took place farther north, where the German Fourth and Sixth Armies attacked the Ypres salient, but the area of Armentières, while not in the line of the main German thrust, was by no means unimportant. 'C' Company was decimated in the fighting at Le Maisnil and the Battalion's casualties overall were more than 200. During a German attack on the line south of Armentières on 30 October, a platoon of the 93rd cleared 'the enemy at the point of the bayonet out of a nullah (ravine), killing 56 and taking 94 wounded prisoners', but a deliberate battalion attack on the German line on 9 November was a failure, when 130 were killed, wounded or missing from the 330 whowere engaged. After a lull the Germans continued the battle with a major attack on 10/11 November, their thrust line being towards Ypres, but again it failed to penetrate the defences.

From then onwards the line was to remain static throughout the winter, with only desultory fighting and shelling. There was soon established a system by which battalions rotated from front line to rear lines, reserve lines and then to the rear areas for fatigue duties and rest. The BEF's boundaries were altered, but the 93rd remained in the area of Armentières, which was now more nearly in the centre of the sector.

Gradually during the winter the British Army was reinforced, both with individuals for battalions already in France, and with fresh battalions reaching the front. The 1st Battalion, 91st Argylls, arrived from India in December, forming part of 81 Brigade in 27th Division. Their initial spell in the trenches was in January 1915. The first of the Regiment's Territorial battalions, the 7th from Stirlingshire, also reached France in December 1914 and they too quickly joined the line. The 9th

Battalion, from Dumbarton, arrived in February 1915 and joined the 91st in 27th Division.

The first major battle of 1915, known as the Second Battle of Ypres, began on 22 April. The 2nd Battalion, 93rd, stationed some twelve miles south of the town, were not as involved as they had been at the beginning of the month. The 1st Battalion, 91st, had already taken over some French trenches on the edge of Polygon Wood, four miles east of Ypres on the right of 81 Brigade's front line, with the 9th Argylls nearby on the left of their brigade. The attack actually hit the French to the north of the Ypres

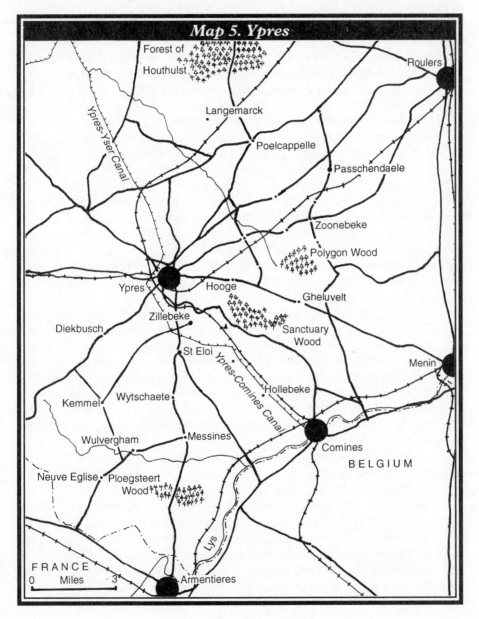

Map 5. Ypres

salient first, and they were immediately forced to withdraw. The Germans used poison gas for the first time, and although it caused only limited casualties, being dispersed by a strong wind, its psychological effect was most damaging to the Allies. Rightly or wrongly, the British themselves were to use it later in the year against the Germans, and to greater effect.

For the first few days of the battle 27th Division was not attacked, but their trenches were frequently shelled and the 2nd Argylls took a number of casualties. By early May the Germans had forced the French and Canadians to withdraw, and the British 27th and 28th Divisions of V Corps were by now holding a dangerously exposed line. On 3 April 2nd Argylls withdrew with their brigade some two miles westward to the edge of Sanctuary Wood, and patrols were left behind to deceive the enemy with activity going on throughout the night. Lieutenant Neill, commanding one patrol, reported that the enemy discovered the withdrawal by 6 a.m. on the following day, but the secrecy had allowed a clean break. Soon Sanctuary Wood was under savage enemy shellfire.

On 8 May the Germans launched a massive attack on the V Corps area. By the middle of the morning it was clear that they had penetrated the line to the north of 81 Brigade. Two companies of the 91st Highlanders were rushed to the assistance of a Canadian battalion, Princess Patricia's Canadian Light Infantry, in the area of Railway Wood. Two more companies were sent to plug a gap during a counter-attack by 80 Brigade, but then the Argylls were ordered to return to their own 81 Brigade area south of the Menin Road (the inter-brigade boundary) and occupy trenches there during the night. The following day the Argylls were again called upon to relieve 80 Brigade to the north, and during that day and night the Battalion suffered from extremely heavy shelling. The Germans had been halted, but it was reported that several of them had been seen wearing British and French uniforms including the kilt, attempting to infiltrate the British line clandestinely.

On 10 May the 9th Argylls bore the brunt of a heavy bombardment and attack while holding trenches in their 81 Brigade area, losing twelve officers, including the CO, Lieutenant Colonel Clark, and 300 men. On successive days the casualties mounted. Meanwhile the 91st, manning trenches on both sides of the Menin Road, also 'received a tremendous hammering' from the bombardment, even though they were not in the front line. There the 4th King's Royal Rifle Corps and 4th Rifle Brigade were being blasted out of their trenches. They, however, effected a partial withdrawal and the CO, Lieutenant Colonel Kirk, ordered the 1st Argylls forward to their assistance.

'Their advance across an area of a mile in depth, swept by shellfire, was magnificently carried out. Casualties were few, due to the excellent formation of each company. No time was lost and discipline was perfect. It was an inspiring sight.'

This enabled the Green Jacket battalions and the 2nd Cameron Highlanders to go firm, with the Argylls' companies in intimate support along a new front line.

On 11 May some trenches changed hands in several attacks and counter-attacks on this part of the front line, and gas was used again by the Germans, fortunately with little effect. On 12 May there was another determined attack on the front, but this was repulsed. The bombardment continued for a few more days and on 18 May the 1st

Argylls were at last relieved. They had been under continuous fire for 36 days and had sustained 488 casualties.

Farther north the 7th Argylls had been in action with 4th Division, fighting in the vicinity of St-Julien north-east of Ypres. Later in the battle they were ordered south to the area in front of Armentières, and during an attack on Ploegsteert they suffered 500 casualties.

The 9th Argylls also remained in the same sector for several more days. On 24 May a German gas attack caused disastrously high casualties when the Battalion moved forward to relieve 2nd Royal Dublin Fusiliers. Later in the day the 9th were finally withdrawn, but only two officers and 85 men remained fit. The 7th and 9th Battalions were then ordered to amalgamate under the title 'Composite Battalion' of the Regiment. Some reinforcements were forthcoming over the months, and while 7th Argylls in due course were reconstituted and joined 154 Brigade in 51st Highland Division, 9th Battalion became a base holding battalion.

Second Ypres had been a severe test for the British troops, but the German offensive had been effectively halted at last. It would be several months before they launched another attack on such a scale in the British sector.

LOOS 1915 — SUMMER 1916

After the battle the 91st moved to the Armentières area where the 93rd had remained relatively unscathed. At the end of May the 91st and 93rd found themselves manning adjacent sectors of the line, and this was the first time that they had ever met and served together.

Also in May 1915 two more Territorial battalions arrived in France as part of 51st Highland Division, the 6th from Renfrew and 8th from Argyllshire. They were soon involved in the Battle of Festubert. Although alternating between reserve and front-line trenches in a defensive role, 8th Battalion lost eight killed and 53 wounded. Three of the new 'Kitchener' battalions followed during the summer, 10th, 11th and 12th, respectively in 9th Scottish Division, 15th Scottish Division and 26th Division.

The newly arrived battalions had a gentle initiation. Typical comments in the records read:

'... proceeded to take over the line [10th Argylls] ... The enemy mortared us rather severely, when Lieutenant Ewart and several men were buried but were dug out.'

And:

'It was Maj Jim Brown of Campbeltown [8th Argylls] the Medical Officer, who was awarded the first DSO in the battalion, for his gallantry in attending to and bringing out a mortally wounded man when battalion HQ was heavily shelled.'

Then, for the older battalions:

'On 6 June a draft of 150 men arrived, [91st] and on the 11 June the officers of the 1st Battalion lunched with the officers of the 2nd Battalion, after which a photograph was taken of the Regular officers of both battalions.'

And:

'Captain Irvine was killed, Captain and Adjutant J. Kennedy and Captain H. J. D. Clark [later to command the 91st] severely wounded, other ranks killed 5 and 3 wounded by shell fire on billets on 8 July.'[93rd]

There was never any guarantee of safety from ubiquitous artillery fire — which caused two out of every three casualties during the war. In August 10th Battalion were off duty:

'Béthune was a delightful place, plenty of amusement and the Shell Cafe and Hotel in the Square were often frequented for dinners and the 2nd Divisional concert party shows every night in the theatre.'

On another level of entertainment, it would be fairer to draw a veil over the proclivities of individuals. Armentières was after all a French town, and the British soldier was nothing if not human.

Later;

'Two unarmed lance corporals of the 93rd went out on the 8th August to bury a dead body, and seeing two unarmed Germans, attacked them, and after a stiff fight brought in one as a prisoner.'

It was not recorded whether Queensberry Rules were adhered to. Then:

'On 16th the GOC III Corps carried out a detailed inspection of the Battalion and expressed himself as very satisfied at the fine turn out and bearing of the men.'

The General had said as much to another battalion of the regiment a month earlier, and no doubt to many more battalions. Such are the rituals of military life.

In September the 91st left the French/Belgian border area, 27th Division being redeployed to the Somme, some fifty miles south. The remainder of their tour of duty in France was uneventful, and in November 1915 they entrained for Marseilles to embark for Salonika and the Bulgarian front.

By the autumn of 1915 there were thirty-seven British and Dominion divisions in France. On 21 September a massive British bombardment began against the German front at Loos, some thirty miles south of Ypres, coinciding with two French offensives, the northern one being at Lens, contiguous with the Loos sector. Six British divisions (three Regular, one Territorial and two New Army) were involved in the attack on 25 September, a force inadequate for the task and hampered by bad staff work, ill-organized troop movements and ammunition replenishment, and a lack of reserves. Gas was used by the British during the battle.

The 93rd were on the left flank of the attack and were caught by the lingering gas which had not blown across the German trenches as planned.

'The ground was flat, except for mine craters thirty or forty foot deep, with sides eight or nine feet high, screening from view and fire the heavily fortified German trenches eighty yards distant ... A Company lost all its officers as soon as it moved, and as our machine-guns had been brigaded so as to fire well behind the German line, the attack was a hopeless failure for lack of support. Only eleven men of the two leading platoons succeeded in getting back ... many officers and men .... had to remain between the trench lines, until they could crawl back in the evening.'

In the one day of battle fourteen officers and 315 rank and file of the Battalion were killed or wounded.

The 10th Argylls were in a subsequent wave of the attack. After making slow progress through blocked trenches and lines of German prisoners:

'The advance continued ... skirting the south face of the Hohenzollern Redoubt across Big Willie [another redoubt] and the German main line trenches ... once over [them] the battalion, in addition to being heavily shelled, had come under enfilade fire from a machine-gun ... A Company ... was badly mauled ... we now found our left flank was frightfully exposed with a gap of 300 yards, there being no troops on our left. The enemy fortunately did not pursue his advantage and the front was reorganized.'

But the position was untenable and with no orders from Brigade HQ (the Brigadier had been captured and his Brigade Major killed), the CO decided on a withdrawal over the hard-fought country, back to the original British front-line trenches. The Battalion's casualties were 489 killed, wounded and missing.

The llth Argylls, in 45 Brigade of 15th Scottish Division, were also in reserve at the start of the battle, but as all the leading brigades swept through the village of Loos they were blocked in the area of the infamous Hill 70, which meant that the reserve was urgently needed. The llth first occupied and held German third-line trenches and then moved up to defend the line that had been established across Hill 70 itself, the summit being in German possession. But the momentum of the Allied advance had been checked and successful German counter-attacks all along the front brought the battle to a standstill. It was one of the fiercest battles of the war and the new battalions had 'fought like lions'.

The disaster of Loos, with 60,000 British casualties (the French lost 190,000 and the Germans 178,000), resulted in the replacement of the CinC, Sir John French, by Field Marshal Haig, to some commentators a man of great determination and pragmatism and to others a commander lacking boldness and imagination. Unlike his German adversary, Ludendorff, Haig was no gambler and preferred to fight according to probabilities rather than possibilities on the Western Front. History records that the former was the loser.

Reorganization and retraining was urgently needed and valuable lessons had been learnt at all levels. During the winter and spring the various battalions of the Regiment spent their time holding the line, resting or training for future offensives. A new battalion, the 14th, arrived in February.

Along the British sector there were sporadic attempts to disrupt the defences of each side, with mining operations and local attacks. The 10th Battalion guarding 'The Bluff' alongside the Ypres-Comines Canal had such an experience one morning:

'At 6 a.m. the enemy blew a large mine on "the Buff" where we lost 70 men, 30 killed and 40 wounded and unhappily several of the draft just arrived from home. All the dugouts were blown in and many of the men buried.'

An attack by the 93rd took place:

'On the night of 15 April, following the explosion of two mines, 2nd Lts Calder and MacKay, each with twenty men, penetrated the German trenches, killed several of the enemy, and brought back valuable material and information much wanted. Three men were slightly wounded.'

Even if holding a 'quiet' sector of the line, as Colonel George Malcolm of Poltalloch reported:

'You were normally living in dangerous proximity to your opponent, and daily and nightly engaging in close combat with his patrols ... a "quiet" week in the front line trenches could cost fifteen casualties.'

While in command of the 93rd, Major H. de B Purves was killed outright by a stray bullet on 19 June, such misfortunes being as much a part of the war as death or injury in deliberate attacks or while defending the front line.

During the spring and early summer 1916 preparations were under way for a massive Anglo-French offensive to be launched in July in the River Somme area. It was designed to end the war no less, now that Britain's New Armies were fully operational and tested. Plans were upset, however, by the urgent need to reduce the French contribution in order to meet a huge offensive by the Germans at Verdun during May and June.

It is necessary to look to the Eastern theatres of the war in the meantime, to learn of the contribution there of three battalions of the Regiment.

CHAPTER 7

EASTERN THEATRES, 1915–1916

GALLIPOLI

In order to assist the Russians fighting on the Eastern Front, open up the Dardanelles Straits and the Bosphorus to the British and Russian fleets and take the war to the heart of the Ottoman Empire, pre-empting any attack against Egypt and the Suez Canal, it was decided to send an Anglo-French naval force to seize the Dardanelles. It was thought that naval *force majeure* would effectively unnerve the Turkish government in Constantinople, cause them to sue for peace and allow the Allies use of the Straits.

Had there been ground troops to land in conjunction with the bombardment from the sea in February 1914, the venture might have succeeded. Kitchener, however, would not release troops at the time, despite the insistence of the former cavalry officer, now First Lord of the Admiralty, Winston Churchill. In the event three British battleships were sunk by mines and the Allies were forced to reconsider their whole strategy. In the same month an attack by the Turks on Egypt and the Canal from across the Sinai Desert was launched: fortunately it failed. Each side now had declared their intentions and learnt the nature of their weaknesses.

The amphibious assault, with Kitchener's reluctant blessing, took place on 5 April 1915, a Regular British Division, the Royal Naval Division, Australian and New Zealand divisions all landing 'with murderous losses' on the Gallipoli peninsula, and a French colonial division landing on the Asian side of the Dardanelles as a feint. The Turks, stiffened with German staff officers and weaponry, contained this invasion and the Allies held on with great difficulty to their own beachheads at Cape Helles, the southern tip of the peninsula, and Suvla Bay, fifteen miles to the north-west.

During the summer three new British divisions including 52nd Lowland Division, with 5th Argylls from Renfrew in 157 Brigade, landed at Cape Helles, Gallipoli:

'To this disease-ridden place,' records the divisional history, 'where myriads of pestiferous flies tormented the living; where the supply of water was lamentably inadequate; where men's throats were parched with heat, dry and breathing a foul atmosphere; where the Turks by this time had all important points ranged to a yard; which possessed every possible military defeat for the Allies, came the Division full of life and expectation, to do battle for the first time.'

The 5th Argylls joined the British defence lines on 2 July and spent several days acclimatizing themselves to the weather, disease and enemy fire.

Although other brigades in the division had fought major actions, 157 Brigade's first attack with 52nd Lowland Division took place on 12 July, the task being to capture three Turkish lines on the dominant feature known as Achi Baba Nullah. The enemy held the whole area in enormous strength with an intricate system of trenches covered by artillery support and heavily wired.

The 5th Argylls were in the centre of their Brigade in four company waves and after a massive British bombardment, answered by a Turkish bombardment which caused many casualties in the battalion:

'Then, with a burst of cheering and to the skirling of the piper, 157 Brigade scrambled over the parapet, and went forward. Again the Turks turned on the assaulting troops every machine-gun and piece of artillery that they could bring to bear, and the din was terrific. Line after line pushed steadily forward through the bursting shrapnel ... until each wave of men in turn disappeared into the inferno of dust and smoke that smothered the Turkish trenches.'

Words cannot truly describe the heroism and slaughter on both sides.

'Lt J Rowan fell mortally wounded by a bursting shell, but, holding up his shattered frame as best he could, never ceased to cheer on his Highlanders until he died ... The leading waves of 7th HLI and 5th Argylls now joined in one surge of men, rushed forward for the third Turkish trench, but found nothing except a few detached pieces of empty trench. Some went on to look further, and most of these never returned.'

A hole had been punched in the Turkish Front, but the Division had insufficient strength or artillery cover, and could only consolidate, dig in and prepare for enemy counter-attacks. The Argylls were holding an area known as 'the horseshoe', and enemy counter-attacks were launched during the night and throughout the next day, when another British attack was mounted alongside by the Royal Naval Division. On the whole the operation was a qualified success, but the Argylls lost 333 officers and men killed and wounded.

After a further reinforcement and attack in August, chiefly in the Suvla Bay area, the entire campaign stagnated. The Argylls were in and out of the front line during the next few months and in December took part in an action at Krithia Nullah. There was fierce fighting and a number of bombing raids were successful; the operation had the effect of diverting enemy attention from the withdrawals then taking place at Suvla and Anzac Bays. During freezing weather at the beginning of January, 5th Argylls took part in the only successful phase of the whole campaign, the withdrawal from Cape Helles, an operation in which the secrecy was so perfect that there were no casualties at all.

EGYPT AND PALESTINE

After recuperation at Lemnos the 52nd Lowland Division sailed for Egypt. In February 1916 5th Argylls found themselves guarding the Suez Canal from fortified outposts in the desert, notably Canterbury Hill and Hill 70.

The Turks frequently raided the Canal defences, but were easily beaten off on each occasion. Their last attempt was in August 1916, but they were decisively defeated at Romani, twenty miles east along the coast of Sinai, and 4,000 prisoners were taken. The Argylls were involved in the pursuit, but the Turks retreated faster than British and dominion troops could follow, and soon the whole of northern Sinai was clear of the enemy. It was not until January 1917 that there were sufficient troops and enough confidence to begin the offensive against Palestine, which was held in great strength by the Turks with a German command structure and assistance. Their main positions were along the ridges between Gaza and Beersheba, the natural gateways.

During the first battle of Gaza in March 1917, 5th Argylls held a defensive position while other formations went into the attack. There was an unfortunate lack of co-ordination between the infantry and mounted troops, and the British lost nearly 4,000 casualties from 16,000, against a similar number of Turks. The withdrawal was covered by the Argylls and their Brigade at In Seirat.

The second battle of Gaza in April, launched by an overconfident Commander-in-Chief, backed by an optimistic war cabinet, was also a failure. The Turks had devoted enormous energy in strengthening their fortifications. The frontal assault was blocked easily and the Argylls' neighbouring brigade was severely cut up. The Argylls' 157 Brigade was engaged in a subsidiary thrust which depended for its success on earlier objectives being seized by other troops. As a consequence of the latter's failure, the Argylls had to dig in on a feature nicknamed Lees Hill, under heavy fire and close to Turkish positions:

'They dug unceasingly throughout the night, but the ground was very hard, and the trenches were only two and a half feet deep by dawn ... when day broke the Turks opened on the ... trenches ... with machine-guns, rifles and later trench mortars.'

52nd Lowland Division lost more casualties than any other division in this disastrous battle, and it was little comfort to them at the time that the two commanders responsible were removed from their appointments.

General Allenby, however, was duly appointed as the new commander and he was one of the most imaginative leaders that Britain fielded during the war. With his practised cavalry knowledge and experience in command on the Western Front, he was the man who unlocked the situation and enabled the Turks to be ejected from Palestine. But first he waited to build up his numbers and ensure that his supporting troops could prepare to meet the logistic problems of a rapid advance, particularly sufficient water supplies. In late October Allenby was ready to smash through the Gaza positions with his 88,000 troops against 35,000 Turks.

While the British infantry appeared to be mounting a frontal attack on Gaza, the Desert Mounted Corps swung wide to the east and captured Beersheba with its vital water wells. This forced the easternmost of the two Turkish armies to withdraw rapidly. The feint against Gaza was turned into a real attack, with the Desert Mounted Corps sweeping in from the east in support. But the battle was by no means a pushover.

The 5th Argylls were in reserve for the first few days of the battle, but on 7 November were called forward with their Brigade to seize the Wadi Hesi valley close to the sea, after a night march against strong enemy opposition. Continuing the advance, the Brigade then attacked the strongly defended Sausage Ridge, their final approach to the objective in failing light was particularly exposed to a tremendous weight of enemy fire. Even on the objective the Argylls were severely cut up by small-arms fire, but used their bayonets to good effect in the hand-to-hand fighting. The battle raged back and forth over the ridge for several hours. Captain A.C.King and RSM Monteith both won the Military Cross for '...the manner in which they kept gathering men together, restoring their cohesion and trying to consolidate what had been gained.' It needs little imagination to comprehend the difficulties they faced in the darkness in achieving this task. By 9 p.m. the Turks had been chased off the ridge completely, at a cost to the Argylls of 113 casualties.

The pursuit through Palestine towards Jerusalem was extremely arduous, and 5th Argylls played a full part in the actions at Kumman, an attack similar to those on Sausage Ridge, Esdud and Nebi Samwil. After three weeks the 52nd Division were replaced, and it was a great disappointment to the Argylls that they were not included in the final advance and entry into Jerusalem.

After a rest, they continued to advance to the west of the Holy City and fought in numerous engagements in miserable December weather, until they reached the River Auja. Eleven days after Jerusalem fell on 9 December, the whole of 52nd Division carried out a night assault over the river, and achieved complete surprise. The reconnaissance was excellent, the plan daring if somewhat complicated, and the silence of movement and crossing the river by wading and rapidly constructed bridges, truly commendable. The 5th Argylls reached to within twenty yards of the enemy before charging with the bayonet. The Turks abandoned their positions rapidly and there was no counter-attack.

It was 5th Argylls' last major engagement of the campaign. Thereafter they spent their time manning the front or in reserve. In April 1918 they sailed for France, where as a result of the German spring offensive, they and their division were needed urgently.

SALONIKA

Remaining in the Mediterranean theatre of operations, the story of the 91st Argylls must be resumed. In November 1915 27th and 28th Divisions had left France for service in Salonika, once part of Turkey-in-Europe and now restored to Greece. The purpose was to stiffen the resolve of the Greeks and prevent the Bulgarians, who had joined Germany, Austria-Hungary and Turkey, from seizing independent Serbia alongside. But before the arrival of the 91st Highlanders in 27th Division, Serbia had actually fallen to the Central Powers.

Despite this setback it was decided to establish a front to defend Greece, for all her claim to neutrality, and maintain pressure in the East as a diversion. This task, however, also placed an extra strain on Allied resources, and the Germans caustically suggested that it was an Allied 'concentration camp' devised for the Kaiser's benefit.

The two British divisions were both Regular Army divisions, hardened by the fighting at Ypres and Loos, but short of artillery support and transport. They were joined later by other troops including 12th Argylls in 26th Division. Greece is a beautiful country to visit, but not to fight in, and the Mediterranean climate varies from extreme heat to freezing cold and bitter rain storms. In cold weather the ground was nearly as bad as in Flanders; in warm weather a fine dust was raised and penetrated literally everywhere. Communications were bad; roads and tracks had constantly to be kept in repair by the troops, in addition to their full-time job of entrenching, wiring and maintaining the Front.

After sizing-up the situation, the Allied command decided to build a defensive perimeter (known as the 'birdcage') across the narrowest part of the peninsula, some 35 miles long, 20 miles of which followed the shore line of two lakes.

The 91st took its first turn in the line in January 1916 with the remainder of 81 Brigade, comprising The Royal Scots, Gloucesters and Cameron Highlanders. It was arduous and tedious enough just to man the trenches, carry out routine maintenance and survive. With time to reflect, many an officer and Jock wondered at his being there and the wisdom of this seemingly negative activity, particularly as the Greeks were suspicious and resentful of the Allies' presence.

The Bulgars had superb defences along the frontier forty miles to the north. They became active during May 1916 and although the British were not involved, seized a strategic mountain pass and infiltrated towards the Allies' line. At one stage it was feared that they would strike against the British line at Stavros, and the Argylls marched hurriedly to the town to act as a reinforcement. The attack never materialized.

To relieve boredom and harden the troops, route marches became a frequent occurrence and if the regimental history is to be believed, the Argylls had the best record for not 'falling out'. Gradually the battalion acquired a useful number of pack mules to carry equipment and supplies, which greatly assisted movement.

In June the 'birdcage' was completed and it was decided to extend the Allied presence northwards. A new defensive line in the River Struma—Lake Dorain area close to the Bulgarian border was marked out and construction work was begun. The Argylls joined in this task, but:

'Working in extreme heat, the troops soon began to suffer from the debilitating effects of the Balkan climate ... malaria and dysentery taking a heavy toll. The Bulgars sprinkled [sic] their detachments along the base of the opposing Beles [mountain] range ... also suffered considerably.'

In subsequent summers, both sides withdrew into the hills to get away from the insects and disease.

While construction of this new line progressed, there were no brushes with the enemy. Towards the end of September 1916, however, a limited brigade offensive was planned, to capture the twin villages of Karadzakoj Bala and Zir, so that a bridgehead on the north side of the Struma could then be established. On 30 September the Gloucestershire Regiment and the Cameron Highlanders took Bala at dawn, and from there the attack by the Argylls and Royal Scots was launched at 11.30 a.m., with two companies in the leading wave supported by two companies in the second. The distance covered in the advance was some 1,000 yards and the leading companies met heavy fire, including machine-guns, particularly from enemy positions in defile. When all 'A Company's officers had been wounded, the Company was withdrawn; 'A' and 'B' Companies then attempted to work their way forward covering each other, but were unable to move. They remained pinned down throughout the afternoon and the, CO, Lieutenant Colonel Henderson, persuaded the Brigade Commander that a new plan of attack should be drawn up. This was done; attacking from a different direction, with extra artillery fire, Zir was captured. Despite Bulgarian counter-attacks over the next two days, accurate artillery fire broke up their formations, and Zir was held. One officer and 20 other ranks were killed; twelve officers and 87 men were wounded.

During the winter no offensives were mounted by either side. Manning trenches in turn with other battalions became the routine, relieved by active patrolling in the two-mile depth of no man's land. By dint of further construction work the line was re-shaped to allow two battalions to man the brigade front line, with two in reserve. In the summer the front along the Struma was abandoned for positions in the hills some six miles south, but malaria struck the Allied troops and more than 80 per cent succumbed to the disease.

In October 1917 the original Struma line was re-established, although in the chief engagement with the enemy the Argylls played only a minor supporting role. During the winter a large number of the less fit men, many of whom had been with the Battalion in France, were sent home and replaced with new drafts. In the spring there were a number of large-scale raids against the enemy in the area of Homondos, and in July 1918 the whole of 27th Division moved fifty miles west to take over from the French in the River Vardar sector. The Argylls' position was alongside a tributary with an unfortunate name, the River Slop. There the Battalion was responsible for trenches close to an important strategic route which gave access northwards towards Bulgarian-held territory, and southwards along the railway and river running through a steep ravine.

The concept of operations was 'to attract the enemy to our own front on the Vardar and hold him there, in order that the task of breaking through his line elsewhere might be accompanied by Allied troops'. For reasons of security, however, the troops were not informed of this point. Patrolling was conducted as before, but with more purpose, because the River Vardar was to be the thrust-line of the forthcoming offensive to drive the Bulgarians back over the northern border of Greece.

On 2 September 1918 27th Division advanced to seize limited objectives, to their front. Despite spirited fighting by the Serbs and their allies the Bulgarians, there was a general advance over the next three weeks, although the Argylls' strength had been reduced to 237 all ranks by incipient malaria and now influenza. By the time the depleted battalions of 27th Division had crossed through the Serbian enclave and into Bulgaria, it was apparent that the enemy's will to continue the fight had been broken. On 20 September an armistice was agreed. In the Special Order of the Day, General Sir George Milne asserted that:

'Thanks to your gallantry, determination and devotion to duty, the Bulgarian Army is now defeated and the Bulgarian nation has sued for peace. This result has been obtained only by your extraordinary exertions, after three summers spent in a malarious country and against obstacles of great natural and artificial strength.'

The march into Turkish-held territory to the east was a somewhat distressing affair; the Allied troops were so weakened by disease that they gave little appearance of a conquering army. Nevertheless the Turkish resistance collapsed. In December 1918 the 91st were sent to Constantinople as occupation troops and in May 1919 they were reduced to cadre strength for the return home to Scotland.

The whole experience had been comparatively inglorious. Was their task useful? Cynicism suggests not, but then an earlier generation than ours was not strong on cynicism. The 91st Highlanders and 12th Argylls had contributed to the war effort as required of them, their casualties were lighter than those of the battalions in France, but many otherwise unscarred men had suffered ill health that would affect them for the rest of their lives. They had done their duty and more.

CHAPTER 8

THE SOMME TO VERSAILLES, 1916–1918

THE SOMME

During the last week of June 1916 the greatest offensive ever mounted by the British Army began with a massive artillery bombardment in the Somme sector. On 1 July the French Sixth Army and British Fourth Army advanced, their objectives being Péronne and Bapaume respectively. Unfortunately the French contribution had been scaled down because the German offensive at Verdun, that battle of 'sheer horror' which had begun in February, was draining the French Army and would do so until December of the year. There was every hope that the Allies would punch a hole in the German defences, the momentum would be irresistible, the Germans would be forced off French soil and the war would end. It was not be and the sad truth is that the first day of battle accounted for 57,450 British casualties, of whom some 20,000 died. Significant advances were made at first, but were quickly checked by the Germans.

The 93rd were not involved immediately, but in their 98 Brigade they mounted an attack in the area of Bazentin-le-Petit and High Wood on 15 July. The momentum of the offensive had long been lost by this time and the attack made little progress, so the 93rd occupied trenches near Bazentin and Mametz Wood for a month. Two further attacks were made during August without achieving any success, and for the following three months the Battalion spent much of the time in the front line, attempting on occasions to make limited advances but with little success. The only impression they made on the German line was the capture of a ridge overlooking Le Transloy.

The 6th Argylls had left 51st Highland Division to serve as pioneers in 5th Division, but the reconstituted 7th and 8th Argylls, in 154 and 152 Brigades respectively, joined the battle when 51st Highland Division were rushed south to the Somme area in mid July. On 21 July the Division was ordered to take over a sector of the line adjacent to the 93rd positions. High Wood, perched on the summit of a 500-foot ridge and the highest point of Picardy, had been taken early in the battle, but the Germans had recaptured part of the reverse slope when the Division arrived.

The 7th Argylls had hardly taken up front-line duties when they were ordered to prepare for a two-brigade attack, beginning at 2200 hours on 23 July, with no opportunity for a proper daylight reconnaissance. The artillery barrage, however, was ineffectual and the '...going within the wood, owing to shell-holes, brambles, dense undergrowth and wire entanglements was extremely bad; to walk ... was a laborious process demanding considerable physical effort'. The attack was not successful, but a German counter-attack was beaten off. The 8th Argylls remained in reserve, and when they took their turn in the front line on 27 July, they suffered greatly from shellfire, including phosgene gas, from which there were 80 casualties. After that a policy of

Above: The 91st arrive in South Africa, 1899. The Colours were sensibly not taken on active service 'up country'.

Below: 91st Argylls on the march in South Africa before going into action. Such drill movements soon seemed inappropriate when the enemy began their work of long-range marksmanship.

Left: Corporal MacKay plays
the pipes to steady the nerves
of the Highlanders caught in
the open in front of
Magersfontein Hill, where the
Boers wrought havoc with the
Highland Brigade.

Below: Charge of the Argyll
and Sutherland Highlanders
across the Modder River, 28
November 1899. A war
artist's view.

Above: Jocks of the 91st manning a blockhouse during a later stage of the Boer War. Such expensive measures in manpower terms, finally defeated the Boers.

Below: The 1st Argylls machine-gun section ready for the march, pose with their weapon and its ammunition, India 1913. The integration of machine-guns within companies and platoons took a long time to achieve, because they were considered to be specialist weapons.

Left: The Territorial Force. 'B' Company 8th Argylls at ease during Camp, the year before the 'Great War for Civilization' began. Grand aims and lofty idealism were brought down to earth in four years of the most appalling horror and bloodshed on an unimaginable scale.

Left: 93rd Highlanders make good their defences during the unofficial armistice, Christmas 1914. The German front line is by the trees on the left of the picture. (Imperial War Museum)

Left: The 93rd – 2nd Argylls' support line in the Bois de Grénier sector, June 1915. (IWM)

Right: 93rd Highlanders dig trenches in a somewhat thinned-out wood near Ypres.

Right: Two officers of the 93rd Highlanders watch aircraft from their trench. An officer of the Regiment, Lieutenant Liddell, won the Victoria Cross serving with the Royal Flying Corps.

Right: 93rd Highlanders' machine-gunners firing at the enemy from a breastwork, 1915. (IWM)

Above: 12th Argylls, a 'K 3' Service Battalion, taking cover during manoeuvres on the Bulgarian Front, 1916. (IWM)

Below: Jocks of the 12th Argylls resting during a march on the Bulgarian Front, 1916. (IWM)

Above: 12th Argylls' Pipes and Drums, Struma Valley Salonika, New Year's Day, 1916.

Below: 91st practise bayonetting Bulgarians during training in Salonika, 1917.

Above: 91st Highlanders sports day relay race. 'Out of the line', Salonika Front, 1917. (IWM)

Below: The War is over. 91st Argylls gathering weapons, now surplus to requirements, in Constantinople, 1919. (IWM)

Right: Battle of the Lys 1918, outposts of the 11th Argylls alongside the Lys Canal. (IWM)

Right: 'B' Company 7th Argylls retiring along a road near Beaumetz, March 1918. (IWM)

Right: Cheerful 'walking wounded' of the Argylls and Seaforth Highlanders near Frévent during the great German offensive of 1918. (IWM)

Left: Second Lieutenants Bisset (6th Argylls) top, and Buchan (7th and 8th Argylls) right, who both won the Victoria Cross in 1918. 'To hell with surrender,' shouted Buchan, who was last seen alive holding out against overwhelming odds.

Below left: Unveiled by the Duke of Argyll, The Memorial to the 8th Argylls and the 51st Highland Division at Beaumont Hamel.

Below right: The Scottish National War Memorial, built high above the city of Edinburgh at the heart of the Castle, contains memorials to all the Scottish regiments and uniformed services. This bay shows the memorial to all the battalions of the Argyll and Sutherland Highlanders who fought in the Great War.

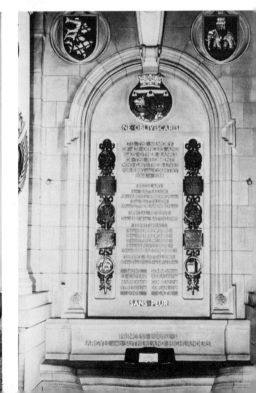

Above: The 93rd Highlanders were on active service in Ireland before Home Rule. Here they are snatching a brief rest after 'driving' Barnalyra woods in search of 150 armed rebels, May 1921.

Below: HRH Princess Louise, Duchess of Argyll, daughter of Queen Victoria and a much-loved Colonel-in-Chief, inspects the 91st Highlanders at Parkhurst, Isle of Wight in 1926.

Above: Guarding the outposts of the Empire. A Jock of the 93rd Highlanders keeps watch on the hills near Golanai Camp, North West Frontier, 1935.

Below: The 93rd Highlanders on the march in India, 1930. Between the wars, field officers were still provided with horses so that they could better direct manoeuvres.

Above: The Regimental Mascot Cruachan I waits with the pioneers and piled drums, ready to head the 91st Highlanders back to barracks after a church service in Aldershot.

Below: 91st Highlanders give a display of Highland Dancing at the Tidworth Tattoo in 1937.

Above: The desert of Omdurman, Sudan 1942. 'C' Company 91st Highlanders training hard after having fought the Germans in Crete and the Italians in Abyssinia.

Below: The 93rd Highlanders were the most effective battalion in the campaign against the Japanese in Malaya, 1942, because their prior training had been both exacting and imaginative. Here they practise drills with their armoured cars. (IWM)

Above: The 93rd on a route march in Malaya, 1941. Much of the countryside in which the Battalion was to fight the Japanese, comprised rubber plantations and not thick jungle. (IWM)

Below: Peter Archer's fine painting of the final withdrawal over the Causeway to Singapore Island. It shows Lieutenant Colonel Stewart, Captain Slessor, Drummer Hardy, Pipers Stewart and Maclean, and Sergeant Nuttall in his armoured car.

Above: 8th Argylls training in beach landing drills on Kintyre, October 1941. The Battalion was to be landed by sea on four separate occasions during the next three years. (IWM)

Below: The 51st Highland Division at the battle of El Alamein, advancing in open formation towards the enemy positions. The 7th Argylls played a major part in the battle, while 1st Argylls were held in reserve. (IWM)

Bottom: A patrol of 7th Argylls capturing some Italians who were hidden in an olive grove near Gabes, 6 April 1943. The Argylls' diced shoulder flash and Highland Division sign is seen on the Jock's sleeve. (IWM)

'sapping forward' was adopted, which meant stealing forward and digging in furiously during the dark in order to establish a new forward trench line. On the night of 3 August the whole Division managed to advance the line by some 200 yards unbeknown to the Germans.

It was small successes such as this that, for all their apparent insignificance, strengthened the morale and determination of soldiers on the Western Front throughout the war. By 7 August more than half High Wood was in British hands, although as originally conceived, such a frontal attack really needed much more

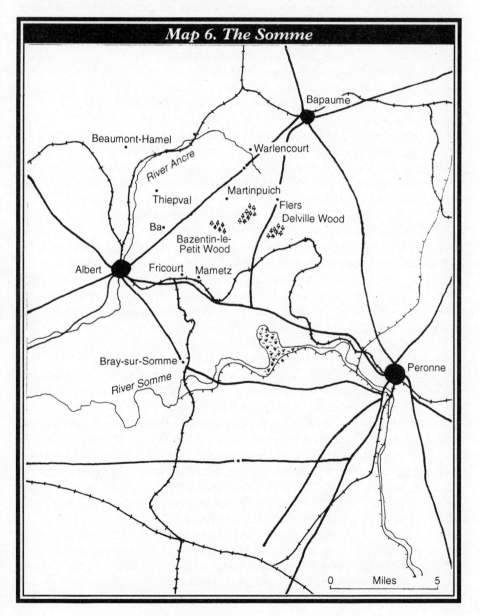

Map 6. The Somme

preparation and far better concealment of intentions. These two necessities were all too often mutually exclusive on the Western Front.

The 10th Argylls in 9th Scottish Division were also in reserve for the first part of the Battle of the Somme. At dawn on 14 July a 'deliberate attack' from a taped forming-up area was launched against Longueval, and this was a complete success despite high casualties

'... with the pipers playing the regimental march and the charge ... C Company under Captain McQueen 'bombed' westwards to assist the 27th Brigade and killed 120 Germans, driving the remainder into the arms of the brigade ... A Company had only 40 men left when they were relieved by C Company. A patrol of 50 men under Lieutenant Leggatt was caught north of the village between two machine-guns and nearly wiped out, 10 men dribbling back in the morning.'

But the enemy were active in nearby Delville Wood, held by the South Africans who had been severely mauled. The 10th Argylls and the remains of their 76 Brigade were then heavily involved in the very confused fighting over the next two days. The tide of war was against them and they lost 59 killed, 300 wounded and a further 76 missing. The officially expressed thanks, 'a feat of arms which will rank high amongst the best military attainments of the British Army', while no doubt sincere, scarcely conveys the real extent of their suffering and achievements. Later the Battalion moved to the sector opposite Vimy Ridge, but returned to the Somme in early October to fight an inconsequential engagement at Flers.

The 11th Argylls in 15th Scottish Division also arrived in the Somme sector well after the battle had begun. On 12 August 15th Division launched a deliberate night attack. The Argylls' brigade was entirely successful in seizing their objectives south of Martinpuich, due largely to:

'The super-excellence of the artillery barrage. The leading wave advanced right under the barrage and .... there was hardly a [small arms] shot fired, and no casualties resulted from our artillery fire. All describe it as a wall of flame and steel, behind which we felt quite secure.'

It is worth remembering that of all the combat casualties suffered by all the armies in the Great War, two-thirds were caused by artillery fire.

The 11th Argylls formed part of Haig's new offensive on the Somme on 15 September, with an attack of twelve divisions on a ten-mile front. The Argylls' objective was the right-hand side of the village of Martinpuich. On this occasion there was no preliminary bombardment and '...the enemy taken completely by surprise and surrendered freely'. The Argylls witnessed the new weapon of war in action for the first time, four tanks of the Heavy Branch Machine Gun Corps, later the Tank Corps. On this occasion the tanks contributed more by the element of surprise than material assistance, but that was sufficient. The three objectives were quickly seized, and by 1600 hours the whole of the village was in British hands. The Division was relieved four days later, having held their gains without difficulty.

At this point it is necessary to mention other battalions of the Regiment who indirectly contributed to the momentous happenings on the Western Front. The 13th and 15th (Reserve) Battalions never served overseas, but sent numerous drafts to the front. Second-line Territorial Force battalions were also raised, together with 16th and 17th Argylls TF, whose purpose was the training and holding of manpower. Although numerous other British battalions were tied up as garrison troops in Ireland, and were much in need at the time of the Easter Rising in Dublin in 1916, no Argyll battalions served there.

The 14th Argylls had formed in early 1915 and joined the new 40th Division in September of that year. They reached France in June 1916, were not involved in the Somme offensive, but took their part in holding the line in various sectors during the following months.

The Somme offensive ended with an ambitious operation by ten divisions north and south of the River Ancre, a tributary of the Somme. The 51st Highland Division's objective was the town of Beaumont Hamel, but because of foul weather the attack was postponed day after day, the Germans suffering the bombardments that were to be a prelude to each attack.

On 13 November 8th Battalion went into the attack with their Division, two brigades up and two leap-frogging past. The state of the terrain was appalling.

'The men floundered in the dark in mud over their ankles; the weight they carried was enormously augmented by the moisture that their clothing had absorbed and by the mud which glued itself to their kilts ... to charge was out of the question. In some places men even became bogged up to their waists, and were unable to extricate themselves from the morass.'

Drowning in mud was a horrible and not uncommon death on the Western Front. The attack was successful insofar as the line of exploitation was reached, and some two thousand prisoners taken. The 8th lost 86 killed, 176 wounded and ten missing.

The 7th Argylls were brought up from reserve and two companies took part in a very successful bombing operation, but two fresh companies of the Battalion got ahead of the programme and suffered from British artillery fire during an advance on the second day of the operation. Overall the battle was a notable victory for 51st Highland Division in the most appalling conditions of weather and terrain.

1917

The 93rd remained in the Somme sector throughout the winter and in March 1917 they were withdrawn to train for the new spring offensive against the Hindenburg Line on the River Scarpe. The Battalion was not involved initially, but later in the battle moved up to the Hindenburg Line, evacuated in part by the enemy, and with their Brigade took part in the fighting on 23 and 24 April.

The attack went in at 0445 hours, the objective being a position overlooking Fontaine-lès-Croisilles. The action by the Brigade was successful, and they linked up with the neighbouring brigade before the Germans counter-attacked. It developed into an extraordinary situation, as 'A' Company of the 93rd and some companies of 1st Middlesex Regiment were cut off at the final objective. 'We were taking prisoners in front and being attacked from behind,' explains the battalion record. There the survivors remained throughout the night and fought off German attacks with great success, before they were relieved. Captain A.C. Henderson was awarded the VC posthumously for his part in the battle, the citation reading:

'For most conspicuous bravery. During an attack on the enemy trenches, this officer although almost immediately wounded in the left arm, led his company through the front line until he gained the final objective. He then proceeded to consolidate his position ... By his cheerful courage and coolness he was enabled to maintain the spirit of his men under the most trying conditions.'

Henderson was killed with 60 others of the battalion. Sporadic attacks and counter-attacks followed during the next few weeks, and at one stage Lieutenant J. MacKellar and 'D' Company captured and held more than half a mile of the Hindenburg Line.

The 8th Argylls took part in the Arras offensive on 9 April, mounting a crisp attack on the second and third line systems of trenches near Roclincourt, which was entirely successful. Five weeks later their Brigade took up defensive positions north of Arras in the chemical works at Roeux. There they were attacked by the Germans in great strength and a tremendous fight developed over a space of five days, with the Highlanders of 152 Brigade just maintaining control over the situation. Individual acts of heroism were numerous, notably by Captain Murdoch MacTaggart and the CO, Colonel Robin Campbell. The Colonel and his Battalion HQ had launched:

'...an immediate counter-attack against the Germans north of the railway ... by 6.45 p.m. he had killed or captured all Germans ... Colonel Campbell sent his adjutant to tell the 6th Seaforth Highlanders to deliver a frontal attack, while he enfiladed the Germans from the embankment. This operation was carried out with complete success. Colonel Campbell then joined the 6th Seaforth with his party, advanced through the chemical works, and dug in just east of them.'

The CO personally shot six Germans in rapid succession. Success in combat, however, is relative. When 8th Argylls were eventually relieved only five officers and 200 soldiers were fit for further action; some 670 men had been killed or wounded.

The 7th Argylls had played only a minor part in the battle so far, but were in the front line as the fighting died down. There they witnessed:

'Hostile shelling, intermittent but accurate. Enemy aeroplanes for the past week have had an uninterrupted survey of our lines. Between 3 p.m. and 3.30 p.m. an aeroplane registered the right brigade headquarters, scoring several direct hits, and causing several casualties.'

This activity was a portent of what another generation of Argylls would face in a future war.

The 10th Argylls had been in the Arras sector for some months already, manning trenches, carrying out patrols and raids, and between times living in the man-made tunnels and caverns under the town. Their 9th Scottish Division attacked on 9 April and, although at first in reserve, the Argylls were quickly leap-frogged through 8th Black Watch and 7th Seaforth Highlanders, to capture the second objective, which they did successfully. Consolidating on this line, a railway embankment, the engagement became so confused that composite companies of Highlanders had to be made up quickly in order to attack the final objective, the village of Athies, which was taken fortunately with few further casualties.

The 10th were also involved in the fighting in Roeux, but their attack went wrong in the darkness and two companies were surrounded by the enemy and destroyed. Very few of the wounded managed to get back to the British lines. Private W.G. Taylor was one of them; he had been shot through both thighs but remained for five days in no man's land with his Lewis gun, picking off targets. Eventually he dragged himself back to the British line, and was awarded the Distinguished Conduct Medal.

The 11th Argylls in 15th Scottish Division also fought in the latter stages of the Battle of Arras, taking part in some very confused fighting, which ended with the seizure of GuBBBmappe on 23 April.

THIRD YPRES

A new offensive had been planned for July 1917 in the Ypres sector. In part its purpose was to take pressure off the French at the lowest point of their war, which included the mutiny of some of their troops. Once again there was a long bombardment before the attack went in on 31 July. Initially there were some successes, but heavy rain and massed German counter-attacks prevented the British Second and Fifth Armies and the French First Army from holding their gains. The offensive continued, as had the Somme offensive the previous year, over a period of months until winter set in.

The 8th Argylls had gone into action with 51st Highland Division on the first day of the Battle of Ypres. Their Brigade was involved in two separate and well-organized attacks, showing '...extraordinary initiative. Whenever a point of resistance disclosed itself it was attacked immediately by the troops in the vicinity with great dash — not, however, by wild frontal and expensive charges, but by the skilful use of ground'.

Such tactics kept the casualty rate as low as possible. The 7th Argylls remained in reserve at this time.

The 7th and 8th took part in the Battle of Cambrai in November, when the initiative was seized from the enemy, with the use of massed tanks to punch through the German trench systems and allow the infantry to exploit. In this battle 7th Argylls played a more prominent part than the 8th, and had the satisfaction of not only making a great leap forward geographically speaking, but rounding up droves of German prisoners. Unfortunately a massive breakthrough was not achieved by the Allies.

The 93rd Highlanders meanwhile had been moved to a position near the coast at Dunkirk. Their Brigade was due to attack along the coast, should the Ypres offensive farther south be successful, but this plan was suspended and the Battalion was moved to the Ypres area in late September. There they took over responsibility for the second-line trenches west of Hooge, alongside the Menin Road. Their Brigade was to advance and seize Polygon Wood, but due to a massive enemy bombardment the battalion in front of the 93rd, had great difficulty in advancing and were carried by the advance of the Highlanders, the two waves of the attack merging. The ground from the south-western edge and along the southern boundary of Polygon Wood was secured.

'A' and 'C' Companies held their ground during German counter-attacks and throughout the night their right flank was exposed to further attacks, artillery fire, and gas. The following day British and Australian troops advanced, relieved the two companies and swept on to clear Polygon Wood of the enemy. The 93rd were withdrawn and went into reserve in Ypres, being billeted by a quirk of irony in a lunatic asylum. They were spared further fighting, but after the third battle of Passchendaele, captured with enormous cost by the Canadians, New Zealanders and Australians, the 93rd assumed responsibility for the line in the village for several weeks.

The 10th Argylls' contribution to the Ypres offensive was with 9th Division at Havrincourt, many miles to the south; they held the front and took part in several raids. In September they were summoned to return to Ypres, but were not involved in much fighting until 12 October, in the desperate battle for Passchendaele. The attack began at 5.25 a.m., and the start-line was,'...a sheet of water ... it was pouring with rain ... every man was drenched to the skin and very cold, and so we lay in the water'.

'A' and 'C' Companies were frustrated in the attack by a carefully sited enemy pillbox with four machine-guns, but it was captured by a concerted effort by the Jocks of all four battalions of the brigade who had got somewhat mixed up. A further advance of 600 yards was made under heavy fire, but casualties were numerous — several men drowning in the mud — and the final objectives could not be reached. After prolonged suffering their 26th Highland Brigade was relieved during the night.

The 10th were employed in quieter sectors for the remainder of 1917, but on 30 December at Gouzeaucourt were raided by a 60-strong party of Germans, who got into their trenches. Captain Bonnyman, commanding 'C' Company, and his officers reacted immediately and led their soldiers in first clearing the trenches and then went over the parapet and fought the enemy in no man's land in the snow. Bonnyman was awarded the DSO, and several others were given awards for their 'prompt action and gallantry'. There are times when the vocabulary describing men's actions in combat is totally inadequate.

The 11th Argylls had also taken part in Third Ypres, where 15th Scottish Division fought a particularly fierce battle on 31 July. On the following day the 11th were ordered into action:

'It was at the end of the second day of very heavy fighting,' read the Brigade record, 'and for the whole of that day they had been "resting" in torrents of rain in waterlogged trenches. Officers and NCOs had not been able to make any previous reconnaissance of the ground, and darkness set in almost immediately after the start. The ground in the vicinity of the objective was similar to that of the Somme area in the wettest time of winter. In spite of this the objective was reached, well consolidated, and patrols sent out ... next morning ... heavily laden and exhausted as they were, alert and cheerful in spite of a night of incessant rain ...'

Such business-like operations often worked and with few casualties, but not without a severe test of the moral fibre of the troops. In an attack three weeks later, two companies of 11th Argylls with two companies of 13th Royal Scots were wiped out in a similar advance. The division was relieved at the end of the month.

The 14th Argylls were not involved in the Ypres offensive until the Battle of Cambrai. They acted as follow-up troops after the Hindenburg Line had been penetrated, their 40th Division being given the objectives of Bourlon Wood and Bourlon village for an attack on 23 November. The Argylls were in reserve, but were soon called forward and had some stiff fighting in the wood itself. The Division held on tenuously to some parts of Bourlon Wood, and members of the 14th took part in skirmishing during the next day and night. Eventually a line was secured and defences dug before the Division handed over the sector.

Mention must be made of three Argyll officers who had distinguished themselves serving with other arms. Captain John Liddell in the Royal Flying Corps had won the VC while fighting in the air and performing extraordinary feats of airmanship.

Lieutenant John Graham won his VC with the Machine Gun Corps at Istabulat in Mesopotamia. The citation reads: 'He was four times wounded ... His valour and skilful handling of his guns held up one strong counter-attack which threatened to roll up the left flank of the brigade.' Lieutenant David Macintyre was to win his VC while attached to 6th Highland Light Infantry at Henin in France during the summer of 1918.

1918

During the first part of 1918 there was sporadic fighting on the Western Front. Early in March 10th Argylls had a lively period in the line at Houthulst forest near Ypres. The enemy carried out several raids, using the wood as cover. Many of the battalion were wounded and a particulary brave and resourceful stretcher-bearer, Corporal Wilkes, was especially commended:

'He carried wounded without ceasing from 7 a.m. until night, performing fifteen journeys without halting for food, often through heavy shellfire and at night went out searching for wounded.'

He received the Médaille Militaire and the Military Medal.

On 21 March 1918 the German Army launched an all-out offensive on a front fifty miles wide. This had not been unexpected, but there was little immediate warning. 'His objects', reported Field Marshal Sir Douglas Haig, 'were no less than to separate us from the French, to take the Channel ports and destroy the British Army.' More than a hundred divisions were thrown into the battle, twenty of them against the Arras sector alone, held by eight British divisions. The famous Order of the Day was subsequently given by Haig:

'There is no other course open to us but to fight it out. Every position must be held to the last man. There must be no retirement. With our backs to the wall, and believing in the justice of our cause, each one of us must fight to the end.'

It says much of the British citizen soldiers that this order was faithfully carried out; as St John said: 'Greater love hath no man than this, that a man lay down his life for his friends.' This 'Great War of Civilization' may be judged differently now, but in 1918 the choice was simple.

The 7th Argylls' Brigade was in reserve at the time of the offensive and they were hit hard as the enemy penetrated 'the front and support lines by parties "bombing" along the trenches'. It took a huge effort to block the enemy. In this battle the 7th gave 'one of the finest performances of the Division', but some of their sub-units were also overwhelmed, while others fought a tactical withdrawal with the remainder of 51st Highland Division.

Meanwhile 8th Argylls' officers, after a good dinner in their hutted camp behind the lines, had been woken by artillery fire at 3 a.m. on 21 March. 'C' Company's officers were all wounded by a direct hit, but the Battalion mustered and marched forward as rapidly as possible. They were in the direct line of the advancing enemy, and for twenty-four hours they held their allotted positions against the most terrible pressure. 'C' Company was quickly surrounded and destroyed; the handful of survivors were captured. A general withdrawal was ordered for both battalions and in a bitter rearguard action, fought over several miles for four days, 8th Argylls suffered a further 542 casualties. Lieutenant Buchan:

'...when he saw that the enemy had practically surrounded his command, he collected his platoon and prepared to fight his way back. At this point the enemy, who had crept around his right flank, rushed towards him shouting "surrender". "To hell with surrender," he replied and shooting the foremost of the enemy, he finally repelled this advance with his platoon ... later cut off, he was last seen holding out against overwhelming odds.'

Buchan, originally of 7th Battalion, was awarded a posthumous VC for his incredible courage. Reduced to company strength, the 8th miraculously managed to remain an entity, until reinforced by large drafts from 11th Argylls two months later. They were constantly in action in the meantime.

The 11th Argylls in 15th Scottish Division were not hit so hard in the offensive: they were able to carry out an orderly withdrawal, one of the most difficult operations in war, and one that helps to conserve forces for a future offensive. By the end of the week, however, they were fighting as hard as any battalion, intent on blocking the massive weight of the German advance. They held the designated 'Army Line' in the spirit of *'ils ne passeront pas'*.

The 10th Argylls were not involved in the offensive at first, but were rushed to the front on 27 March for the protection of Arras, which fortunately was not reached by the enemy.

The 14th Argylls in 40th Division were also ordered forward to take blocking positions near Guémappes, where the Germans had broken through the front. But the enemy's strength was too great and their Division was severely tested. At one stage on the second day of battle, it was reported that, '...the Colonel said the Argylls would stand firm .... and by God they did stand firm, our gallant little party and we were not idle: true we had no machine-guns but we had rifles.' It became more and more difficult to hold on long enough before an orderly retirement, and the fighting for the 14th became more and more confused, before the Germans were eventually halted.

The 93rd were not in action during the offensive, but throughout the period were constantly shuttled around as a reserve. Their chance came on 17 April when they were holding the line at Méteren: 'B' Company were hard pressed, particularly as they came under British artillery fire in error, but they held out until relieved. A fortnight later they were involved in holding positions where the Germans had penetrated parts of Kemmel Ridge. They fought the enemy off until two battalions of the Cameronians counter-attacked successfully and drove the enemy away. The British Army's old battalions, Territorials and New Army battalions had faced the severest test of the war in this offensive. It is not an overstatement to say that it was their strength of character as well as the physical effort of fighting for an Allied cause on foreign soil, that had prevailed against the worst the enemy could do.

Sporadic fighting continued during the spring and summer of 1918, but while the Germans had forced the Allies back almost to their 1914 limit of advance, the effort undoubtedly had weakened them. The arrival of more than a million American soldiers, chiefly as reinforcements to the French sector where the Germans had made the greatest advances, turned the scale against the Germans. Moreover when a unified command of all the Allied troops had been agreed at last, under the Frenchman Marshal Foch, the initiative passed to the Allies.

The last German offensive was launched against the French on the Marne in June. It was partially successful, and British troops, including 5th Argylls, newly arrived from the Middle East, were rushed to the assistance of the French. At first they helped to defend Beuguem Ridge near Senlis, and in a famous attack on 'Hill 158' the CO, Lieutenant Colonel Barlow, was killed while personally leading the Battalion.

In July the Allies began what was to be the last major offensive on the Western Front. It was first confined to the French sector, where the 51st Highland Division with 7th and 8th Argylls in 15th Scottish Division were deployed there. Fierce fighting took place at Soissons and Buzancy which proved the value of the closest co-operation of formations from different nations in fighting together.

For the next three months the Allies pressed their attacks right across the front and the pressure proved irresistible. Every battalion of the Regiment had a part to play. The 5th assisted in the Ypres sector, capturing objectives on Kemmel Hill and Wytschaete Ridge. The 93rd met strong opposition at Villers-Guislain in mid September. Intelligence had failed to take account of a whole German division and for many hours there were attacks and counter-attacks, the Battalion suffering numerous casualties but taking scores of German prisoners. Soon the notorious Hindenburg Line was breached. The farther east the Allies advanced, the more water obstacles they met which had to be crossed and captured, but at least they were now crossing open country away from the terrible trenches. The 6th Argylls had resumed the infantry role during the advance and, during a spirited bayonet charge, Lieutenant Bisset won the VC for his outstanding courage and leadership. The Germans fought very gallantly and time and again the British had to deploy for attacks such as for the St-Quentin Canal, the capture of Cambrai, the pursuit to the River Selle, and an offensive over the River Sambre. Although thousands of German prisoners were being taken as the Allies advanced, there were still thousands of Allied soldiers being killed and wounded as well. The 10th Argylls, for instance, suffered 350 in October at Joncourt.

By early November the British were back in the area of Mons, where they had been in August 1914. On 11 November the Armistice was signed, ending the most terrible war in history, the war of mass involvement and massive destruction.

In due course the Treaty of Versailles was concluded. The war and the Treaty had checked the ambitions of Germany to become the continental superpower. The ambitions, however, remained dormant for a while, until sinister forces emerged ready for a new conflict. The world was kept waiting for two decades, and as time progressed the late war seemed to have been of diminishing value for Britain and her Allies.

Before closing this episode, mention must be made of the Regiment's contacts with dominion troops. The first affiliation actually pre-dated the Great War by nine years — with the 91st Regiment of Canadian Highlanders (formed in 1903). In 1920 they were renamed the Argyll and Sutherland Highlanders of Canada. Another Canadian regiment, the 103rd Regiment, Calgary Rifles (formed in 1910), became the Calgary Highlanders in 1921 and were affiliated to the Argyll and Sutherland Highlanders in 1924.

An Australian battalion, the 12th Infantry Regiment, dating from 1914, was affiliated to the Argylls in 1927 by which time it was titled the 4/5 Byron Regiment.

Their cap badge was the same boar's head and wild cat, but with the name 'Byron Regiment' encircling these devices. They are now the 41st Battalion, Royal New South Wales Regiment.

At the end of the war the Regiment shrank to its pre-war size. All the Service battalions of the Argylls were disbanded, while 3rd and 4th Special Reserve Battalions were amalgamated and placed in suspended animation, until their final deletion from the Order of Battle in 1953. Of the Territorial battalions, 5th and 6th Argylls from Renfrew amalgamated in 1922 (to be separated again later), while 7th, 8th and 9th continued in service between the wars, until they were required once more at a time of crisis.

The Regular battalions reconstituted themselves quickly and both were soon on as near active service as can be experienced in peacetime.

CHAPTER 9

DEFENDING THE EMPIRE, 1919–1942

BETWEEN THE WARS

The 1st Battalion returned to the Indian sub-continent in 1919, but for the few old soldiers remaining India was not going to be the same as hitherto. Given the partial reorganization of the world political balance caused by the Great War and focused at the peace conference at Versailles, together with a growing awareness of a weakened hold over the Empire by the home government, and a realization that the exertions of Indian troops during the war reflected military strength which could be translated into political power, the demand was beginning to grow for a greater say in government by the Indians themselves.

Life for a resident battalion was pleasant enough, however, and apart from an increase in internal security duties, which took the form of a deterrent presence most of the time rather than an active role, the pattern of life was much as before. There was a constant requirement for field training and musketry practice, route marches, formal parades, guards and Durbars, but off duty there was sport and recreation in abundance, particularly for the officers. Poona was after all one of the best stations in India.

In 1921 the name of the Regiment was altered from 'Princess Louise's (Argyll and Sutherland Highlanders)' to 'The Argyll and Sutherland Highlanders (Princess Louise's)'. Another event which was designed to draw the two battalions closer together was the amalgamation of the two 'regimental' journals, but this publication failed and the two fiercely independent battalions reverted to their former practice.

In 1923 the 91st moved to Egypt and were stationed in Moascar garrison, close by Lake Timsah on the Suez Canal. After a few months they were rapidly dispatched to the Sudan by sea and on landing entrained for Khartoum where a mutiny had broken out. At that time the Sudan was a joint Anglo-Egyptian protectorate, which in effect meant that both the administration and military command was the responsibility of the British. The Argylls assisted in quelling the mutiny before it got out of hand, but lost one officer and four men killed. For some weeks the Battalion was engaged in detachment duties in various parts of the Sudan before returning to Egypt in January 1925. There they remained until 1928.

The 2nd Battalion, the 93rd, had been serving in Scotland and Ireland during the 1920s. The period of service in this part of the United Kingdom was both exciting and frustrating. The war had arguably delayed solving the 'Irish problem', until it was too late to reach a position whereby home rule could have meant acceptable dominion status, rather than full independence. It was the 1916 Easter rebellion which determined the future. Before independence in 1922 a large force was needed to keep the peace all over the island, and the 93rd were extremely busy in both static and mobile roles.

A pleasant time was spent in the West Indies, unfortunately marred by an incident of ill discipline against the civil police, before the Battalion moved to the Far East — rumoured to be as a punishment - and served in Shanghai on mainland China . For a hundred years and more British troops had been stationed in China, where large expatriate civilian populations lived and British commercial interests were strong. For the Argylls it was a mixture of 'real' guard duties and training for war, the possibility of which sometimes seemed remote and at other times imminent.

'During the month of May, A (MG) company provided river guards on the Yangtze, and from all accounts this appears to be quite a popular duty,' reported the *Thin Red Line*. 'It is certainly quite a change to learn the rudiments of the Lewis gun and in fact we guarantee to strip and assemble one of these weapons without having any spare parts left over.'

Another station in which the 93rd served for a while was Hong Kong after which, during the 1930s, they returned to India. There the pace was leisured, although the mumblings of constitutional change were concentrating the minds of the governments in Delhi and London. Massed Scottish bands took part in the Simla Jubilee Tattoo in 1935, the Pipes and Drums' complaint being, 'the lack of football' for four weeks; the '...Tattoo ground, which was the only football ground in Simla, was jealously guarded by the polo fraternity'. The 93rd had two periods of active service on the North West Frontier. They joined a 'Column' named Mohforce to restore order in the Mohmand area in 1935. There was some shooting, but the Battalion was never close enough to take an active part in the fighting.

In 1937 the Battalion was ordered to Waziristan 'due to unrest promoted by the Fakir of Ipl'. This was in the same area of the River Tochi where the Battalion had served in 1897. During March and April the 93rd were constantly on the move and were frequently sniped at while on the road and manning picquets. On 22 and 27 May there were deliberate attacks on the Battalion. There were casualties on both sides and in all the 93rd lost thirteen dead in the campaign. The Fakir's base was destroyed on 28 May and the British force gradually withdrew. It had been an arduous campaign and officers and men suffered considerably from heat, marching, septic sores and lack of rest. They still found time, however, to celebrate the coronation of the new King Emperor, George VI.

The 91st served at home from 1928 to 1939, initially at Shorncliffe, Kent and then in Edinburgh. There the resident battalions to this day perform the same function in the northern capital as the Household troops in London. The regimental records go into much detail of ceremonial routine, regimental events and domestic matters, including the provision of drafts for the 93rd which was serving overseas. The grand old lady, HRH Princess Louise, maintained her interest in the Regiment and in 1928 presented to the 91st a Shetland pony which was appropriately named 'Cruachan' after the lofty mountain dominating north Argyll and the war cry of her husband the Duke of Argyll's clan Campbell. Cruachan served faithfully in the Battalion for eleven years before retirement, although it must be said that regimental mascots often have as many vices as virtues.

With organizational changes in the Army, the 91st was at one time converted to a machine-gun battalion (simultaneously with the 93rd in India) and training of regimental drivers became a high priority too, in view of the developments in mobile warfare. It was a memorable day when at Tidworth in 1935 the Battalion paraded for what was to prove to be the last time in full dress, with red jackets and feather bonnets.

Portents of war had of course been evident since the early 1930s, but with the benefit of hindsight, preparations in the Army had not been as enthusiastic or as advanced as they should have been. Government, Army and nation were all at fault and without doubt this was because of the willing suspension of belief that the Germans could be contemplating military action on a large scale after the horrors of the Great War. In the East there was little indication of the extent of future Japanese expansion and the threat to India and the Far Eastern possessions.

In 1939 the Britain woke up fully to the military dangers of the time. The Territorial Army was rapidly expanded, and for the Regiment this involved various changes. The 9th Argylls (reconstituted in 1920) had already converted to 54th Light Anti-Aircraft Regiment RA in 1938, and 5th and 6th Battalions became machine-gun battalions in 1939: they were converted in 1941 to the anti-tank role as the 91st and 93rd Anti-Tank Regiments RA. All three of these artillery regiments were allowed to retain the suffix 'Argyll and Sutherland Highlanders'. The TA infantry battalions both formed twin battalions, 7th providing the nucleus for a new 10th Argylls, and 8th a new 11th Battalion. The 15th Argylls were re-formed in 1940, and their future was to take an unexpected turn later in the War.

MIDDLE EAST

The 91st were expecting a move from Aldershot to Fort George, but on 1 April 1939 they sailed for Palestine as an 'emergency' measure to join 16 Infantry Brigade in the British 6th Division. While other momentous events were occurring in September 1939, the Argylls' time was chiefly taken up with training and security duties in the townships, where both Arab and Jewish political groups were maintaining a level of violence in pursuit of their respective goals. In June 1940 the whole brigade moved to Egypt to man defences east of Mersa Matruh and two months later the Italians launched an attack across the western border of Libya and Egypt; they seized Sidi Barani, but advanced no further. The Argylls spent the next six months in intensive desert training in preparation for the British counter-attack.

In December 1940 a large-scale surprise attack was mounted against the Italians at Sidi Barani. This involved the British force of two divisions with Australian and Indian formations and supporting troops in a three-day advance in desert formation, along a route well inland so as to maintain secrecy. Travelling in troop-carrying vehicles, the brigade's task was to circle round to the south of the Italians and sweep in from the west. Their attack was to follow that of Indian troops in the first phase of the battle on 9 December, but 16 Brigade had to wait for artillery and tank support to join them for the second phase of the battle. Despite the delay and loss of surprise, the attack went in at dawn on 10 December with a dash across the desert towards the Battalion's objective, a hill overlooking Alam El Dab and the coast road.

'Immediately after starting, the battalion came under heavy artillery and machine-gun fire from the front and right flank ... there was no way to counter this fire while travelling in vehicles ... there were many casualties, and vehicle casualties were also heavy.'

Ordered to halt and debus, it was soon very obvious to the CO, Lieutenant Colonel R.C.B. Anderson, that it would be better to advance rather than hold intermediate positions under fire; so the Battalion embussed and continued the advance, covered by a few remaining tanks of 7th Royal Tank Regiment. After another halt during a sandstorm, the advance continued with 'A'and 'C' Companies in the lead. They seized objectives at bayonet point after facing a heavy weight of fire from machine-guns, and entered Alam El Dab. Other battalions passed through and Sidi Barani was quickly captured. The British victory was the more remarkable since the Italian ground troops and air force greatly outnumbered the British. It was the Battalion's major achievement of the early phase of the war.

The 91st remained in Egypt for several months of defensive work and training while awaiting a possible German invasion of Egypt. In May 1941, however, with the Germans sweeping through mainland Greece, the Argylls were ordered to embark for the defence of Crete.

Landing on the southern coast, the 91st's task was to defend the Plain of Messara from an invasion which was expected any day, while other British and Greek battalions were defending Heraklion and its harbour and airfield, twenty-five miles north across the mountain backbone of the island. On 20 May German paratroops were dropped on Crete and the situation immediately became very confused, because neither antagonist knew the whereabouts of the other's dispositions. Hunting for the larger groups of Germans was the Argylls task and when they were located and reported over an intermittent communications network, various attacks were ordered by Battalion HQ. These were often: '...nothing more than a gamble ... involved attacking at night an enemy of unknown strength, over rough and un-reconnoitred ground, with no supporting arms'.

More paratroops were arriving daily and their strength was mounting at an alarming rate. Casualties in the Battalion were also mounting with every engagement; by 24 May the Argylls had been ordered to march north to help in the defence of Heraklion, leaving a strong detachment at Ay Deka on the Messara Plain. Plans for the evacuation of Crete were announced and the Argylls in the north embarked in ships of the Royal Navy on the night of 28 May. The ships were bombed as they sailed away from Crete the following morning, and there were further casualties. The 300 Argylls who were expecting to be taken off the island from the southern beaches could not be rescued and in due course most were rounded up by the Germans, with only a few escaping. Less than half the Battalion reached Egypt, and a high proportion of the specialist officers and soldiers were missing. This was a disaster for the Battalion, whose fighting effectiveness could not easily be restored even with fresh drafts arriving and bringing it up to its full complement. For this reason it was left behind when 16 Brigade was sent to Syria and, in the words of Lieutenant Colonel Anderson:

'For the next two and a half years the battalion was destined to pursue its lonely way over a very wide area of the Middle East, performing many and varied tasks, some dull and monotonous, but no less essential, and it was not to find a permanent home again until February 1944.'

Internal security in Alexandria was their role for a time, before moving to Asmara in Eritrea, which four months earlier had been occupied by the British, during the final part of the Abyssinian campaign against the Italians. The Argylls joined 26 East African Brigade as the only British battalion, and on 17 November they were ordered to attack Venticinque on the road between Asmara and Gondar, close to Lake Tana. 'A' Company was delegated this task with support from the King's African Rifles; the intelligence summary stated:

'A Company A & SH advanced up the slopes of Venticinque under MG, rifle and mortar fire and the leading troops reached the summit at 1730 hours. The section and platoon formations of the A and SH drew the rapt admiration of those of our African troops who were lucky enough to see the attack.'

Most tactics with a real enemy do not follow the pamphlet drills, but this clearly did. Despite a number of further obstacles, British progress continued and Gondar was surrendered by the Italians, as the last engagement of the campaign. The job done, a few days later the Argylls returned to Eritrea, shortly to be sent to the Sudan.

FRANCE 1940

The 7th and 8th Argylls had been mobilized with 6th Black Watch in 154 Brigade as part of 51st Highland Division. Early in 1940 the Division was sent to France during the 'phoney war' period before German ground forces first engaged the Western Allies. In March, after a succession of tactical exercises, 51st Highland Division first moved to the Belgian border, and then to positions near Metz in Saarland to assist in guarding the Maginot Line, the massive line of concrete defences and gun emplacements on the Franco-German frontier. Except for occasional small-arms contact with German patrols when on concealed picquet duty in forward positions, the troops, if not totally relaxed, had much time to contemplate the beauty of the countryside in springtime and the rural life which seemed so peaceful that it was as if no human agent could have the temerity to disturb it. The initiative was firmly with the Germans.

On 10 May they invaded Holland and activity immediately increased, including the shelling of the French and British troops in this part of France. Elsewhere the main body of the British Expeditionary Force was ordered to advance rapidly through Belgium towards the German frontier, but was unable to resist the momentum of the German armoured thrust through the Ardennes forest. The 6th Argylls, having been in France for some months already, had been rushed forward with their machine-guns to the area south-west of Brussels; there they were separated into machine-gun sections to strengthen a number of British battalions. They fought gallantly during the delaying battle as the BEF conducted a fighting withdrawal across Belgium to Dunkirk. Their casualties numbered 400, but 270 all ranks escaped from Dunkirk to re-form and convert to an anti-tank regiment, the 93rd Anti-Tank Regiment, Royal Artillery.

Similarly 9th Argylls, as 54 Light Anti-Aircraft Regiment RA, served in France with the BEF from September 1939. They too were deployed forward to provide defence against the Luftwaffe which was maintaining an unrelenting series of air attacks each day of the campaign, causing tremendous damage, disruption and a high rate of human casualties. In the retreat to Dunkirk, one battery became detached, but the remainder of the Regiment did its best to give protection to the troops concentrating at Dunkirk. Their guns were destroyed deliberately when the ammunition ran out, and the members of the Regiment took their turn for the passage across the Channel. The remaining battery continued in support of French troops and a British division that landed in Cherbourg after Dunkirk, as a final gesture to the French allies. The battery managed to escape in June via the west coast, when French resistance collapsed.

The whole of 51st Highland Division, including 7th and 8th Argylls, had continued to be detached from the BEF during the retreat, and for a number of days both battalions took their turn in manning successive lines of the Maginot complex: the *'Ligne de contact'*, *'Ligne de soutien'* and *'Ligne de recueil'*. Enemy shelling and patrolling became more intense and it was perhaps fortunate that the Argylls were unaware of the fate of the BEF, feeling only the frustration of not being properly committed to battle. The French Command requested that the battalions should be moved by road on 23 May, first to a concentration area near Verdun and, three days later, to the Somme estuary. This latter journey was made by train on a very circuitous route. The tedium and uncertainty of the future was relieved when 8th Battalion, whose rations had run out, came across a forlorn BEF ration train with nowhere to go, and willing fatigue parties seized upon the contents in no time; 'one van was found to be full of enormous cheeses, which were bowled across the railway line by company quarter-master-sergeants,' runs the Battalion record.

The situation for 51st Highland Division, however, was very serious indeed. The Government at home was reluctant to leave France to its fate, but it also needed to salvage as much of the British Army as possible; these two aims were obviously incompatible. Thus the sole remaining British division in France after Dunkirk was now required to face six German divisions.

On 1 June the 51st was ordered to take over a 14-mile sector south and south-east of the town of St-Valery-sur-Somme on the estuary of the river, with elements of British 1st Armoured Division. It was relatively quiet: only a few German units having reached this far, the situation was very fluid and there was no clear 'front'. But the Germans were rapidly advancing across northern France with powerful forces, and it was only a matter of time before this British component of French Tenth Army would be overwhelmed.

The 7th Battalion's positions were five miles south of St-Valery; 8th Argylls were on their left, south-west of the town. Both battalions had to guard their front which was some four times as extended as normal. Enemy activity was evident in front of 7th Argyll's position on 1 June, with patrols and shelling building up over the next few days. On 4 June an attack on the Germans at Abbeville was launched to the south-east of 7th Argylls, but it was unsuccessful. A day later all hell broke loose and the enemy advanced with great speed and firepower straight towards 7th Battalion.

'A' and 'C' Companies were quickly overrun and elements from 'D' Company in reserve moved forward in support, but the companies were too dispersed to permit mutually supporting firepower and withstand the enemy's advance. Even Battalion HQ was soon under attack by forward elements of the enemy but these were defeated by the remainder of 'A' Company, who had withdrawn under severe attack. 'B' Company, however, were able to hold their positions when the attack came in. Each company of the Battalion was surrounded and besieged by enemy formations, and were thus unable to hinder the main flow of the enemy westwards. Enemy mortar fire was particularly effective and casualties very heavy by the end of the morning. A counter-attack by The Black Watch to assist the Argylls was called off at the last minute, because it was recognized that the situation was by this stage beyond redemption. Battalion HQ was entirely powerless to control the battle, the ammunition for their own self-defence was by now exhausted, and the CO, Lieutenant Colonel E.P. Buchanan, was captured. The remainder of 'A' Company kept the enemy at bay during the night, but 'B' Company, which by now was exposed well behind the enemy advance, was surrounded and compelled to surrender during the afternoon. 'D' Company, the only relatively unscathed sub-unit left, managed to make contact with 8th Argylls to their left and came under their command. In all the Battalion lost 23 officers and 500 other ranks killed, wounded or missing and most of the latter categories were captured.

The 8th Argylls' forward platoons had been hit at dawn on 5 June. Friendly artillery fire had at first been effective against both infantry and their accompanying tanks, but later in the morning this artillery support was no longer available and enemy mortars were being used with devastating effect; some of the Argylls' forward sections were lost. As a consequence of the Germans overwhelming 7th Battalion to the south, the situation for the 8th became more critical during the day and orders were given for their withdrawal. Fortunately 'A' and 'B' Companies were in contact with Battalion HQ and, by skill and some unaccountable good fortune, still at considerable strength; they avoided meeting the enemy during the evening and night.

'C' and 'D' Companies, however, were out of contact and far forward, and on the morning of 6 June they were attacked in considerable force. By sheer determination and courage they held out for another twenty-four hours, but the Germans moved up close and then rushed their positions, to discover only a very few Argylls still able and fighting to the end. They were captured.

'A' and 'B' Companies, however, assisted by tanks of 9th Lancers, were able to defend themselves and had reached the coast at Ault. It became obvious to Major Lorne Campbell that a position could not be held at Ault for any length of time because the remainder of the Brigade had withdrawn west of the next river, the Bresle. Campbell conducted a march over two nights, hiding-up during the daylight hours of 7 June, and successfully brought in his 200 men to rejoin Lieutenant Colonel Grant at Battalion HQ on the morning of 8 June.

While the main body of 51st Highland Division were surrounded at St-Valery-en-Caux farther up the coast, and most of 7th Argylls had been destroyed, 8th Argylls were still a fighting force of three companies (one being 'D' Company of the 7th). The immediate plan was to move the Battalion back to Le Havre where a bridgehead was to be established. This was achieved quite quickly on motor transport, despite enemy interference, but orders were soon given for all British troops to be evacuated. This was achieved overnight on 15/16 June in the appropriately named SS *Duke of Argyll*.

Thus the weakened 8th Argylls were saved, and a nucleus of 7th Battalion also returned home, around which a new 7th Battalion could be formed.

MALAYAN CAMPAIGN

The 2nd Battalion, the 93rd had been in the Far East all this while, having left India and moved to Singapore in August 1939 as part of 12 Indian Infantry Brigade. The concept of the defence of the island of Singapore had been worked out long before,

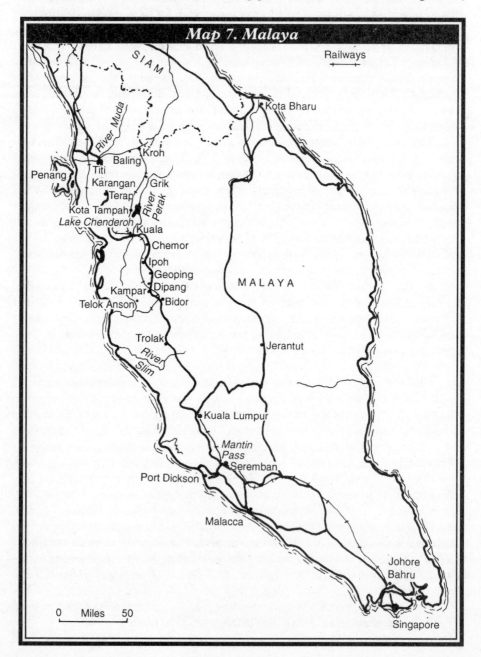

based on the supposed impenetrability of the mainland Malayan jungle by large enemy forces, and the protection by the Royal Navy and Royal Air Force of the seaward approaches. The extent of the Japanese intentions, however, even in 1939, was severely underestimated: China, where the Japs were already fighting and in control of large areas, was after all a long way off. The war in Europe was already two years old before the Japanese attacked the British and Americans.

Hitherto jungle training had never featured much in the training of the British Army. The 93rd Highlanders, however, were commanded by a very great soldier, Lieutenant Colonel Ian Stewart, who devised for the Battalion a complete system of jungle tactics. In the Great War Stewart had been severely wounded at the Battle of Le Câteau, and served with the Tank Corps as a staff captain at the Battle of Cambrai. On the Battalion's arrival in Malaya he had commandeered six armoured cars, which were to prove invaluable in the subsequent fighting.

The Jocks responded with alacrity to life in the jungle, the 'tiger patrols' and the scheme to 'fix frontally - encircle' at every level, from three-man patrols to battalion. Another tactic was 'to fillet' the enemy advance along the line of a road, and there were times when control was vital, which meant concentration of troops and fire (including artillery) on the road through the jungle, and other times when the jungle could be dominated for a while by small groups acting on their own initiative. High morale and an aggressive spirit could maintain the troops' effectiveness for an extended period, but overwhelming numbers were eventually the deciding factor. During the period before hostilities began, the 93rd were so highly trained that they became known as the 'Jungle Beasts', although a changeover of personnel in 1941 meant that not all the Battalion had gained as much experience as the original members.

On 8 December, the day on which both Britain and the USA formally declared war on Japan, Japanese forces landed at Khota-Bahru on the north-east coast of Malaya, and the 93rd were put at 48 hours' notice; on the 10th the Japanese Navy sank the battleships *Prince of Wales* and *Repulse* off Kunatan, and on the same day the 93rd with 12 Brigade were ordered from Port Dickson to Jerantut as part of the Command mobile reserve. No decision had been reached as to their task; this depended on the whereabouts and success of the Japanese advance, and how well the enemy could be resisted. By 12 December it was decided that the 93rd should assist in the defence of the western settlements and lines of communications and the Battalion moved forward by train and road to Ipoh to reinforce the hard-pressed 11th Indian Division.

On arrival 'C' Company under Major Kennard with two armoured cars, was sent forward to Grik to meet an attack from the east, while the remainder of the Battalion were ordered to Baling, twenty miles north but on a different road, to meet another possible threat from the east through Kroh. By 16 December, with the defeat of 11th Indian Division, the 93rd had to face the prospect of an enemy threat from the north-west as well as from the east; so far there had been no contact with the enemy although the Battalion's task was to delay, rather than to defend. They were kept on the move as a reserve, however, which was a most exhausting and frustrating experience, until they received orders to defend Titi-Karangan near the River Muda, where an armoured threat was expected. They arrived at 2200 hours on 16 December:

'It was a pitch black night with continuous heavy rain, and reconnaissance of the ground in daylight had, of course, been impossible ... few could find cover. The armoured cars and part of the transport that had been sent off southwards before our destination was changed were recalled, and to their credit all ... turned up in time for the battle next day ... No artillery or anti-tank guns were available.'

Thus the 93rd faced their first battle.

Contact was made at 1000 hours on 17 January and 'A' Company managed to contain the enemy's attempt to encircle them, despite some losses of their own. Japanese pressure increased for the next two hours and the CO was about to order the companies to attack, when a message advising withdrawal was received from Brigade. The companies extricated themselves one by one, the armoured cars on the road, with their twin Vickers machine-guns, proving of great assistance. Moving some twenty miles south to hold Terap, gave the Battalion a welcome break. Meanwhile 'C' Company was heavily involved with the enemy at Grik, successfully ambushing the Japanese and inflicting numerous casualties. Their armoured car, commanded by Corporal King was invaluable in giving mobile fire support, but sadly the Company lost a platoon in the fighting before they too were ordered to withdraw.

The battle for Malaya, as far as 2nd Argylls were concerned, continued for a further three and a half weeks. 'C' Company had rejoined the Battalion, and the axis to be denied the enemy was now the road leading south from Grik. On 19 December the forward company, of another battalion, but under command of the Argylls, was ambushed and suffered heavily.

'The Argyll armoured cars of D Company group arrived, and in turn smashed into and surprised the Japs in close area, in large numbers and at short range. Under such circumstances the fire of well-served machine-guns is devastating.'

Captain Boyle's 'D' Company restored the position while 'A' and 'B' Companies held tactical features along the road in linear defence. Although this was the only way to hold the road, the companies were susceptible to an encircling attack, to prevent which tiger patrols went into the rubber plantations alongside the road. The numerical odds against the 93rd were five to one, and as the whole of 11th Division was withdrawing there was no way in which the 93rd could seize the initiative and attack the Japanese. By now the enemy were also moving by river craft on the Perak which flowed parallel to the road and could not be guarded as well.

The defence of a causeway over the River Perak was a key engagement in this part of the withdrawal, and despite the difficulties of communications, the Argylls held positions at Kota Tampan a mile north and brought up a reserve company to defend the causeway. 'The Argylls', reported the CO, 'were able to halt completely the Jap threat, and nowhere did it get nearer than 500 yards from the vital artery of the road.' The Battalion had adopted a particularly successful tactic of 'filleting' the enemy's advance along the axis of the road, and causing delay by dividing his force. Even so, it appeared that the planned fighting withdrawal had been allowed to be too long delayed, since reports were coming in that the Japs had encircled to the south, cutting off the Argylls' withdrawal route completely. Fortunately this intelligence was incorrect, and by moving 'A' Company quickly southwards, the Argylls were able to set up ambushes to prevent the Japs seizing the road. 'Shouts and screams answered the Argylls' fire, and that was the end of the pursuit.' Artillery fire was available and successfully prevented the main body of the enemy from following up. When the causeway itself was attacked, the same determined fire succeeded in beating the Japs off. The

Battalion's casualties had been relatively light. The same tactics were repeated over the next few days. 'Companies were slowly leap-frogged back so as to invite a repetition of the encircling attack, and ambushes were laid to catch the follow up.'

In due course the Battalion was pulled back into reserve, but on 27 December the Argylls planned for a counter-attack through 5/2 Punjabis, which could have succeeded had that battalion managed to hold the ground for a while longer. The operation had to be cancelled, however, and later that night, with the 93rd as rearguard, the Brigade withdrew twenty-five miles, breaking contact with the enemy.

Despite the successful fighting withdrawal, the Japanese managed to follow up with amazing speed and maintain pressure at all times, rendering impossible further opportunities for counter-attacking. There were, however, scores of engagements and incidents along the way — Chemor, Gopeng-Dipang, Telok-Anson, being the chief ones. At Kota-Bahru Captain Hendry, commanding 'A' Company, CSM Bing and Private Anderson were involved in a fight with a strong Jap patrol, which had entered the railway station. Under cover of an armoured car

'They at first tried the right flank. Here they met a couple of Japs, whom they shot, but their further progress was stopped by a swamp ... tried the left approach ... and assaulted. The Japs were completely surprised and had little chance in the shooting match which followed ...

Pte Anderson got "running" practice at one or two who tried to escape ... Captain Hendry belaboured two ... into insensibility with his steel helmet ... CSM Bing, who had by this time run out of ammunition, held his tommy gun by the barrel and clubbed the last one over the head.'

As a large number of Japs were by now approaching, Captain Hendry seized one of the 'least dead-looking Japs' as a prisoner and the three Argylls then withdrew.

The final and most desperate engagement on the mainland for the Argylls was the Battle of the River Slim from 4 to 7 January 1942. This position was to be denied to the enemy until the night of 7/8 January by two weak brigades, but it was hoped that artillery would destroy the Japanese, forced out of the jungle because of its extreme density in this area. The 93rd were reinforced at the last minute by 100 men, many of them having been drafted for duty in Singapore until this time, and their task was to form a reserve for whichever brigade flank was attacked.

Enemy armour was much in evidence during the battle and the Argylls' armoured cars were early casualties; there was an extreme scarcity of anti-tank weapons on the British side. The first tentative enemy advance was held back, but soon pressure became far too great and the battle became extremely fluid as companies of Argylls tried to cut off Jap probing attacks. But the Japanese were in overwhelming strength and they infiltrated the area rapidly. 'Heavy and confused fighting now took place with the Japs swarming in from all sides.' Accounts, while full and detailed, give the impression of a general mêlée which lacked tactical coherence on both sides, despite all efforts for control. Captain Boyle with 'D' Company was cut off, and while collecting:'the remnant of his company, did a wide detour nearly a mile to the west ... The party, encumbered by their wounded, ran into impossible country and were left far behind the tide of Jap advance. Some days later they were surprised by a Jap patrol and captured.'

Other groups were captured, the wounded were shot, and those who could walk were marched away to captivity. Thus with the fighting effectiveness of the Battalion and other battalions in the Brigade lost, it was a miracle that Captain Tom Slessor managed to gather three officers and some 90 other ranks, together with the two remaining armoured cars and a few transports under the command of Major David Wilson. They were not involved in any further action as they motored south in the general withdrawal to Singapore island.

On 13 January this small group reached Singapore, but within days the battalion had grown to 250 all ranks. Lieutenant Colonel Stewart, who had been in temporary command of 12 Brigade, returned and the new second in command, Major Angus Rose, who had been on a clandestine operation behind Jap lines after landing from the sea, arrived and they set about reorganizing the Battalion as a fighting unit. Intensive training resumed, there being many new men who had little experience of fighting, and it was fortunate that some 200 Royal Marines, survivors from *Prince of Wales* and *Repulse*, joined the Battalion to increase its strength considerably. This cemented the 'Plymouth Argylls' connection (8th Argylls had served with a Marine division in 1940) and it had to be acknowledged that the Marines were superior footballers, in the odd moments that were free from training.

Meanwhile the Japanese advance on the Malayan peninsula continued unabated and was forcing the remaining British, Indian and Australian troops back towards Singapore. But there was time to plan a withdrawal for the by now greatly depleted formations, through a defended bridgehead of which the Argylls formed part. The Battalion was given the task of holding the Singapore 'causeway', the only link to Singapore Island.

The withdrawal of all the British and Dominion troops took place on 31 January. Thirty thousand troops crossed the causeway without incident or further casualties during the night, and this was achieved faster than had been expected. By 0730 hours on 1 February the operation had been completed and the Royal Engineers had placed demolition charges; the Argylls were then ordered to withdraw from their positions on the mainland:

'With their pipers before them and in extended order they marched out of Malaya ... The morning sun was already hot when the still air was broken by "A hundred Pipers" and "Hielan' Laddie", and the remaining Highlanders, with steady bearing and heads held high, marched from the lost campaign into a doomed island.'

The last man out was Drummer Hardy, the CO's batman. He had a near insubordinate obstinacy about him, it being the nature of his race, and, as on previous occasions, the CO could never induce him to 'double away' from danger. 'He just walked, slowly, all the way over.'

Apart from artillery shellfire and bombing by the Japs, there was a lull of a week after the evacuation of Malaya. Singapore Island measures 25 miles by 14 miles and was largely covered by rubber plantations, jungle and swamp. The population numbered more than 700,000 and the city is on the southern coast facing the sea. The Argylls spent many hours reconnoitring possible sectors where they might be deployed as part of the reserve brigade.

At 2000 hours on 8 February 1940 the Japanese invaded the island on the north-west sector held by the Australians. Twelve hours later the 93rd were ordered forward to assist the Australians, but they were 'well and truly' bombed on their arrival at the concentration area. By nightfall on 9 February the Japanese had consolidated their bridgehead and captured an airfield, while the 93rd had taken up a position some two miles to the east to block further advances. An Indian battalion was bombed, shelled and driven back by a Japanese attack and an Australian battalion was ordered to withdraw; this left the Argylls in the front line and with no depth to their defensive position. Nearby oil tanks were burning furiously and steady rainfall brought the vaporized oil down to earth, covering everything. As the British artillery fire was extremely thinly spread, any plans to counter-attack the Japanese had to be abandoned.

Fighting on 9 February was spasmodic, however, and the Argylls easily resisted Japanese forays until some fifty medium tanks appeared after dark, driving along the main road in the 'filleting' movement of slicing the defenders down the middle, a tactic that had been used with some success by the Argylls on the mainland. There were virtually no anti-tank weapons forward to deal with the armour, but an Argyll armoured car with the redoubtable Sergeant Nuttall in command, gallantly opened fire but to no avail; the car was quickly knocked out. The tanks were delayed by the Battalion for a while during the night, however, and one was immobilized by a mine. But they were virtually invulnerable to the lightly armed British infantry, although they were successfully blocked farther down the road.

A withdrawal of two Argyll companies was then ordered, while 'A' and 'D' Companies, now out of touch with Battalion HQ, were left to carry out the previous order to delay the enemy thrust as much as possible. Their final orders had been to withdraw to the building at Dairy Farm and a pipeline some miles along the road to Singapore city. 'B' and 'C' companies had been given orders to withdraw behind British lines; the remainder fought on along the line of the Japanese advance. On 11 February a final order was given to Lieutenant Colonel Stewart to lead the remaining Argylls and Marines in a counter-attack, but this order was cancelled as it was now recognized that the position was beyond hope. Ordered back to Tyersall camp, the Argylls awaited fresh instructions; on 15 February they were ordered to surrender.

Many of the Argylls had got through the Japanese lines on the mainland and a good proportion actually reached safety. A handful were ordered to leave by sea (there was very limited shipping space) to take with them the hard lessons that had been learned. Two men remained in Malaya for the rest of the war, instructing local Malays and Chinese in the art of resisting Japanese occupation. A total of 244 Argylls died in this campaign and a further 184 died in captivity.

Field Marshal Sir Archibald Wavell must have the last word on the campaign; as Commander-in-Chief he was in the best position to judge the events:

'There was one battalion — a battalion of the Argyll and Sutherland Highlanders — commanded by a remarkable commanding officer — which he had trained most intensively in jungle fighting. There was no doubt whatever that this battalion was as good as and better than any of the Japanese, and naturally that battalion did quite magnificent work until they were practically wiped out in the battle of the Slim River on 8 January after a gallant fight.'

'Ne Obliviscaris', 'Do not forget'.

CHAPTER 10

MEDITERRANEAN THEATRE

ALAMEIN AND THE DESERT

The re-formation of 51st Highland Division was a matter of national pride in Scotland, and was to vindicate the wartime expedient of battalions of famous regiments, forming brigades and divisions of extraordinary strength and resilience in battle. It is only in peacetime that special pleading is necessary for the British 'regimental system', because people forget or find difficulty in imagining what it is to gamble with death or, perhaps worse, anticipate and feel pain. Identifying with a local regiment helps most members to combat the fear within and express true selflessness, the two human emotions most needed in battle.

The 7th and 8th Argylls were both quickly rebuilt, the former being an amalgam of the survivors from France and 10th Argylls, their twin battalion; indeed for a while the battalion was known as 7/10th Argylls. They joined a new 51st Highland Division and spent the best part of two years in intensive training in Scotland. For a time they were preparing to go to Norway, but the speed of the German advance northwards through Scandinavia led to the cancellation of this plan. The 8th Argylls trained as part of a Royal Marine Division, involving amphibious landings in Loch Fyne where many of the Jocks were instantly and literally at home. Later serving with the 1 Guards Independent Brigade, there were advanced plans to assault the German-held Azores, and carry out raids on the French coast, but none took place.

The 51st Highland Division including 7th Argylls, with Lieutenant Colonel Lorne Campbell (late of the 8th) in command, left the Clyde bound for the Mediterranean theatre in June 1942. They sailed via the Cape of Good Hope to Port Tewfik to join Lieutenant General Montgomery's Eighth Army in Egypt.

Allied plans had already been laid for British and US troops to expel the Germans and Italians from North Africa in a pincer movement: the British advancing from Egypt through Libya, and a landing of Allied troops nearly 2,000 miles to the west on the Algerian coast to sweep into Tunisia. Rommel, however, with his twelve divisions was within 70 miles of Alexandria and the Nile and on 31 August launched an offensive against the British and Dominion troops on the Alam Halfa ridge. This battle was arguably the turning-point of the campaign, as the Axis forces failed to break through and were thrown back. At this juncture 7th Argylls arrived in theatre.

Montgomery allowed time for the newly arrived divisions to train intensively for the coming battle, and exercises followed a pattern of breaching minefields, following closely behind friendly artillery fire, rushing enemy positions, and digging in ready for a probable counter-attack. The Eighth Army comprised armour and infantry from Great Britain, Australia, New Zealand, South Africa and India. During the few weeks before the battle, the Argylls spent much time in the front-line trenches overlooking the vast minefield which marked no man's land between the armies. British deception plans had convinced Rommel that the breakthrough would be to the south of the line towards the Qattara Depression —ground itself unsuitable for any fighting and hence the southern boundary of the battle zone.

At 2200 hours on 23 October 1942, with the advantage of a full moon, the Battle of El Alamein began. There was an advance on all fronts, but the main armoured thrust took place in the north in the area of the village of El Alamein. The 51st Highland Division's tasks were to capture three objective lines: Green, Red and Black; 7th Argylls were in the lead of their 154 Brigade with 1st Black Watch to their right. Twenty minutes of artillery fire was the prelude to battle:

'The noise was one thunderous roar ... the distant horizon appeared to be on fire. The desert was flooded by brilliant moonlight which made it easier for our troops to make their way through the extensive enemy minefields ... The Battalion advanced at the speed of 100 yards in three minutes.'

The enemy joined in the firing with a vengeance.

'C' and 'D' Companies were in the lead with the sound of the pipes in their ears; within the hour they had taken their first objectives, nicknamed 'Paisley', 'Mons Meg', 'Renfrew' and 'Falkirk'. 'A' and 'B' Companies moved through 'C' Company and they suffered a number of casualties from enemy shellfire, booby-traps and mines. Despite this good progress, some British artillery shells were falling too close and the Argylls had to dig in during a pause of an hour. Enemy artillery, mortar and machine-gun fire increased, but by 0200 hours on 24 October 'Greenock' had been taken, although plans to capture 'Stirling' were delayed until tank support was available. Surprisingly there was no enemy counter-attack during the day, but 2nd Seaforth's (152 Brigade) attack on 'Stirling' failed during the afternoon. Enemy artillery fire was kept up all the while which emphasized the absolute need to be dug in at all times, when not actually on the move.

The plan for the second night of battle was to advance a further mile to a position known as 'Nairn', with three companies up and the somewhat weakened 'C' Company in the rear with Battalion HQ. Although there were many casualties, including all the officers of 'A' and 'D' Companies, the operation was entirely successful. The enemy were in considerable strength, however, and there were large expanses of uncleared minefields, so the battle had many days to run. Indeed for the Argylls until 26 October it remained a holding operation in their sector, and replenishment of ammunition, rations and water was becoming problematical.

The arrival of friendly armour and lorried infantry relieved the position, which allowed the Battalion time in reserve. Active patrolling in front of the positions was necessary, and enemy shelling was continuous until 7th Argylls were fully relieved by a South African battalion on 30 October.

A second phase of battle started for the Argylls on 2 November when they relieved a New Zealand battalion in the front line north of the 'Nairn' position. A day later the Battalion was ordered to attack a hill 'Point 44' at Tel el Aqqaqir, close by the line of the proposed armoured breakthrough. It was a battalion objective and seven regiments' worth of artillery were to fire in support, giving an indication of the importance of the operation. The approach was some 2,200 yards, and although there was much difficulty in locating the start-line in the dark, artillery fire helped to identify the objective. 'A' Company under Captain Seymour and 'C' Company under Captain Young were in the lead:

'After we had advanced about 1,000 yards C Company disappeared in the smoke ... laid for us in order to cover our advance. The line of [telegraph] poles was crossed at 6.15 a.m. according to schedule ... Unfortunately some of our guns were firing short, and in consequence caused a number of casualties.'

Inevitably some of the sections got lost in the smoke but half an hour later the position was cleared — most of the enemy had remained until the last minute and then rapidly departed. On arrival the Argylls discovered the hill had been an enemy divisional headquarters. In a mock ceremony, the CO was awarded an Iron Cross, of which a store had been found, and several of the Jocks also awarded themselves the same distinction. There was also a large quantity of champagne and chianti, which was also fair game for a cheerful battalion. Sadly 72 men had been killed and 203 wounded.

On that day the Allied armoured broke out and began the pursuit across more than a thousand miles of desert. Tripoli was the main objective since it offered port facilities which were of fundamental importance to the supply lines of Eighth Army. During the advance rations, water and ammunition had to be dumped on beaches from lighters. A week later the British First Army, in an Allied invasion force, landed in French North Africa.

During the first stage of the advance 7th Argylls were not committed to battle, and indeed Rommel, who had lost most of his tank force and abandoned his Italian divisions, was not able to establish a position any farther forward of El Agheilla some 600 miles to the west. Thus on 5 December the Division reached to within twenty miles of Agheilla, and the Argylls joined the front line at Mersa Brega. There they remained for a week, but when the neighbouring Black Watch launched an attack the enemy abandoned the position. There were a number of casualties from mines and booby-traps when the Argylls searched and cleared the village. Then the advance continued rather more cautiously for a further two hundred miles to Beurat, where enemy resistance was again met. Casualties were suffered from shelling and mortar fire during the next few days, but Beurat was cleared and the advance to Tripoli continued.

The 51st Highland Division was responsible for clearing the coast road, and despite a shortage of petrol good progress was made. At Corradini near Homs, 7th Argylls were ordered to mount a flanking attack after taking a roundabout route through the desert. The enemy positions could not be attacked in daylight because of lack of artillery cover, and when the attack went in after dark the enemy had withdrawn. Several more similar operations were planned, but the Germans were not in the mood for waiting. Tripoli was captured on 23 January: it had taken precisely three months from the attack at El Alamein. There was a 'Victory Parade', the first one for British troops during the war, when Prime Minister Winston Churchill visited and inspected Eighth Army. The Highland regiments and their pipes and drums were of course much in evidence.

TUNISIA

In the mean time 8th Argylls had landed with First Army to the east of Algiers. The Army was a somewhat skeletal formation, and the Battalion was in 36 Brigade. They landed direct from the troop ship via assault craft, adopting techniques they had practised dozens of times during training, but encountered no resistance from the French troops nominally under Vichy French command and therefore 'hostile'. The 93rd Anti-Tank Regiment Royal Artillery, formerly 6th Argylls, also landed with First Army as V Corps anti-tank regiment. Within a few days the whole of the invasion force had moved east towards the Algeria-Tunisia border.

The Luftwaffe was much in evidence and it was obvious that the Germans and Italians were intent on holding Tunisia at all costs. On 18 November, some twenty miles east of the border, 8th Argylls' 'X' Company came into contact with the enemy at Djebel Abiod, and the following day a particularly daring raid was carried out by two platoons under Lieutenants R.G. MacKay and R.A. C. McClure, on what was thought to be a tank harbour area. When holding the *jebel* (hill) alongside the village on 21 November, they were infiltrated by Italians and some Argylls were captured; fortunately they were spotted being led away and the tables were turned on the Italians, forty being taken prisoner.

A week later 8th Argylls were part of a brigade advance with 6th Royal West Kents and 5th Buffs along the road to Mateur. The weather was wet, the wind appalling and the approach move by infantry carriers was frequently delayed. Then the enemy made their presence known by firing at the Argylls from hills on each side of the railway, nicknamed 'Green Hill' and 'Bald Hill'. It was an ideal ambush position and 'A' Company in advance were quickly brought under intense machine-gun, anti-tank rifle and mortar fire. Lieutenant Colonel MacKellar ordered 'Y' Company to seize the northernmost 'Green Hill', while 'X' Company was to attack 'Bald Hill' to the south, covered by fire from the centre. 'Y' Company were soon pinned down and progress could not be made on 'Green Hill' until 'B' Company could be moved up; 'X' Company were more successful, but later they were threatened from the rear. 'A' Company were then counter-attacked by the Germans and only eight men managed to escape, the remainder being captured. The other three companies lost a third of their strength in the battle, before Brigade HQ issued orders to withdraw after dark. The Germans succeeded in holding these hills for several months until the final assault on Tunis in May 1943.

During the next few weeks there was little movement. The rain continued, it was cold; the hills of Tunisia proved formidable obstacles and well suited to defence in depth. Throughout the winter 8th Argylls were constantly on operations, chiefly patrol work rather than deliberate raids or attacks. On Christmas Day 1942 they were moved to join 1 Guards Brigade in the area of 'Longstop Hill' which dominated the western approach to Tunis through the town of Medjez el Bab. There aggressive patrolling was carried out against the constant enemy movement in the hills. Sergeant Sandy MacKinnon and his platoon did excellent work:

'One night he was holding an outpost position when about sixty Germans approached; so he quickly moved his sections in order to set a trap for them, and held his fire until they were almost on him. At this close range they killed twelve and

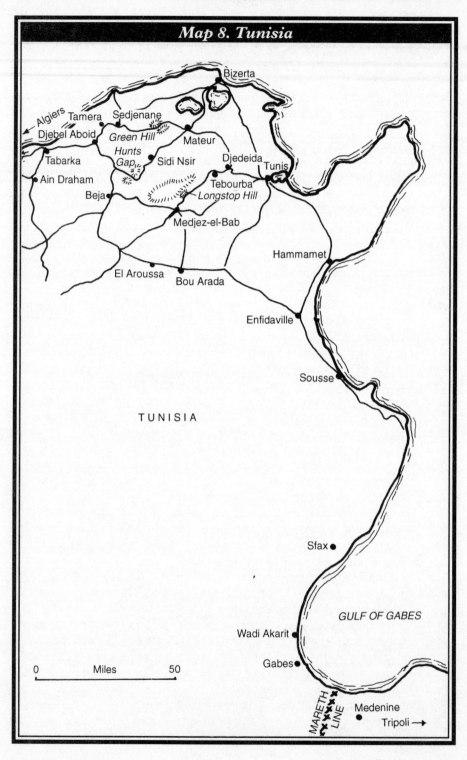

Map 8. Tunisia

Bizerta

Algiers
Tamera   Sedjenane
Djebel Aboid
Green Hill   Mateur
Hunts   Sidi Nsir   Djedeida
Tabarka   *Gap*   Tunis
Ain Draham   Teboutha
Beja   *Longstop Hill*

Medjez-el-Bab

Hammamet

El Aroussa
Bou Arada

Enfidaville

Sousse

TUNISIA

Sfax

GULF OF GABES

0   Miles   50

Wadi Akarit

Gabes

MARETH LINE
Medenine

Tripoli →

wounded many more ... and captured an officer and two NCOs who were carrying a powerful radio set.'

For this exploit he was awarded the Distinguished Conduct Medal.

The 6th Argylls (93rd Anti-Tank Regiment, RA) were kept similarly active during the period in Tunisia, although much of their time was spent divided between various formations. In February 'J' Troop prevented a major enemy tank thrust from breaking through at Thala, and later in the month 'Q', 'S' and 'T' Batteries were rapidly brought together to block a German advance which had broken through near El Aroussa, a task which was successfully accomplished.

In early March 8th Argylls were involved in the fiercest fight they had yet encountered, in the area known as 'Hunt's Gap'. This brigade battle lasted several days, the fortunes of individual companies fluctuating tactically, and the resupply situation in the mountainous terrain always precarious. By dint of sheer determination the various company positions were held despite numerous raids and counter-attacks. Miraculously telephone communications were efficient, enabling Battalion HQ to be kept informed and orders to be passed, while the artillery support was most effective and well controlled despite the difficult terrain. On 19 March 8th Argylls were relieved for a few days.

In April it was possible for large-scale operations to begin in the advance on Tunis, and a number of engagements were fought by the Battalion with great success, involving much close-quarter combat. Progress was slow, however, because the enemy had to be defeated in detail.

To the east Eighth Army had crossed from Libya into Tunisia in late February, and it was apparent that a large enemy force was advancing towards the forward troops in positions at Medenine. The British worked furiously to strengthen the line by digging, wiring and laying minefields. The 7th Argylls were holding part of the front line in early March. Sure enough, on 6 March enemy infantry were seen and fired on. They then inched their way forward in dead ground, and got close before being successfully attacked by platoons carried forward on tanks of 'B' Squadron, 40th Royal Tank Regiment. Elsewhere enemy armour was defeated and they retreated behind their own defensive positions, the 'Mareth Line'.

On 20 March the offensive began against the Mareth Line. At first all the objectives were taken by Eighth Army, but most of them were lost in furious counter-offensives. On 23 March 7th Argylls were called out of reserve to hold a position overlooking part of the line, at Wadi Zigzaou. Here they protected mine-clearing parties from the Royal Engineers and on 28 March patrols discovered the enemy had withdrawn. The line was then occupied before the Battalion moved westwards to the next German stop-line at Wadi Akarit.

At dawn on 6 April the British attacked with three divisions up, 51st on the right and 7th Argylls in the front line of their 154 Brigade. After an hour of artillery bombardment, the Battalion advanced and made good progress despite enemy artillery and machine-gun fire. The minefield and an anti-tank ditch were crossed successfully, and 'A' and 'B' Companies seized the front objectives, while 'C' Company passed through. Casualties were considerable, and when the counter-attacks came in the Argylls had a very hard fight on their hands.

The integrity and subsequent success of the Battalion was due almost entirely to the inspired leadership of Lieutenant Colonel Lorne Campbell who 'read the battle' with the greatest skill and imagination as it progressed.

'In spite of heavy machine-gun fire,' the citation states, 'in the early stages of the attack, Lt Col Campbell skilfully accomplished this difficult operation.' Later 'realizing the vital necessity of quickly establishing a gap for the passage of anti-tank guns, he took personal charge of this operation ... He inspired his men by his presence in the forefront of the battle, cheering them on and rallying them as he moved to those points where the fighting was heaviest ... He went forward alone into a hail of fire and personally reorganized [a company] position remaining with the Company...:' and much more besides to embarrass a modest man. The citation is longer than most, and mentions his neck wound almost as an aside. To his two DSOs won in France in 1940 and at Alamein in 1942, was added the Victoria Cross for this action.

Fortunately enemy armour was broken up by artillery fire during the afternoon, and at 1800 hours two enemy battalions with armour in support mounted a very strong counter-attack, some getting to within 50 yards of 'C' Company HQ. Whereupon the Company Commander, Major John Lindsay Macdougall, charged the enemy with five other men, uttering the cry 'No surrender "C" Company"!', killed some of the enemy, captured a further twelve and saw off the remainder. Overall this engagement had been 'the most vicious and furious the battalion had yet to endure' in the campaign. The Battalion took 700 prisoners in all, seventeen anti-tank guns, fourteen artillery pieces, eight anti-tank rifles, 33 machine-guns, ten mortars and much else besides in the way of ammunition and stores.

A fortnight later 7th Argylls were in action again, holding part of the front line at Enfidaville. Although thinly spread, a full programme of active patrolling was necessary as the campaign closed for Eighth Army.

Meanwhile, with First Army 8th Argylls had further tasks to achieve while advancing through the mountains to the west of Tunis. It was hard going and much close fighting was necessary and many casualties were sustained by the Battalion over a period of a fortnight. Their final battle was for 'Longstop Hill' which had been held by the Germans since the start of the campaign, because it dominated a major route into Tunis. Detailed and elaborate plans for a brigade attack were made and reconnaissance was carried out by the commanders.

The 5th Buffs took positions on the high ground to the left while 6th Royal West Kent Regiment took intermediate positions on the approach to Longstop. At daylight on 23 April the Argylls edged forward and at 1030 hours the CO, Lieutenant Colonel Macnab, was ordered to attack, supported by a squadron of North Irish Horse with full artillery support. They moved forward in a box formation and despite enemy fire managed to keep their relative company positions in the open ground, where they could be clearly seen by the enemy. But on the hill:

'... the going was so bad that we carried out the assault more as a body of men than as individual sections. Generally speaking the Boche stayed put and fired until we were right upon their positions.'

Thus read Major Jack Anderson's account. Battalion HQ in the centre of the box had been destroyed in the fire fight and Anderson was leading not only 'Y' Company but the whole Battalion by this stage.

'Gradually more officers and men arrived all exhausted by the heat, the stiff climb and the previous fortnight's fighting. In the end we had collected about 4 officers and 30 men, and casualties had been so heavy that it seemed unlikely that many more would materialize. Finally we advanced again to the last height ... and we set about reorganizing at the top.'

His citation for the Victoria Cross mentioned his '...leading the battalion through intense enemy machine-gun and mortar fire' for five hours and that he '...personally led the attack on at least 3 enemy machine-gun positions and in every case was the first man into the enemy pits', and captured four mortars defended by more than 30 of the enemy.

A new CO, Lieutenant Colonel J. Scott Elliot, arrived to take command, and the Battalion was reorganized with drafts from other regiments. Within a week 8th Argylls were back in action in their last engagement of the campaign. On 7 May 1943 7th Armoured Division swept into Tunis, and to the north the Americans were equally successful. Both battalions then began training for their next task which was the invasion of Sicily. In this they were to be joined by 1st Argylls, albeit in a different role.

SICILY

The invasion of Sicily was the first major amphibious operation mounted in Europe (other than the Dieppe Raid), and provided lessons in joint operations that were to prove invaluable when planning the Normandy invasion eleven months later.

The 1st Argylls had had a most frustrating period in Egypt since they had returned there from Eritrea a year earlier. They were in reserve during the Battle of El Alamein, but not called forward to fight. Later they trained for the role of No 33 'Beach Brick', a formation designed to follow up assault troops during an amphibious landing and organize all the administrative tasks, including the landing of stores and vehicles.

They landed at 0330 hours on 10 July 1943 to carry out this role and their casualties on the first day were eight dead from enemy air activity. On that first day more than 11,000 troops landed through the Brick, with 556 vehicles and 91 tons of stores. A few days later their record was 2,350 tons of stores brought ashore in one day.

It was 7th Argylls, in their original 154 Brigade, however, who were the first Argylls ashore in the reconquest of Europe, landing at 0245 hours on 10 July on a beach at the south-eastern tip of Sicily, their initial task being the formation of a brigade bridgehead stretching one mile inland. This was achieved against slight opposition and they remained there for just under twenty-four hours. Two days marching northwards followed, until the Battalion's transport caught up with them. In the evening of 14 July they were ordered to attack two hills at Bucheri held by the Germans, after a first and unsuccessful attack by another brigade. Mounting a deliberate brigade attack with 1st Black Watch and 7th Argylls up, the operation met no opposition and the objectives were quickly taken. The Italians had presented very little opposition, but the Germans held strong positions overlooking the Plain of Catania, and were much more formidable opponents. A ridge was seized by 'A' and 'C' Companies who lost a number of casualties, and during the night of 17/18 July a rapid divisional operation to cross the Plain was carried out, with battalions leap-frogging one another to seize various objectives. Stiffer opposition was met the closer they got to the town and important airfield of Gerbini at the foot of Mount Etna.

So on 20 July a night attack on the airfield was mounted by 7th Argylls with two squadrons of tanks and full artillery support. 'C' and 'D' Companies were in the lead and both suffered a number of casualties, including all the officers of 'C' Company. 'A' Company moved through them and beat off a counter-attack while the tanks defeated another counter-attack. But during the morning of 21 July 'A' Company ran out of ammunition, were surrounded by enemy infantry supported by armour, and had no choice but to surrender. On the left 'D' and 'B' Companies fought hard through the night and were counter-attacked during the day until, having lost eighteen officers and 160 men, they were withdrawn. Gerbini and its strategic airfield were then abandoned by the enemy.

With great speed the Battalion was reinforced and retrained under a new CO, Lieutenant Colonel A. Dunlop replacing Lieutenant Colonel Mathieson who had been killed at Gerbini. On 1 August 7th Argylls were back in action at Pietraperciata, an attack which worked so smoothly that it was nicknamed the 'Field Day' battle. The enemy withdrew as the attack went in, and there was no counter-attack. One final operation was fought on 5 August, but after that 7th Argylls merely waited for the end of the Sicilian campaign. In September they returned to the United Kingdom.

The 1st Battalion were suddenly called forward on 28 July as a reserve for 51st Highland Division, and for three days they held positions while 7th Argylls were being reconstituted. On 11 August the 1st were withdrawn again to prepare for Beach Brick duties on the Italian mainland.

The 8th Argylls had arrived on 25 July on the beach south of Syracuse. They were moved forward around the southern foothills of Mount Etna to capture Centuripe, the last major battle fought by the British in Sicily. It was an extremely difficult operation; the terrain was extremely hilly, covered with ravines and bristling with enemy positions all exceptionally well hidden. The town itself was on top of a precipitous ridge with spurs stretching out in many directions. No vehicles could follow the troops and mules had to be employed to carry the machine-guns.

'X' and 'R' Companies in the lead reached the top of the ridge some 800 yards from the village. The Germans waited their moment until both companies were in view and opened fire. Taking some casualties, 'R' and 'Y' Companies manoeuvred to establish positions on two high points from which they could return effective fire, and 'R' Company were involved in hand-to-hand fighting. Lieutenant-Colonel Scott Elliot ordered the Battalion, which by now was at about half strength, to remain in their positions during the rest of the day until another battalion, 1st East Surreys, could come up. He received orders to attack across the valley at night, with artillery support, while the East Surreys attacked along the ridge. Although 'B' Company managed to cross the valley they were unable to reach the top of the precipitous ridge under enemy fire before first light; thereafter it would have been suicidal. The East Surreys were also unable to traverse the ridge and 'R' Company, already in weakened strength, was attacked by the Germans and its personnel either dislodged or captured. The impossibility of the task was underlined when the following night it took a whole brigade to capture the village and clear the ridge of enemy.

Right: Lieutenant Colonel Lorne Campbell, whose brilliant leadership while commanding the 7th Argylls during the battle at Wadi Akarit earned him the Victoria Cross. He had already won the DSO and Bar in earlier battles.

Below: The 8th Argylls move up to relieve the Coldstream Guards on Longstop Hill, Tunisia, 25 December 1942. (IWM)

Above: Invasion of Sicily, July 1943. A 7th Argylls bren gun carrier and crew are towed ashore while other troops handle the stores. (IWM)

Below: A Jock of 1st Argylls looks out over the River Lamone, close to the battle for Monte Cavallaro, October 1944. (IWM)

Right: 1st Argylls enter Ferrara just before the surrender of all German troops in Italy, May 1945. (IWM)

Below: The Pipes and Drums of 8th Argylls lead British, French, American and Russian troops in the Allied Victory Parade in Vienna, 8 May 1946. (IWM)

Left: Led by a piper, 2nd Argylls march towards the battle at Cheux, France, 26 June 1944.

Left: 2nd Argylls and 10th Highland Light Infantry move up to Tilburg in Holland, 27 October 1944. (IWM)

Left: 2nd Argylls take over captured trenches near Nijmegen, February 1945. (IWM)

Above: 2nd Argylls advancing behind tanks on their way towards the German border near Cleve, February 1945. (IWM)

Right: 2nd Argylls dig in beside the road on the way to Cleve, 11 February 1945. (IWM)

Right: The Prime Minister, Mr Winston Churchill, speaking to a group of Argylls near the Rhine, March 1946. Field Marshal Sir Bernard Montgomery looks on. (IWM)

Left: A section of 7th Argylls passes through Mittesbosch, Germany. (IWM)

Left: A bren gun group of 2nd Argylls dug in near Uelzen, Germany, 14 April 1945. (IWM)

Left: Pipers of 7th Argylls march into Bremerhaven past German soldiers, May 1945. (IWM)

Left: Dominion troops played an important part during the Second World War. The Argyll and Sutherland Highlanders of Canada march through Berlin, 1945.

Right: Colonel of the Regiment, General Sir Gordon MacMillan of MacMillan and Knap, KCB, KCVO, CBE, DSO, MC, DL. He had a distinguished regimental career in the First World War and commanded successively 15th Scottish Division, 49th Division and 51st Highland Division during the Second World War.

Right: A patrol of 1st Argylls in Tel Aviv during the troubles with Jews and Arabs. Private Logan is on the left; he was later killed at Jaffa.

Right: A Company of 1st Argylls on exercise 'marry up' with a squadron of 4th Royal Tank Regiment in the New Territories, Hong Kong, 1949.

Top left: A Vickers machine-gun (water cooled) being manned during the Korean War by members of 1st Argylls.

Centre left: Members of 'C' Company 1st Argylls take a leisurely paddle in dug-out canoes in British Guiana, 1954.

Left: Major G. P. 'Timber' Wood, MC, briefs the Jocks during the period of ceasefire before the withdrawal from the Suez campaign.

Above: Anti-tank guns of the 1st Argylls await eventualities in the Suez campaign of 1956. For the Battalion, the campaign was a frustrating 'non-event'.

Below: This wintery photograph of the early 1960s shows a joint Passing Out Parade at the Regimental Depot, Stirling Castle. By this time The Black Watch Depot, formerly at Perth, had amalgamated with that of the Argyll and Sutherland Highlanders.

Opposite page, top: Her Majesty the Queen, Colonel-in-Chief, presents Colours to the 7th and 8th Argylls in 1961. Behind her stands Major General F. C. C. Graham, DSO, Colonel of the Regiment.

Opposite page, bottom: Five Pipe Majors of the Argyll and Sutherland Highlanders parade for their Colonel-in-Chief. Pitkeathly (HM The Queen's personal piper), Weatherstone, Smith, McCallum and Hill.

Above: Sergeant Bryan Baty (centre, standing) and the 'B' Company Tracker Team, Borneo, August 1964.

Below: A platoon of the Argylls prepares for an airlift by helicopter during the Confrontation in Borneo, 1965.

Above: 'Argyll Law'. A patrol of the Argylls questioning an Arab in Crater, Aden, 1967.

Top right: Lieutenant Colonel Mitchell and his Headquarters Group in Crater.

Right: Peter Archer's painting of the Argylls' entry into Crater. In the centre are Pipe Major Robson, Lieutenant Colonel Colin Mitchell and the Adjutant, Captain David Thomson, MC.

Above: Members of the Reconnaissance Platoon prepare for a rural patrol in Northern Ireland, 1987.

Below: The Argylls on exercise in Germany 1990. The modern infantry is equipped with the Rarden Cannon-armed Scorpion recce vehicle.

Above: Jocks of 'A' Company, 1st A and SH in their armoured vehicle, Northern Ireland, 1990.

Below: The anti-tank platoon of the Argylls site their Milan missile-launcher during an exercise in Germany, 1990.

Left: The Secretary of State for Defence, Tom King, with the Argylls stationed in Northern Ireland. Lieutenant Colonel Sandy Blackett, the Commanding Officer, is in the centre. The weapon the soldiers carry is the new SA80 rifle.

Below: Vehicle check-point set up by the Argylls in Belfast, 1991. Lance Corporal Keenan is speaking on his personal radio.

Although much weakened in number 8th Argylls were involved in two further operations before the campaign ended on 16 August. Thereafter preparations were begun in earnest for the invasion of the Italian mainland.

THE ITALIAN CAMPAIGN

Both politically and militarily the situation in Italy was ambiguous. Mussolini had been deposed on 26 July and an armistice with the Italians was signed at Syracuse, whereupon their fleet surrendered to the British in Malta. Their army on the mainland was disarmed quickly by the Germans who, having managed to evacuate 60,000 of their own troops from Sicily, now had fifteen divisions serving in Italy. They were determined to hold Italy at all costs, a determination they showed time and again during the next eighteen months of campaigning. The Italian population while warmly welcoming their liberators, often co-operated with the Germans when it was in their interest.

A bold strategic plan had been considered; the landing of a large Allied force on the mainland close to Rome in an attempt to end the war in Italy swiftly, but such an operation would probably have failed. In the event the Americans landed their Fifth Army, which included a British corps, at Salerno just south of Naples on 9 September 1944, six days after the first British troops of Eighth Army crossed the Straits of Messina and landed on the Italian mainland near Reggio. A third landing by air at Taranto by 1st Airborne Division followed, and 8th Argylls were moved by sea to Taranto on 25 September. Their 78th Division was to clear the eastern coastal plain of Italy, but their initial moves by rail and then infantry landing ships ensured that they were quickly transported to where the Germans were actually defending, just north of the River Biferno. On 3 October the Argylls disembarked at Termoli, 150 miles north of Taranto, which had been occupied by a commando force and marked the seaward edge of the German defence line.

Lieutenant Colonel Scott-Elliot was ordered to capture the village of San Giacomo, some four miles inland and held in unknown strength by the enemy. Like the battle for Centuripe, this was a tall order and it was decided to commit only one company ('B' Company) in the advance on the morning of 4 October. Sure enough the Company was heavily engaged by machine-gun and mortar fire. 'X' and 'R' Companies were brought up but no further progress could be made that day. 'Y' and 'R' Companies continued to advance in the early hours of 5 October and discovered enemy armour close to the village of San Giacomo. 'Y' Company attacked the tank harbour with some success, but it was obvious that unaided the Battalion had come across a much larger force than had been anticipated. Indeed it quickly became evident that the Battalion was facing an armoured division preparing to re-capture Termoli. Later in the morning 'X' Company and Battalion HQ were attacked by enemy infantry over a period of two hours.

More enemy armour appeared and it was with difficulty that the Battalion, less the two forward companies, 'R' and 'Y', consolidated and held their positions. With both enemy and, in error, British artillery fire coming down on their position, the CO decided to abandon it and move to a more sheltered area of the hills. 'R' and 'Y' Companies in the meantime remained in forward positions until last light and withdrew in the dark. The casualties numbered 162 all ranks, and among the dead was Major Jack Anderson, VC. Fresh troops took over the advance while the Argylls rested after their gruelling experience.

Progress was very slow for the Allied troops during the rest of October 1943. The next operation in which 8th Argylls took a major part was in the area of the River

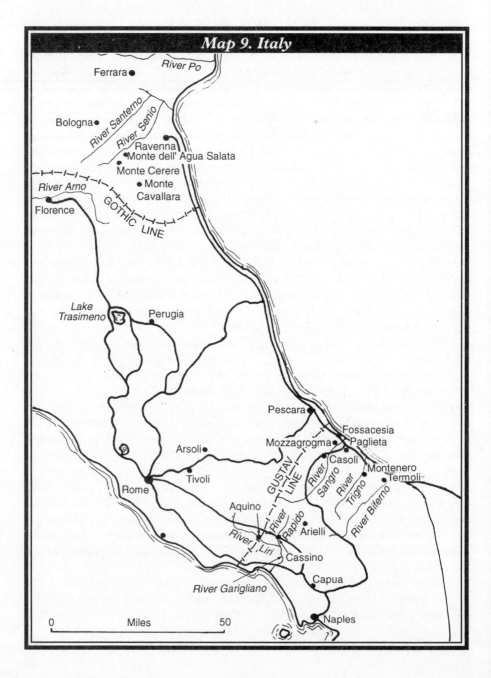

Map 9. Italy

Trigno with 'an advance of five miles by night across unreconnoitred country towards unknown enemy positions'. The official reports stated that during the advance 'the whole situation was generally very obscure', and having been ordered from above to halt and dig in short of the Battalion's objective, one platoon of 'R' Company being out of wireless contact, failed to receive the message and actually occupied the final objective without meeting opposition. Such illustrates the confusion, the luck and the determination which are the experience in war. A more orderly operation on 5 November was equally successful in taking a ridge near Torino.

On 15 November 8th Argylls were moved to Paglieta near the River Sangro behind which the enemy lay in great strength. The Battalion was ordered to carry out extensive reconnaissance of the main German positions and these were found to lie on an escarpment one to two miles north of the river. On 19 November probing attacks by companies within the brigade were sent forward to seize objectives north of the river. 'X' Company under Captain Askwith achieved their task, but were counter-attacked and forced to withdraw. It subsequently took two attacks at battalion strength to capture and hold the objective.

For several days similar operations were carried out, mainly at night, all along the Sangro and the British established a number of positions north of the river. On 30 November it was at last possible to mount a divisional attack with armour across the Sangro, and despite the weather and the mud it was entirely successful. After two months of fighting, 8th Argylls were withdrawn for a month's reconstitution.

The 6th Argylls (93rd Anti-Tank Regiment, RA) had remained in North Africa during the summer of 1943, as they were not required for service in the Sicilian campaign. The main party reached Naples by sea in November 1943. Again the batteries were divided in support of various divisions, including an Italian division which had recently 'changed sides'.

In January 1944 the Allied front was reorganized pending landings at Anzio, thirty miles from Rome and designed to bypass the German 'Gustav Line'. The 8th Argylls took up positions in the foothills of the Apennines in conditions of deep snow. Patrol activities were conducted on a nightly basis.

In March as the weather improved, 78th Division was moved to that part of the Gustav Line where the key feature was the famous monastery at the top of Monte Cassino. Early attacks on Cassino had failed, but by the time 8th Argylls reached the area some nearby features had been captured by the New Zealand and Indian Divisions. From 20 March successive platoons of the Argylls held positions near a castle three-quarters of a mile from the monastery, in dead ground with an enemy outpost only 150 yards away. Relief in daylight was not possible and even by night was difficult and dangerous. There was concern that the enemy could destroy the building in which the platoons lay up, and indeed there were a number of casualties from mortar and machine-gun fire. There the Battalion remained for a fortnight, and returned for a second spell in April.

In March 1944 1st Argylls resumed a combat role, joining 19 (Indian) Infantry Brigade in 8th (Indian) Division. Their first tour of duty was in the trenches at Arielli, just north of the River Moro on the eastern side of the Apennines. On 11 May they took part in General Alexander's successful attack which ended in the final capture of Cassino, and the crossing of the River Liri which opened the way to Rome. The 91st's first task was an opposed crossing in assault craft of the River Rapido, a tributary of the Liri in the 'Saint Angelo horseshoe' five miles to the south of Cassino. Unfortunately some of the boats were swept away in the dark, and an enemy smoke-screen proved so successful that the Argylls were left straddling the river for a while, and had to withdraw during the following night. On 14 May with armoured support and the help of a Bailey bridge, the Argylls crossed the river and took their objective.

By now the battle was progressing well and 8th Argylls, as follow-up troops, crossed the Rapido by Bailey bridge on 17 May and advanced rapidly on the 18th, the day Monte Cassino fell to the Polish corps. The farther 8th Argylls advanced the stronger grew the enemy's resistance. The terrain was quite dense and the accompanying armour, at different times the Derbyshire Yeomanry and Wiltshire Yeomanry, had to move very cautiously. The Argylls were involved in a number of minor operations against German stay-behind parties, bristling with machine-guns. Twenty-five miles were covered in thirteen days, and the Germans were by now in full retreat.

The 1st and 8th Argylls and 93rd Anti-Tank Regiment all took an active part in the advance to the Gothic Line, more than 200 miles to the north, which took a further three months. The 8th were heavily involved in a set-piece battle at Alatri on 2 June, on top of a hill with steep valleys on each side. Their CO, Lieutenant Colonel Taylor, ordered an encircling movement during daylight; behind the town 'Y' Company scaled a 200-foot hill on top of which was a monastery which they seized. But with machine-gun and artillery fire, the enemy effected a fighting withdrawal. At last light two companies of 6th Royal West Kent Regiment attacked Alatri, only to find the enemy had sneaked away without being spotted. The 1st Argylls mounted a similar attack at Arsoli on 7 June, with a similar ending. By the end of the month they had reached Assisi. Rome had of course been liberated by this time.

The 8th Argylls continued to meet firm resistance and on 18 June they had to take the leading position in their Brigade. The battalion record, with complete honesty, states:

'After one of those confusing nights in pitch darkness when officers do not known where the men are, orderlies do not know where headquarters is, and quartermaster-sergeants do not known where to take the rations, the battalion was ready to advance at dawn.'

Objectives were reached after a cautious advance during the day, although they expected stay-behind parties of 1st German Parachute Division to cause delays. An early start on 19 June met resistance at Vaiano and 'R' and 'B' Companies were ordered to attack during the evening:

'They were soon engaged at close quarters among the scattered houses and gardens and confused fighting continued in the dark until midnight, when the companies took up positions outside the town.'

At 0200 on 20 June the enemy counter-attacked and the two companies had to withdraw. It was discovered later to have been a battalion position. After a brief rest in reserve the Battalion continued the advance and took part in considerable skirmishing before they were pulled out of the line with the remainder of the division. They visited Rome in early July and saw the sights of the city, entrained for Taranto and from there sailed to Egypt for a period of rest and recuperation.

The 1st Argylls meanwhile continued their advance to the River Arno which they crossed on 31 August east of Florence, to form a bridgehead just south of the 'Gothic Line'. Fighting for the next two months was intense. The terrain was mountainous and the enemy were capable of a strong defence against troops well dispersed in a general advance, or concentrating to move into a deliberate attack on an identifiable objective. At times whole companies and battalions were tied down for hours when they advanced against positions with dominating arcs of view. At Abertino just south of Monte Rotondo, hampered by forty-eight hours of rain, 1st Argylls fought a fierce battle which cost them eleven dead, 43 missing and 33 wounded. The Germans suddenly evacuated the position. On 7 October at Cavallata, with a well-laid artillery and mortar fire plan and 'C' Company giving machine-gun and rifle support, 'A' Company stormed a hill after a stiff fight and with hand-to-hand fighting drove off the Germans. But the Battalion was engaged from another position and 'B' Company had to mount a quick attack led by Captain D G Wood. Two platoons seized the objective, were counter-attacked and had to withdraw, but the enemy did not hold the position for long.

On 1 December, after a spell in reserve, 1st Argylls returned to the front near Monte Cerere. In thick mist on the 11th the Germans launched a major attack and 'C' and 'D' Companies took the full brunt, a platoon of 'D' Company being overrun. Defensive fire eventually broke up the attack and hearing wireless intercepts Brigade HQ ordered the CO, Lieutenant Colonel Freddie Graham, to mount an immediate counter-attack, which was greatly successful and restored the position. The Battalion was once more in action before the end of the year in support of a US division which was anticipating a major German attack. In the event the Germans seemed to lose heart and only small probing parties were encountered, before the Germans withdrew.

On their return from Egypt 8th Argylls reached Italy in mid-September 1944 and by a circuitous route moved across Italy to join the front near Florence, some ten miles east of 1st Argylls' positions. On 10 October the 8th were in the centre of a divisional advance along the River Santerno, and good progress was made despite a number of changes in plan. On 15 October the Battalion took up positions in the village of Gesso which had been captured by another battalion. The relief was accompanied by shelling and mortaring, was conducted along paths bordered with minefields and slimy with mud, and the supply system was by mule! The nearest German positions were 1,200 yards away. A forward position was occupied pending a battalion attack on the Monte dell' Acqua Salata ridge. Patrols were sent forward to reconnoitre and on the night of 20 October 'R' and 'B' Companies set off in the lead to capture the position on the ridge some 2,000 yards away. The attack went well. 'X' Company passed through, followed by 'Y' Company and gradually the ridge was captured, making a substantial salient in the enemy's line. But the fighting had been at close quarters and enemy shelling was most effective. During the night of 21 October the Battalion was relieved.

For the next four months the line remained static and the wet weather and dreadful mud favoured the Germans rather than the Allies. Later, snow added to the discomfort of the troops, but at least the battalions were relieved according to a plan and allowed rest, dry conditions and reconstitution. The 8th Battalion's record states that 'on balance it was probably the worst four months of the war'. The 6th Argylls were also involved in defending the line with their self-propelled guns used in both anti-tank and traditional artillery roles.

As the weather improved both the Argyll battalions began to train for the final phase of the Italian campaign. In March 8th Battalion took part in operations against the German defences south of the River Senio which flows through the great northern plains of Italy. The 1st Argylls then took part in the first crossings of the Senio on 9 April and the '... operation went like clockwork' according to the Battalion record; '... the speed of the assault had caught the enemy before he was able to get out of his bunkers'. The Argylls and all first-wave infantry carried light wooden bridges — the river was not very wide. They continued to advance, carrying out a number of operations against the rapidly retreating enemy, until 28 April.

The 8th Argylls crossed the Senio on 12 April, being part of a 'battle group' with a squadron of tanks, SP guns and engineers. The Battalion was commanded by Lieutenant Colonel Henry Leask (from the Royal Scots Fusiliers and later to be GOC Scotland), and a very rapid advance was made during the first and subsequent nights. With the momentum of truly mobile warfare, 8th Argylls overcame many obstacles and captured 200 enemy, but suffered 100 casualties. On 2 May the Germans surrendered all their forces in Italy, and the end of the war in Europe was only days away.

CHAPTER 11

NORTH-WEST EUROPE, 1944–1945

NORMANDY

Along sixty miles of the Normandy Coast the greatest seaborne invasion in the history of mankind struck the unsuspecting Germans guarding their 'Atlantic Wall' on 6 June 1944. Thirteen of the forty divisions engaged were British. Soon the Germans would face a total of seventy-two divisions, including those fighting their way up from the French Mediterranean coast. The vast and complex preparations had taken more than three years of work and increasingly realistic training and activity, including the mounting of a wholly successful deception plan. Many of the sixty German divisions were smaller than those of the Allies, but had better and more numerous anti-tank guns and mortars. A good proportion of their troops had been battle-hardened on the Eastern Front and in North Africa.

The first Argylls ashore were 7th Battalion, a few of whom had fought in France in 1940, and many more had taken part in the battles in North Africa and Sicily in 1943. From a 'sealed camp' in Essex, they embarked at Southampton and reached Courseulles on the French coast close to Caen. This city astride the River Orne was the hub of the entire Anglo-US strategy, as the Allied formations were to pivot on Caen before striking for the heartland of France and the capital Paris. In the event, so hard did the Germans fight that Paris was not liberated until late August.

The re-formed 51st Highland Division, in which 7th Argylls were still serving, was initially in reserve, and they were kept waiting in defended localities in the lodgement area north of Caen until 14 June, when they moved to defend bridges over the Orne. Two days later the Germans attempted a counter-attack but it was broken up by artillery. Thereafter for several days the Battalion was responsible for defending a sector of the Bois de Bavent, a long, heavily wooded feature which dominated the eastern flank of the area occupied by the Allies. It was a monotonous but essential task, and the Jocks had to maintain extreme vigilance against snipers and remain under cover from artillery, mortars and *Nebelwerfer*, multi-barrelled projectors delivering high-explosive warheads.

On the night of 24 June 7th Black Watch was attacked in the left forward position of the brigade, while the Argylls had to carry out an ammunition resupply task in the dark and then prepare to mount a dawn counter-attack. The Battalion took over the Black Watch's positions and remained there until 8 July. On several occasions it seemed that the enemy were preparing similar attacks, but apart from shelling on the Argylls' area, there was no attack. 'Our sniper section had many a good bag', according to the record, 'and in one afternoon killed five Germans.' Caen was eventually captured after two assaults, the first on 8 July and during Operation 'Goodwood' on 18/19 July, but 7th Argylls were chiefly in reserve.

In the meantime 2nd Argylls — the new 93rd Highlanders, re-constituted from 15th Argylls in May 1942 — had landed in Normandy with 15th Scottish Division in VIII Corps, after a particularly stormy crossing of the Channel. The division was commanded by Major General Gordon MacMillan, himself an Argyll who later became Colonel of the Regiment. In support were the former 5th Argylls — 91st Anti-Tank Regiment RA. 'Epsom' was a major British operation by VIII and XXX Corps, designed to start the pivotal movement from the west. After concentrating west of Caen the divisional tasks were clear the Germans out of their positions north of the River Odon, a tributary of the Orne, and to seize two bridges over the Odon at Tourmauville and Gavrus.

At dawn on 26 June the battalions of 44 Lowland and 46 Highland Brigades went into the attack, supported by a heavy artillery barrage and some tanks. The enemy resisted fiercely. The Argylls of 227 Highland Brigade were hurriedly committed at first light on the 27th and once past their start-line just north of Cheux, they made good progress despite the sniping by Germans still resisting amid the ruins of that town. Half-way towards their objective, the bridge at Tourmauville, two companies were held up: 'A' Company in the village of Colleville and 'B' Company in some orchards. There was some enemy artillery and small-arms fire , and 'B' Company encountered German tanks and an armoured car, but these veered off after one of the Tiger tanks had been disabled by an Argyll anti-tank gun. On reaching the cross-roads at Tourville 'C' and 'D' Companies passed through, and 'C' Company, under Major Hugh Fyfe, supported by Sergeant King's section of the Carrier Platoon, made a dash for the bridge over the final 1,000 yards of open country.

After clearing three enemy machine-gun positions, '...exactly as if they had been doing a demonstration at the School of Infantry', Major Fyfe's group captured the bridge intact, for the loss of three killed and eleven wounded. It was a notable achievement, and within the hour elements of 11th Armoured Division passed through the Argylls towards the high ground at Point 112.

The Scottish Division now formed a narrow salient —nicknamed by the British press the 'Scottish Corridor' — jutting deep into enemy territory, with the Argylls, six miles ahead of where they had started the previous day, at the very tip of the salient. The units behind them had more fighting to do: Cheux had not been fully cleared and the flanks of the 'Scottish Corridor' were still under persistent German pressure. The next day, 28 June, the 93rd sent out a strong patrol. This found the Gavrus bridge intact and undefended, so late that afternoon the Battalion moved along the river bank and dug in so as to secure the second and larger bridge at that small Norman village, as originally planned.

The Germans, however, were concentrating for a major counter-attack by II SS Panzer Corps against the British and Canadian Armies.This they launched, despite heavy Allied air attacks, on 29 June. The 2nd Argylls, in their exposed positions astride the Odon, were subjected to two days of hard fighting; the forward companies were mortared and attacked by tanks and infantry, but held their ground. The next day, 30 June, Battalion HQ and 'D' Company positions were heavily shelled and much damage was done to vehicles and radio sets. The German attacks against the units in rear of the

Argylls, particularly in the Cheux area, now caused the British higher command to call a halt to Operation 'Epsom', and the armour which had reached Point 112 was pulled back behind the line of the Odon. Fifteenth Scottish Division was withdrawn, on relief by 53 Welsh Division, and 2nd Argylls had a period of rest and very necessary refitting.

The 2nd Argylls' next action was the XII Corps Operation 'Greenline' aimed at securing the high ground, extending 4,000 yards south of the Odon and giving excellent observation over the Orne river-line. A previous attempt to break out in this direction had been thwarted by the Germans.

The operation started on 15 July. The fighting was severe and the Glasgow Highlanders (a TA battalion of the HLI) and 2nd Gordons were held up around Esquay. In consequence the Argylls, who had been heavily and continuously shelled in their assembly area and while moving up through the village of Baron to their start-line, were caught at first light on an open forward slope. The situation was saved by the supporting Gunners who, by firing smoke shells for more than an hour, prevented the Germans from profiting from the target presented to them. The operation was called off and the whole division was taken out of the line.

'Greenline' was truly an ill-starred operation. Although the Argylls were not committed to battle, they lost 71 killed or wounded; and their Brigade Commander, Ronnie MacIntosh-Walker, was killed at his HQ in Baron.

American success in the west at last was forcing the Germans to withdraw eastwards. The 2nd Argylls were moved from the Caen sector over to the boundary with the US Army, and on 29 July moved up ready for Operation 'Bluecoat'. The aim of this operation was to roll back the enemy defensive formations across a wide front. After the enemy positions had been bombed by the RAF early on 30 July, the Battalion advanced and despite coming under fire and becoming entangled in a minefield, soon reached the main enemy position, resolutely defended by infantry, among whom were conscript or volunteer Poles, Yugoslavs and Russians..

The Argyll companies, closely supported by their affiliated tanks of 3rd Battalion Scots Guards, pressed on through the close, rich farmlands and eventually reached the area of Les Loges, '...having advanced nearly 6,000 yards through three enemy battalion positions'. The enemy did not counter-attack the Argylls on their objective, but the Scots Guards lost a number of their Churchill tanks to a sudden and audacious attack by two SP guns which appeared from a flank. Casualties to the Argylls throughout 'Bluecoat' had been fortunately light, and their success had been due in large measure to the skilful planning of Major John Kenneth, their acting CO. Major General John Graham has written:

'The 93rd owed much to its Commanding Officers. Colonel John Bedford-Roberts had instilled into All Ranks very high standards of administration and discipline. John Tweedie, his testy but kind-hearted successor, brought the battalion's tactical skills and confidence to the high level demanded if the German Army was to be beaten in Europe. His cousin, Russell Morgan, who commanded from August 1944 onwards, is remembered to this day as a uniquely admired and beloved officer. Under his leadership the 93rd was rated by many as the best battalion in the finest infantry division in Sir Miles Dempsey's Second Army.'

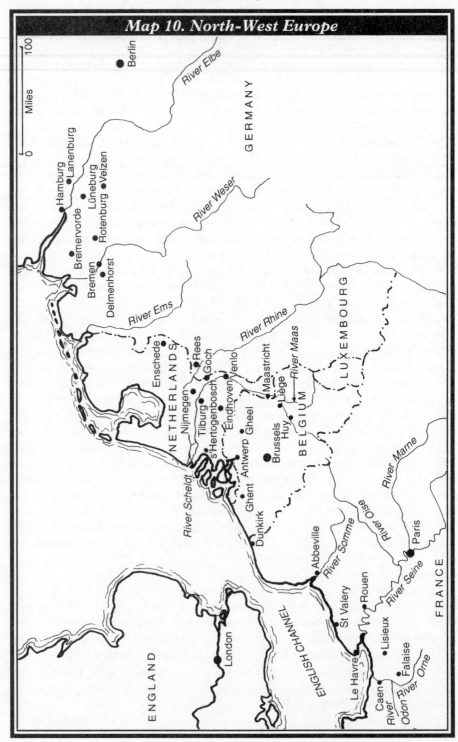

Map 10. North-West Europe

GERMANY

Berlin

River Elbe

Miles
100

0

Hamburg
Lanenburg
Lüneburg • Velzen
Bremervorde Rotenburg
Bremen
Delmenhorst

River Weser

River Ems

River Rhine

LUXEMBOURG

Enschede
Rees
Goch
Tilburg Yenlo
Nijmegen
's Hertogenbosch
Eindhoven
Antwerp Gheel
Ghent
Dunkirk

Maastricht
River Maas
Liège
Huy
Brussels

NETHERLANDS

BELGIUM

River Scheldt

Abbeville

River Somme

River Oise

River Marne

Paris

FRANCE

River Seine

St Valery
Rouen

ENGLAND

London

ENGLISH CHANNEL

Le Havre
Lisieux
Caen • Falaise
River Odon River Orne

A few days later 2nd Argylls moved south towards the battlefield of Falaise. Speed was essential in order to trap the major part of the German forces in Normandy. Each battalion was given cross-roads on the enemy lines of retreat to capture and hold, but German resistance, particularly by pockets of Waffen-SS troops supported by tanks, was fierce and effective. Having reached the line of the road Estry—La Caverie, the Argylls dug in and remained there while German Seventh Army was destroyed in the Falaise Pocket during those dramatic days of early August 1944.

The 7th Argylls had in the meantime been serving in and out of the front-line positions at Caen where, even after a month of fighting, it was proving very difficult for the Allies to dislodge the enemy from their defence line. On 18 July the RAF mounted a huge bombing attack on the city as part of Operation 'Goodwood', but the enemy continued to resist, and their harassing artillery fire caused several casualties to the Argylls at Cuverville. A particularly successful fighting patrol captured thirty-five prisoners on the same day. On 19 July the Battalion took over the Grenadier Guards' objective at Cagny, and at the end of the month the Battalion was back in the Bois de Bavent area.

In early August General Montgomery ordered Operation 'Totalize', a break-out from the Caen area. A meticulous plan was drawn up, reminiscent of El Alamein, timed to coincide with plans to cut off the German armoured divisions in the Falaise Pocket to the south. During the night of 7 August 7th Argylls were lifted into battle, some in armoured personnel carriers and others on the back of 'Unfrocked Priests' (25pdr 'Priest' self-propelled guns with the armament removed), which was to become a familiar mode of transport during the next nine months. They debussed at 0400 hours and within the hour had seized their objectives at Crasmesnil, ten miles to the south-east of Caen. A few hours later enemy armour and infantry appeared in order to counter-attack the positions, but withdrew under hastily called artillery fire. The Canadian and Polish armoured divisions swept past and the advance gathered momentum, although the Germans were nowhere giving up territory without a fight. The advance towards the next large town, Lisieux, took a fortnight. Thereafter the destruction of the German Army was particularly evident, with large quantities of equipment lying abandoned all over the countryside. By the end of August 7th Argylls had reached the banks of the River Seine.

During this period 2nd Argylls were also approaching the Seine as part of a separate Allied thrust against which there was little opposition. They suffered grievously, however, from a surprise bombing attack at Vassy on the night of 20 August, when twenty-five officers and soldiers were killed by low-flying German aircraft.

ACROSS BELGIUM AND HOLLAND

On 27 August 2nd Argylls crossed the Seine against light opposition at Louviers, south of Rouen; 7th Argylls passed through the city on 1 September. The 51st Highland Division's task was to sweep north-eastwards in the direction of Le Havre, but first they were given the opportunity of re-entering St-Valery-en-Caux, near where so many of the original 51st had been killed or forced to surrender in 1940. Le Havre fell on 11

September and the advance along the coast continued during the remainder of the month, until the Belgian border was reached.

The 2nd Argylls' move east of the Seine by vehicle was rapid as the Germans were now abandoning ground with little opposition. On 7 September the Battalion crossed the border into Belgium; although used to the rejoicing of men, women and children of liberated France, the scenes of wild joy in Belgium were unparalleled. After several days during which various plans for assault crossing of canals were drawn up and soon abandoned, the Argylls moved several miles into the Gheel bridgehead where they relieved a battalion of 44 Lowland Brigade.

The whole of the area was developing into a major battlefield as the bold but abortive Operation 'Market Garden' — the seizure of the Rhine bridge at Arnhem — was launched some eighty miles away, the plan being to sweep the Allied armies northwards to join the airborne troops. The 2nd Argylls spent a number of days of grim fighting in the Gheel bridgehead, as part of a diversionary operation by the whole of 15th Scottish Division. Later in the month the Battalion was engaged in a series of fierce encounters in woods near the Wilhelmina Canal close to Eindhoven in Holland. It was a dreary period in gloomy surroundings, during which the Battalion sadly lost — and to little purpose — a number of excellent officers and soldiers.

The 7th Argylls were lifted in transport across Belgium during early October, and they too became involved in the battle for the Dutch canals in the area north of Eindhoven. On 23 October the Battalion took part in a brigade attack to seize bridges over the Wilhelmina Canal. The approach was hampered by a minefield, but a battalion of The Black Watch managed to cross a parallel river and establish a bridgehead. The 7th Argylls passed through and, supported by 1st Northamptonshire Yeomanry and some flame-thrower tanks, were launched into an attack on the town of Vught. They met a simultaneous German attack head on and both sides came to an abrupt halt. After holding positions and then advancing cautiously, the Battalion approached the town, in due course allowing 7th Black Watch to pass through without opposition to occupy it.

At this time 2nd Argylls were also involved in a major operation — the liberation of Tilburg. Although the approach march by their 227 Highland Brigade proved difficult because of mines, blown bridges and broken roads, Tilburg was eventually reached and occupied. Two days later, however, the Argylls were suddenly moved more than forty miles to the Asten area to block a German counter-offensive by XLVII Panzer Corps against American 7th Armored Division. There:

'The villages and farms had all been badly knocked about in heavy fighting and the weather degenerated into almost continuous rain. All the tracks had been thickly sown with anti-personnel mines and movement of the tracks in the waterlogged fields was almost impossible, even for tanks.'

The 2nd Argylls remained in the boggy 'Peel' country of south-east Holland — 'an abomination of desolation' — for three miserable months, slowly closing up to the line of the River Maas (Meuse), where they spent Christmas.

Meanwhile 7th Argylls were involved in several operations at the end of October and November, including the crossing of various waterways and occupying s'Hertogenbosch. They suffered a steady number of casualties as they took part in operations over the Noorder, Wessem and Uitwaterings Canals. At the end of

November they reached the Maas in deteriorating weather and wet conditions underfoot.

During the first three weeks of December 7th Argylls were defending the area of Nijmegen on the Rhine where it flows into Holland. Large areas of low-lying farmland were under water. Although there were fears that the Germans might mount an attack over the river, the Argylls were only fired at while on patrol; but enemy shellfire was occasionally accurate and heavy. Towards the end of December 51st Highland Division went into reserve in Belgium and came under command of the Americans.

The 7th Argylls, however, were to have little leisure over Christmas 1944 and the New Year. The Germans launched their offensive in the forests of the Ardennes in the south of Belgium, and 51st Highland Division were moved to the area of Huy to guard bridges over the Maas; the Argylls initially held two of them. On 6 January 1945 they were ordered south to blocking positions on the River Ourthe. There was much enemy activity including artillery fire. On 12 January 154 Highland Brigade advanced capture the a village of Roupage, but the objective was suddenly changed for Beaulieu. Passing through wooded country in thick snow, they were in considerable danger from the enemy's Panther tanks and self-propelled guns. The Allied counter-offensive, which for the Battalion lasted for three days and covered upwards of fifteen miles, proved successful and German resistance in Belgium crumbled.

The 2nd Argylls meanwhile were performing a defensive role on the River Maas, kept alert by German night patrols which occasionally crossed the river. This pattern continued for two and a half months until the last week of January, interspersed for the Battalion with periods of rest.

Mention should be made at this stage of two other elements of the Argyll and Sutherland Highlanders that were an active service in North West Europe.

The 9th Argylls, as 54 Light Anti-Aircraft Regiment, armed with Bofors AA guns, arrived in Normandy to join Canadian First Army at the end of August 1944. They moved across France and Belgium to provide air defence of the recently liberated port of Antwerp. After an interlude, when they were split into battery detachments at Boulogne and Ostend, they moved to Holland for the protection of the Scheldt estuary. Although the Allies had superiority in the air, the Regiment was frequently required to engage enemy aircraft. Their most notable action was on 1 January 1945, when fifty enemy fighters came over the estuary at 'zero feet'. A number of hits were scored and the enemy formations were broken up. This sortie proved to be the Luftwaffe's last show of aerial force against the British.

The 5th Argylls, nominally 91st Anti-Tank Regiment, Royal Artillery, had supported 15th Scottish Division in Normandy. The Regiment comprised two batteries of towed 17-pounders and two batteries of 17-pounder self-propelled M10s. At times they fought as individual batteries in close support and at other times in a regimental concentration to block possible enemy armour thrust lines. The Germans were still able to mount extremely effective counter-attacks which held up the Allies for days.

In the autumn of 1944 the Regiment took part in a divisional attack in the Overloon and Venraij area of Belgium, followed by two months defending areas on the River Maas. In late October 5th Argylls were involved in defeating the German counter-offensive attempting to seize Helmond.

In December two of the Regiment's batteries were exchanged with 63rd Anti-Tank Regiment, Royal Artillery — the Oxfordshire Hussars — to enable the latter regiment to assume at least in part an operational role, hitherto denied them. The regimental identity of both regiments was of course affected by this merger. During 1945 5th Argylls took part in operations in the Reichswald and later supported the sweep from the Rhine to the Elbe.

INVASION OF GERMANY

The Germans were holding their frontier with Holland in great strength, along defences known as the Siegfried Line. Where 15th Scottish and 51st Highland Divisions were deployed, the frontier followed the high ground, dominated by the Reichswald between the Rivers Rhine and Maas which are some twenty miles apart. Operation 'Veritable', launched on 8 February 1945, was designed to seize this area between the two rivers, and 2nd Argylls in 15th Division were placed in the north, while 7th Argylls in 51st Division were formed up some miles to the south, poised at last to carry the war on to German soil.

The 2nd Argylls were carried to their assembly area on the tanks of 3rd Scots Guards in the early hours of 8 February. They had some difficulty getting through the first minefield, but their phase of the attack was successful because the artillery barrage had neutralized the enemy. In the second phase, more determined resistance together with difficult cross-country movement — wide areas covered by smoke or flooded — slowed the battle considerably. By last light, however, the Battalion was on its final objectives and were digging in; there they remained for two days. On the third day there was heavy and confused fighting in the ruins of Cleve. The 2nd Argylls remained east of Cleve for the next week, clearing woods and farm buildings.

The 51st Highland Division also advanced on 8 February. The 7th Argylls in 154 Brigade followed behind 1st and 7th Black Watch, who first cleared the open ground to the east of the River Maas during daylight, before the Argylls passed through and entered the Reichswald at 11 p.m. There was little opposition until the following morning, when several machine-gun posts were encountered, which had to be dealt with swiftly by the Churchill tanks of 107 Regiment, Royal Armoured Corps. Later that day 5th Seaforth Highlanders passed through the Argylls, and mutually supporting each other as best they could, both battalions advanced slowly, clearing tracts of the dense forest. On reaching the eastern edge, plans were made for an assault on Kessel, in which the Argylls were to pass through other battalions and capture the village during the night of 14 February. They met some resistance in Kessel, but quickly dealt with it. A counter-attack on the following day was defeated. The 7th Argylls left the Kessel area a week later and were sent to Goch where 15th Scottish Division was already operating. The Battalion helped to clear that town. A few days later they were called upon to carry out a similar task in Hulm, which was strongly defended. Their last day of fighting in 'Veritable' was on 28 February, by which time the Battalion had suffered 121 casualties, of which 21 had been killed.

Fighting in and around the Reichswald had proved to be very grim. The 2nd Argylls were next committed to battle on 19/20 February in open country to the east of Goch, their objective being Buchholt, one of a cluster of villages. They attacked in misty conditions, which caused delays in bringing the Battalion forward in Kangaroo carriers. One platoon of 'C' Company, finding themselves in the wrong position, corrected their error by attacking their objective in the village from the rear, although crossing in front of the Battalion. Fortunately there were few casualties and the Battalion quickly cleared Buchholt and rounded up 194 prisoners. The Germans seemed reluctant to counter-attack, but the Argylls were subjected to artillery and mortar fire. After a few days in defence 2nd Argylls were withdrawn into reserve at Tilburg. There the Pipes and Drums of the two battalions combined to beat Retreat in the main square. Thus ended Operation 'Veritable' for both battalions of the Regiment, and preparation began in earnest for the crossing of the Rhine.

The Rhine crossing was an operation of great magnitude. The plan was to launch a British-Canadian attack north of the Ruhr industrial area on the night of 23 March and another by US forces to the south, accompanied by massive artillery and air bombardments together with airborne assaults.

The 15th Scottish and 51st Highland Divisions were on the northernmost flank, and both 2nd and 7th Argylls, mounted in Buffalo amphibious carriers, crossed in the area of Rees north-west of the town of Wessel.

'It was thought', runs the 7th Argylls' History, 'that the river and river banks might be mined ... and countless anti-tank guns well sited along the opposite bank ... It was a thrilling moment when these great clumsy vehicles lumbered into the water and started swimming across to the far bank'

Their crossing of the 300 yards of river, unlike that of other less fortunate battalions, was on time and was directed at the correct river exit site. On landing the Argylls organized themselves quickly, seized their objectives and enabled 1st Black Watch to pass through and reach further objectives.

The 2nd Argylls crossed during the early hours of 24 March, also in the dark. Their river exit site was more difficult than that of 7th Battalion and they had to cross in more than one 'flight'. The countryside immediately ahead of them was more broken up by waterways. 'A' and 'B' Companies stormed ashore, but 'D' Company's Buffalos experienced difficulties and had to make several attempts before landing the Jocks ashore. The Battalion's objective was the village of Hübsch which was held by some determined German paratroops. In the confused fighting in the dark, the Battalion became divided by more than a mile, the left-hand companies making good progress, those on the right meeting strong resistance. Fortunately, well-directed artillery fire cut up a German counter-attack, and Hübsch was captured by dawn. There was further fighting for the Battalion during the first part of the morning, and later in the day the Argylls secured all their objectives, 6th Airborne Division having captured the German rear defences and gun areas.

The 7th Argylls, however, after their less troubled crossing, met greater resistance as they advanced through 1st Black Watch to capture the village of Bienen. They suffered high casualties; eventually it took two battalions of Canadians to capture Bienen. Throughout the day and night of 24 March there were numerous enemy attacks, and one of the strongest efforts by the Germans to dislodge the Allied troops was beaten back. It was at this stage that the GOC of 51st Highland Division was killed by artillery fire and the Argylls' senior soldier, Major General Gordon MacMillan, took command.

On 26 March 7th Battalion took part in another night attack, which included the crossing of a lake in their Buffalos, which was a great success. After a short rest they were sent northwards to join in a brigade attack on Dinxperlo, which meant re-crossing into Holland. This too went well, with few casualties.

The 2nd Argylls were facing much closer terrain as they progressed deeper into Germany, and although units of 6th Airborne Division were ahead, the Argylls had to clear large expanses of woodland as stay-behind parties of Germans could cause much confusion. Fortunately the woods were relatively clear of enemy, but there were moments of anxiety when German troops suddenly appeared at close quarters intent on disrupting the advance. Wood clearing continued for several days, but by now there were few Germans still at large, although sporadic enemy artillery fire was directed to good effect at the advancing Allied troops.

During the first few days of April 1945, 7th Argylls were in Corps reserve and remained near the Dutch border. The 2nd Argylls were part of a rapidly advancing formation which was moving steadily day and night across northern Germany, meeting delays more from broken roads and bridges rather than from enemy activity. On 4 April 2nd Argylls were near Osnabrück, two days later north of Minden and on 10 April north of Hanover before crossing the River Aller at Celle. The fifty miles between the Aller and the Elbe required a deliberate advance-to-contact operation across the high ground of the Lüneburg Heath, and for 2nd Argylls this next phase was characterized by short sharp actions followed by seemingly interminable delays. Attempts to surprise and destroy enemy positions were often frustrated because the Germans were by now pulling out and moving eastwards almost as rapidly as the Allies. At Uelzen, however, the enemy put up a very strong resistance which required a brigade operation to dislodge. By 19 April the Argylls had reach Lauenburg on the Elbe, where the Germans had blown all the bridges and which was thus a major obstacle.

The 7th Argylls' advance in the north was steady and less eventful. Their route took them through Bremen on the River Aller, which they reached at the end of the month, enemy resistance being negligible. Occasionally they deployed from the designated route, to be prepared to mount quick attacks, but this became less and less necessary because the German will to fight was diminishing day by day as their command and control system collapsed. Enemy artillery was sometimes a problem, and minefields and sniping kept the Battalion alert. On 4 May Battalion Headquarters, situated to the west of Hamburg, was visited by German emissaries on their way to Montgomery's Headquarters where their surrender was to be negotiated.

The last Argylls in action were 2nd Battalion. After reaching the Elbe it was discovered that the Germans, squeezed between the British, Canadians and Americans in the west and the rapidly approaching Russians to the east, were preparing to make a last-ditch stand. Thus on the night of 29 April 15th Scottish Division mounted an assault crossing over the River Elbe. The 2nd Argylls crossed in their Buffalos in the early hours of 30 April almost without incident. The Germans were actually deployed well back from the river, with defensive artillery targeted on their own side of the Elbe. Forming up in a quarry, the Argylls were hit by gunfire, which quickly knocked out fifty members of the Battalion. Then, as they moved forward during the morning, the enemy kept up artillery fire and lone aircraft flew sorties against the Allied ground troops causing more casualties. There were still numerous groups of Germans at large, as the battalion history records, intent on '...killing at least one of enemy apiece before the inevitable surrender'. In consequence, a number of Argylls lost their lives in the very last days of the campaign.

The German surrender took effect from 5 May. Immediately the Allied armies became occupying troops with all the attendant responsibilities and difficulties. Both Argyll battalions remained in Germany, taking part in the huge task of sorting out the shambles of a defeated and broken country. The 7th Argylls were formally demobilized in due course, and the 2nd Argylls stayed on in Germany until December 1946.

CHAPTER 12

MIDDLE EAST AND KOREA, 1946–1959

Once hostilities were at an end, a large part of the British Army remained as occupying troops all over the world. The new Labour government in London was soon to discover that more often than not wars fail fully to resolve pre-war problems, and they tend to bring new ones in their wake. The restoration of firm control of the Empire was a Herculean task, and the British government was preoccupied in achieving this while restoring an impoverished economy. The constitutional status of India had been under discussion for many years, and it was soon decided that the sub-continent should be given independence as soon as possible. This was achieved — with partition — in 1947. The future of other possessions was not so urgent a matter, or so it seemed, other than that good rule and prosperity should return, particularly where this had been damaged by the war. This simple concept of Britain's post-war situation could not last long and the Middle East presented special problems almost immediately.

The 1st Argylls returned from Italy to the United Kingdom at the end the war in Europe and the intention was that they should be posted to India. The Battalion consisted of a small, hard core of Regular officers and NCOs, but the majority of officers and soldiers had been conscripted during the war or had been in the Territorial Army in 1939. They were young, tough and very fit, all had seen service in many theatres, and they were looking forward to demobilization. But for them there was to be little respite from active service during the next two years. Staging briefly in Lincolnshire, they embarked for the Middle East in the autumn of 1945.

Since the break up of the Ottoman Empire at the end of the First World War, Britain had been the power responsible for Palestine under a mandate from the League of Nations. There had been trouble before the Second World War, concerning the rights of Jews to own land, a matter naturally hotly disputed by the Arabs. At the end of the war the flood of Jewish immigrants from Europe increased, and British forces found themselves having physically to restrict their entry, and contend with armed force used by both Jews and Arabs, directed at the British and one another. The fierce debate about the idea of a Jewish homeland went on until 1947, when Israel finally became a separate and internationally recognized nation state; but until then the British troops were caught in a situation that required large-scale military containment.

The violence took the form of sporadic but well-planned attacks on British garrisons, and riots, shootings and bombings in numerous towns. The position gradually deteriorated and the Battalion was called upon more and more for guard duties, mobile and foot patrols, cordon and searches, road-blocks and other IS duties familiar to generations of soldiers. When the King David Hotel in Jerusalem was blown up by the Jewish Irgun organization in July 1946, killing and wounding staff of the GHQ and government offices, who worked in a wing of the hotel, the Argylls were first on the scene and did all they could to rescue those still alive in the building; they then assisted in imposing a curfew on the city. It was done quietly and methodically, and despite provocation there was no overreaction.

In October, the Battalion was involved in intensive operations and curfews in Jerusalem which meant manning road-blocks in the streets to control the city. Jewish terrorists had set a timed explosive device just next to where off-duty Jocks were sleeping. In the words of Colin Mitchell:

'All seemed quiet in the street, deserted except for the Argylls ... suddenly there was an explosion. Nobody knew what was happening. Were we being mortared? Nobody knew how to react. All we knew was that there on the pavement lay a dead Argyll.'

Eight more were wounded and one of them, a corporal, died soon afterwards.

It was an extremely trying first year that the Argylls spent in Palestine and it was a great relief for them to spend a month in Egypt. In January 1947 they returned to Palestine under the command of Lieutenant Colonel Cluny MacPherson; Lieutenant General Gordon MacMillan, the Colonel of the Regiment, shortly took over as GOC. The situation in 1947 until the end of the British mandate was even more chaotic, as both Jews and Arabs sought to gain military dominance particularly in Jerusalem, and the signs of an imminent civil war were apparent. For the Battalion, internal security duties increased, and with a policy of minimum force it was as if the British Army were itself under siege. The most trying duty of all was the policing of the demilitarized zone declared between the Arab and Jewish areas, with groups of belligerents in their hundreds ranged on either side. There was constant small-arms and mortar fire, and frequently the Argylls were involved in shooting incidents directed at themselves. Eventually on 1 May 1947 a truce was called, and an orderly withdrawal of British troops took place in the middle of the month. Two more Argylls had been killed in action, and another five died in an accident, while Lieutenant James Masson was awarded the George Medal for great courage in defuzing a bomb at the railway station shortly after the King David Hotel incident.

It was with understandable relief that 1st Argylls left Palestine and staged in Egypt before returning to England. Colchester was their new home, and in October 1948 the two battalions of the Regiment amalgamated in a special parade. The form of words for such events vary and have different connotations: in this first major post-war reorganization 2nd Battalion was placed in 'suspended animation', while its customs and traditions were 'preserved' in 1st Battalion. The Battalion remained in Essex for only a short while, was visited by the new Colonel in Chief, HRH The Princess Elizabeth, for the first time, and prepared for a move to Hong Kong in mid 1949.

Although Hong Kong had been returned to British rule after the Japanese occupation, there was a full-scale war in progress in neighbouring China. The Communists were gaining the upper hand and there were fears that infiltrators from across the border would cause trouble in the colony. The Argylls' chief task, however, was to prepare to defend the border from actual invasion by the Chinese Communists, a threat that was not to be taken lightly. It was also feared that inadvertent straying over the border could result in a major incident. Intensive training in the New Territories was conducted over many weeks, but in October when the Chinese Communist forces reached the border, there was no indication that they intended to invade. There was by that time a whole division of British troops to guard the New Territories' border, including armour provided by 4th Royal Tank Regiment, as well as close air cover from the Royal Air Force. With hindsight one can see that it was in the interests of the Chinese Communists to allow Hong Kong to remain a British Colony until the expiry of the agreement in 1997.

At the end of the Second World War, Soviet troops had occupied nearby North Korea and, in defiance of the United Nations, set up a Communist regime in Pyongyang, thus establishing two Korean states, one on each side of the 38th Parallel. The Soviet troops withdrew from the North, as did US troops from the Southern republic of Korea by mid 1949. The arbitrarily decided border meant that trouble was inevitable, and the very much stronger Northern army eventually invaded the South on 25 June 1950. Five days later US troops under General MacArthur began to arrive in order to support the South Koreans. Because of a Russian boycott of attendance at the Security Council at that time, the US troops had the authority of a UN resolution and were thus acting for the UN. But the Communist troops swept southwards and captured Seoul, and there was a lull before a sufficient force of Americans could launch a seaborne re-invasion. On 15 September the Inchon landing took place near Seoul and to the south the US Eighth Army broke out of the small Pusan enclave which had remained in US hands.

The 1st Argylls and 1st Middlesex in 27 Brigade, had been warned for active service in Korea in mid August, and within days the Argylls had embarked in the cruiser HMS *Ceylon*. The British troops disembarked at Pusan to a great welcome from the inhabitants, and by the end of August the Argylls had reached their concentration area close to the 'perimeter' of the Pusan enclave, some fifty miles from the town. They came under US command and on 5 September took responsibility for part of the line in very rugged country overlooking the River Naktong. There was a certain amount of enemy activity and a recce patrol was fired upon from an enemy company position. Captain Neil Buchanan and Private T. Taylor were hit and mortally wounded. The remainder of the patrol were ordered by the wounded officer to return to friendly lines, but five more were wounded. Buchanan was awarded posthumously the American Silver Star.

Meanwhile preparations for the breakout from the Pusan Perimeter were being made. The brigade's task was to cross a river and capture an enemy position at Songtu eight miles north, at the same time protecting an American formation's flank. To the Argylls' immediate front, and between the river and Songtu were three peaks forming a triangle. The Argylls were on the left and the Middlesex on the right; the Middlesex had an intermediate peak as their first objective, and this they captured on the morning of 22 September. During the afternoon the Argylls' 'A' Company seized the southernmost hill, which they achieved with fire support from two US Sherman tanks. But there was not enough time before last light to be sure of capturing the other two hills to the north — Hill 388 and Hill 282 — forming two ends of a ridge about a mile in length, so the battalion held their ground overnight.

At dawn, with 'C' Company on the left and 'B' on the right, the advance on Hill 282 began. 'B' Company, under Major Alastair Gordon-Ingram, surprised the enemy 100 yards from the summit and, killing fifteen, drove them off the hill in a 'Highland charge'; the Argylls suffered ten casualties. The company dug in, while 'C' Company were ordered to swing to the left and occupy the summit of Hill 388, to the west of the same ridge. By mid morning, however, fresh enemy troops appeared to be advancing from Hill 388 towards the two companies of Argylls, who by now were being shelled and mortared, and sustaining several more casualties. To the south 'A' Company in reserve with Battalion HQ were dealing with the enemy on their west flank, and Major Kenneth Muir, the second in command, came up with stretcher-bearers to collect the wounded. Seeing that the situation was getting worse by the minute, he decided to take charge of the by now weakened companies on Hill 282. 'Muir moved around the forward elements ... continuously under fire, and despite entreaties from officers and men alike, refused to take cover'. After a while it became clear that probing attacks by hundreds of North Korean troops and their artillery fire were making the position untenable; there was no friendly artillery support.

The CO, Lieutenant Colonel Leslie Neilson, then decided to ask for an air strike by the US Air Force on the enemy-held Hill 388, in order to relieve the pressure on the Argylls' positions. At 1215 hours three USAF Mustangs arrived, circled three times, and to the horror of the witnesses and victims, began to attack Hill 282 in error with napalm and machine-gun fire. Major Muir tried to stop them by standing up and waving air recognition panels, but this failed to prevent a second strike. The top of the hill was soon blazing furiously and those that could escape moved rapidly off Hill 282; five officers and 35 soldiers were the remaining effective strength of the two companies. Although he was given permission to withdraw, Major Muir gathered the remainder of the soldiers and led an attack to seize the summit against the advancing enemy despite a shortage of ammunition. OC, 'A' Company, Major David Wilson, was the last person to talk to Muir on the Battalion command net:

'He said he was going to get the summit back to give the wounded a chance ... and in the style of the North West Frontier somehow got back to the top. I have never seen anything like it. From perhaps 2,000 yards away I watched through my glasses, impotent to do anything.'

The Argylls retook the hill and Muir and his soldiers held it for more than half an hour. His personal courage and leadership in the chaos of the situation inspired the defenders to superhuman efforts. At one stage Muir and Gordon-Ingram were firing the 2in mortar as a team, but the former was mortally wounded by a burst of machine-gun fire, his last reported words being the 'Gooks will never drive the Argylls off this Hill'. With only ten men and three Bren guns left, Major Gordon-Ingram asked for permission to withdraw and Lieutenant Colonel Neilson reluctantly gave the order.

The 1st Middlesex and US troops in the area worked feverishly to recover, treat and move the wounded back, in an endeavour to alleviate their suffering; but seventeen Argylls had been killed or were missing and 79 had been wounded during the initial attack on the hill, the air strike and the subsequent defence of the hard-won position. Kenneth Muir was awarded the Victoria Cross posthumously as well as the US Distinguished Service Cross. During the following weeks efforts were made by the US authorities and private individuals to make amends; the reputation of the Battalion was if anything enhanced by this tragedy.

The enemy themselves withdrew later on in the day, and the remainder of the Battalion concentrated in 'A' Company's position. Having occupied Songtu, they remained there for a few days, as US troops smashed through the Koreans' resistance and effected a rapid break-out from Pusan, linking in due course with the Inchon Landings.

At the end of the month the Battalion was reinforced with fresh drafts, and 3rd Battalion, Royal Australian Regiment joined to complete the newly designated 27 British Commonwealth Brigade, which was then lifted by air 200 miles north to Kimpo airfield near Seoul. In mid October the advance beyond the 38th Parallel began, in the direction of Pyongyang, and 27 Brigade's task was to 'spearhead' US 1st Cavalry Division. In the advance the leading company was customarily mounted on US Patton tanks, dismounting when trouble was met, or when moving through close country which required clearing on foot. The speed of advance was brisk against disorganized opposition, which meant that from time to time the forward platoons had to dismount from their tanks to deal with road-blocks and snipers. Five miles south of Sariwon a position on a ridge defended by the Koreans necessitated an attack by the whole of 'A' Company with its tanks, mortars and machine-guns. Two platoons led by 2nd Lieutenants Light and Cunningham managed to assault the position from a flank, and in a sharp engagement drove them off leaving fifty dead. The road to Sariwon was open. The Commanding General of 1st Cavalry Division described the attack as a '...marvellous military feat' and the men of 27 Commonwealth Brigade as 'fine fighting soldiers'. Enemy resistance grew stronger the deeper the UN troops advanced, but by 30 October the Argylls had reached Chonju, nearly three hundred miles from Seoul, and fifty miles from the River Yalu, the Manchurian frontier.

By now Chinese Communist 'volunteers' had entered the war, and this radically changed the conduct of the fighting. They were soon able to mount large-scale operations to dislodge the forward UN troops, and after holding the North Koreans and Chinese volunteers for a month, a rapid withdrawal had to be ordered. The Argylls were frequently in action both in the holding operation and then the withdrawal during December 1950. The 27 Brigade covered the rearguard at Seoul in January. Often movement was difficult because of the confused situation, lack of a clear 'front' and the sheer number of Chinese Communists. A break of contact was eventually achieved, and the Argylls re-crossed the 38th Parallel, before going into reserve positions twenty-five miles south-west of Seoul.

The winter weather was bitterly cold, and survival took up much of the soldiers' energy on both sides. In the new year the Chinese established a strong line south of the 38th Parallel, and the Argylls were called forward to perform numerous tasks even when nominally in reserve. In mid-February they were in action again, as the UN force slowly advanced to re-assert control of the border. This was a particularly difficult operation because the broken terrain made forward movement slow and resupply was an additional problem. In March the Argylls had a break from operations, but towards the end of the month they moved forward to the border in defence of a particularly mountainous area before being relieved by 1st King's Own Scottish Borderers after a three-week spell in the front line. Even while they were waiting to be called forward for embarkation at the end of their tour in Korea, a large-scale battle was in progress nearby, which nearly involved their immediate reactivation and return to the front.

It was with great sense of relief that the Battalion sailed for Hong Kong. It had been a very hard eight months, and the Battalion had lost 35 killed and 136 wounded, to which were added a further nine killed and 45 wounded among a large number of men who remained in Korea to serve with 1 KOSB.

Of the Argylls' further service in Hong Kong, there is little to relate. They resumed garrison and border duties, trained hard, played sports and lived a life of relative ease — interspersed with ceremonial events, all of which was a welcome respite from active service.

In August 1952 the Argylls returned to the United Kingdom and their next duty was as the public duties' battalion in Edinburgh. The routine of such tours has become fairly standard over the years, although the variety of tasks is wide and important in terms of civil-military relations — that intangible spirit which keeps the Army and civilian life in harmony. On 29 June 1953 Her Majesty the Queen, as Colonel-in-Chief of the Regiment, presented new Colours to the Battalion.

GUYANA — SUEZ — CYPRUS

It is a historical fact that in the early 1950s there were strong pressures mounting within the colonies against Britain's continued imperial role. The huge financial strain of imperial obligations on the home government should have been obvious, but withdrawal from Empire was only beginning to be accepted, and with the greatest reluctance. There was also political pressure of course from ideologues in the USA and the UN for decolonization, while ominously the growing challenge of Communism in even quite remote corners was becoming a military threat.

The small colony of British Guiana (later Guyana), with a multi-racial population then of about half a million living mainly on the coast, had become unsettled during 1953 and a coup by the left-wing People's Progressive Party had only been prevented by troops rushed from Jamaica to the aid of the police and local Volunteer Force. The US government had encouraged this British reaction for strategic reasons, proving not for the first or last time the ambivalence of US foreign policy. The Argylls arrived in December 1953, travelling most of the way in the aircraft carrier HMS *Implacable*. They were ready to face any internal security operational demanded — from patrols, picquets, cordon and search, to riot squad drill. This latter was a formal manoeuvre, akin to the British Square on a parade ground, complete with a representative of the civil power to read the Riot Act. It was attempted in the first months of Northern Ireland IS duties, but has now been long forgotten.

The battalion was based at Atkinson Field, a US airfield in cleared jungle alongside the River Demarara, and at Georgetown, the colonial capital at the mouth of the river. The first few months passed quietly and without incident. In February some fifty families were flown out to join the Battalion, and were billeted wherever room could be found in hotels and houses in Georgetown. Further evidence of growing confidence was the replacement of the Argylls' duty of guarding Government House by the civil police — 'It is desirable', reads a formal letter to the CO, 'that normal conditions should be re-established in the Colony as soon as possible.' The situation, however, was still unsettled.

In April 1954 the PPP leader and Prime Minister, Dr Jagan, broke the restriction of movement order placed on him, and was arrested. There were demonstrations by some hundreds of his supporters, and the police made further arrests. 'A' Company was put on one hour's notice, but in the event not called out to assist the police. Strikes were reported in some of the sugar plantations, and minor acts of sabotage occurred. But life quietened down again, the soldiers were given passes to walk out in plain clothes. The diary reminds us that this was always a privilege, which could be removed for bad behaviour, low standard of walking out dress ('the wearing of patterned shirts is forbidden, *loud* ties are not to be worn') or 'for contracting VD'.

Life in a colonial station continued in the time-honoured fashion. A parade to celebrate the Queen's Birthday was held in Georgetown, with the Governor taking the salute. In the programme of music for the Governor's reception afterwards, the Argylls' 'Sword Dance' was sandwiched between a certain Jack Casimir and guitar performing 'Luna Rosa' and Daphne Bebidin singing Handel's 'Let the Bright Seraphim' — such was entertainment of the times. One of the problems reported in the Battalion diary was the '...marriages of soldiers to Guyanese girls ... Many of the girls ... are very attractive and the young soldiers fall for them'. Many of the girls who married into the regiment proved to be very loyal regimental wives in the years ahead. PT and sports aplenty was the antidote to overmuch contact with the locals and kept the Jocks occupied. On one occasion two soldiers 'vanished', and in this connection the diary notes that 'there certainly is a great requirement for junior officers to be advised before attempting to make statements of any sort to the press'.

Sporadic trouble with PPP supporters, including incendiarism and explosions occurred, and increased security measures were taken by the police. But the necessity of retaining one regular battalion in support of the police when they were so infrequently needed, was being openly debated by the middle of 1954 in both London and in Georgetown. In October the Argylls were relieved by 2nd Battalion, The Black Watch, and the Battalion, taking part in an air relief test-exercise, was flown from Atkinson Field to Trinidad, quite a novelty for the time. There they embarked on HM Troopship *Dilwara*, by all accounts a most comfortable ship, and for the officers and families such a sea voyages was as good as a cruise, with a call at Las Palmas on the way. A memorable celebration of the centenary of the Battle of Balaclava was held at sea on 25 October.

The winter weeks which the Argylls spent at Pinefield Camp, Elgin were in marked contrast to their life in the tropics. Surviving a Scottish winter in a hutted camp is not a matter that concerns the soldier of the 1990s, but the winter of 1954-5 was not a pleasant experience. A certain amount of training was carried out such as 'attacking the airfield defences of RAF Kinloss':

'The weather was quite atrocious; gale force wind and sleet hindering all movement. It was therefore disappointing that ... the greater part of the force then discovered no opposition ... '

But the RAF had no difficulty in defeating the cross-country running team that the rear party had fielded, to the Argylls' great annoyance. In February there was a 'Parade in commemoration of the Regiment's raising on 10 February 1794 ... The parade was taken by Major General Scott Elliot in a blinding snowstorm. The Battalion was formed up in kilt order (appalling new white sporrans!) in four companies'. The General had commanded 8th Argylls in North Africa, Sicily and Italy.

There was snow too awaiting the Battalion in Berlin, when they travelled to the city halfway across Europe in two trains, via the Harwich ferry. The 'red' and 'green' trains were matched by two continental trains on the other side of the North Sea. Battalion moves by train are not experienced by the modern soldier, and they deserve a book to themselves. But the Argylls found a 'most luxurious and well-appointed barracks' in Montgomery Barracks. The officers and warrant officers were duly impressed by the GOC's introductory lecture. 'There is little doubt in anyone's mind', he told them, 'that this is a place of vast political importance and a place where at all costs we must maintain the highest standards.' This was of course the uneasy period between the time of the Berlin Airlift when the Russians had sealed off the city by land, and the building of the Berlin Wall by the East Germans to staunch the flow of their countrymen seeking freedom via West Berlin.

The Argylls' duty was to provide an alert system with a platoon at fifteen minutes' notice to move anywhere in West Berlin, a company at 45 minutes' notice and the remainder of the battalion at a maximum of three 3 hours'. The first test exercise, under the auspices of the full brigade staff, '...was a moderate success' — one can infer from the words of the Battalion diary the full implication of the statement. 'As they practised time and again the tempo was one of breakneck speed, everything must be done immediately if not before.' The Battalion trained hard in street fighting techniques, shooting, radio procedures, and border patrols, as well as rapid movement and map reading in an urban setting. They also had to find the Spandau prison guard from time to time, where high-ranking Nazi war criminals were held.

Then there were ceremonial parades, notwithstanding a reported 'shortage and continual change of blanco'. On 9 June the Queen's Birthday Parade was held on the *Maifeld*, the Argylls providing Nos 1 and No 2 Guards with the Colour Party. The parade consisted of 'the troop' and march past, followed by a *feu de joie*, advance in review order and march off. The *feu* required an inordinate amount of practice, and invoked some degree of concealed hilarity. The first time it was tried, the Battalion fired as one man, as if artillery, instead of the controlled and even ripple of rifle fire. A full sporting calendar was also resumed — there had been no opposition in British Guyana to speak of — and on 17 April the visiting BAOR football team was beaten by the Argylls 4 goals to 3. Training in the Grünewald in Berlin was somewhat restricted, so training was from time to time carried out in Putlos and Sennelager in the British Zone of West Germany. General Sir Gordon MacMillan, affectionately known within the regiment as 'Babe', and his wife visited the Battalion, an annual event the Colonel of the Regiment is always keen to maintain, and a parade was mounted for the General, with the CO, Lieutenant Colonel Barclay Pearson, commanding the parade.

Then there was more sport. '18 February [1955] was a wonderful day,' reports the diary. 'The battalion won the Rhine Army Football Cup, beating the 9th lancers 2-1.' 21 March 'Another great day for the battalion. By beating the RA the 1st XI football team enter the final of the Army cup.' Sadly the Royal Signals won the cup 3 goals to 2. The challenge is still open to this day for the Argylls to carry off the Army Football cup for the first time this century: the 93rd last won it in 1889.

The pattern of Berlin life repeated itself in the second year before the Argylls returned to the UK. Their next station was Blenheim Barracks, Bury St Edmunds, in Suffolk, which they reached in August 1956, and field training began in earnest after the somewhat confined duties in Berlin. But within weeks it became apparent that the Argylls could be called up for active service in the Middle East, the situation in Egypt having taken an ominous turn with the nationalization of the Canal by the Egyptians. On 27 August all the Battalion transport and anti-tank weapons painted sand coloured, were moved to Newport, Monmouthshire for loading into the support ships. The officers were warned that mobilization was likely, reservists were called up and the Battalion was brought up to war establishment. Leave was cancelled in September and training by both day and night was resumed with a purpose. Meanwhile the Suez Crisis was being debated in the House of Commons.

The wrongs and rights of the Suez campaign cannot be exercised here, although events in the Middle East when viewed from outside are always underestimated, the complexities of the situation obscured and the consequences of any action hard to anticipate. The Argylls, after taking part in a Brigade test exercise at Stanford in late October, were ready for war.

Carrying weapons, ammunition, full kit, steel helmets and blankets, the advance party under Major G.P. 'Timber' Wood left for Southampton by train, followed by Battalion HQ and the companies. There they embarked in HMT *Dilwara*, which many knew from their Caribbean cruise two years earlier, numbering 37 officers and 794 other ranks; a further 73, having arrived late from a short leave pass, joined later. The traditional loyal greetings had been sent to HM the Queen, to which she replied conveying her '...sincere thanks for their kind and loyal message of greetings which as Colonel-in-Chief I greatly appreciate'. The Argylls were 'ready for whatever task may be demanded of them', as the typical British understatement had it. Whatever their feelings of apprehension, they were scarcely prepared for the few and pathetic tasks they actually were called upon to fulfil.

The *Dilwara* called at Gibraltar, Malta and Cyprus before anchoring at Port Said on 14 November. Transhipping proved a dangerous procedure, the battalions being carried ashore by landing craft in a heavy swell. Orders from above were scanty. The Battalion first moved into the area of some apartment blocks to the west of the town. Fortunately both their landing and occupation, much of it carried out in the dark, had been unopposed. Then 19 Brigade, in which the Argylls were serving, relieved the Paras and Royal Marine Commandos of the responsibility of holding the airfield and the Arab shanty town. For the most part this involved patrol and search operations; only once were the Argylls fired upon.

On 21 November the first UN troops arrived to signal the end of the war between the allies (UK, France and Israel) and the Egyptians. The purpose of the assault, which was to reoccupy the 'Canal Zone' (given up one year earlier by the British), had been thwarted chiefly by US pressure, and a ceasefire was accepted. At this juncture the Argylls took over the responsibility of guarding the power station, gas works and sewage works — scarcely a task to warrant travelling from the UK to carry out.

In early December life became more interesting as there was a drive against Egyptian 'terrorists' and in particular a search for some printing presses which were turning out propaganda material. There were also several shooting incidents. Then on 7 December at Quabati, 'B' Company: '...discovered, in the grey light of dawn two small ships being unloaded on the shore of Lake Manzala. On being challenged, the occupants fled, and despite a subsequent search of the village, remained undetected. In the boats were found some 20,000 rounds of ammunition, grenades, detonator sets, rockets and gelignite.'

The Argylls were also called in to assist the Royal Scots when shooting broke out on 9 December, and 'A' Company came under fire. On 16 December 'B' Company were also under continuous automatic fire from the shanty town.

Plans for the British withdrawal were drawn up during December and in the vicinity of Port Said a large area was wired off with a perimeter fence. This was the 'defended locality' from which an orderly and defended withdrawal was to be conducted. The operation took place during the night of 21/22 December, and the Battalion sailed for the UK which they reached on 31 December. Sadly the race for a proper Hogmanay at home was lost for most of the Battalion, the two special trains leaving for Scotland at 0230 and 0300 on 1 January 1957. The general feeling was naturally one of thankfulness that a somewhat futile operation had not been of long duration or resulted in casualties, but the Battalion felt somewhat fed up by the whole performance.

The Argylls remained at Bury St Edmunds until January 1958. Lieutenant Colonel 'Chippie' Anderson took command in what proved to be a quiet period in the Battalion's history. They held the 3rd Division Rifle meeting in May, trained at Thetford in a test exercise and ran a camp for large numbers of cadets from contingents of the Combined Cadet Force between May and August. In September they were training on Salisbury Plain, returning to Bury for the Balaklava Day and Lucknow parades. They were then warned off for duty in Cyprus in the early new year.

Cyprus had erupted in violence in 1954. The Greek Cypriot terrorist organization EOKA were intent on achieving '*enosis*' or union with Greece, by removing the British presence from the island and denying power to the considerable Turkish population. EOKA was led by the legendary General George Grivas, a most resourceful commander who caused immense trouble to the British security forces over a long period, employing tactics reminiscent of Palestine in the late 1940s.

On 21 January 1958 reveille was called at the uncomfortable time of 0200 hours at Bury St Edmunds and at 1830 hours HMT *Devonshire* sailed from Liverpool. The traditional musical welcome on the quayside at Limassol was provided by the band of 1st Battalion, Middlesex Regiment. Limni Camp was the Argylls' home on the island, situated near Polis on Khrysokon Bay; two companies were at Polemi Camp on the western slope of the Troodos mountain range. The operational area was partly cultivated and partly rugged mountain, while the roads were tortuous and in many places formed a series of hairpin bends on the steep mountainside.

The Battalion quickly got into the routine of active service; in turn two companies provided guards, duties and fatigues in camp, while the other companies spent a week at a time on patrol, cordon and search, manning road-blocks, setting up observation points and conducting snap checks in the expectation of hampering the terrorists' activities, if not actually catching them. On 7 March the Battalion carried out a major cordon exercise 'involving a 7-mile approach march and a climb of 2,000 feet' taking place between 0130 hours and 0800 hours. The search proved fruitless. But for light relief there was time for the battalion football team to make its mark on the Cyprus football scene, beating 1st Oxford and Buckinghamshire Light Infantry 5 goals to 1. The team then carried off the Cyprus Cup 10 goals to 1 against a Royal Signals team.

EOKA operations flared up in April 1958. A series of company operations code-named 'Village Green' had the deterrent effect of keeping the operational area free of terrorist incidents, although elsewhere there was activity to keep other British battalions busy. Often security forces are unaware of their own success in denying terrorists freedom of action. In mid-May orders were anticipated for a British landing in the Lebanon, but this never occurred.

A major operation was then mounted in the summer in the hope of catching Grivas and other EOKA commanders. On 16 May Operation 'Kingfisher', involving some 1,500 troops began. Helicopters airlifted OP parties of the Battalion into position on high features, while the cordon troops were moved by truck to various points; no recce had been carried out for fear of compromising the operation.

'"Across country" means a precipitous climb', records the Battalion diary, 'and a drop over a razor-backed ridge ... a long clamber over rocks and thorny scrub before C Company reached their start line'. Other companies had no easier an approach before the cordon was in position by noon. Some close searching was possible, but the area was far too large to control and search effectively. There were, however, several sightings: Corporal Robson and the Pipes and Drums fired on some EOKA who approached their positions, and 'A' Company did likewise, but no hits were recorded or intelligence gathered as a consequence. The cordon remained in place for several days, and assault pioneers and Royal Engineers were called in with blasting equipment and heavy plant to try to discover EOKA hides, which were usually most skilfully concealed, but to no avail. There is little doubt that the terrorists had melted away as soon as they realized what was happening. The operation was not finally called off until 3 July.

Forthcoming constitutional talks were expected to cause trouble all over the island, but prevention or cure is all much of a muchness in an internal security situation. In July there was a spate of attacks by Greeks against Turks and bombs were thrown at two Argylls' patrols. This proved to be a new campaign by EOKA throughout the island and Operation 'Matchbox' was invoked to arrest all EOKA suspects. The Battalion quickly pulled in seventeen of the 22 named suspects in the Battalion area and a curfew was imposed. A second operation code-named 'Spray Sparkle' was mounted three days later, which involved setting up snatch road-blocks throughout the island. In these operations 1,500 EOKA supporters had been put in the bag, but there were dozens of incidents in the following weeks against the security forces and between the Greek and Turkish Cypriots. During August the Argylls scored a number of successes in preventing terrorist activities and making further arrests.

Gradually the situation eased in the autumn of 1958 as British operations were obviously greatly hampering EOKA activities. 'A' Company were sent to Tobruk in Libya for a few months, while the remainder of the Battalion continued operations both inside their area and, on occasions, in support of other troops. New tactics involving designated 'Danger Areas' were mounted; anyone seen moving in them could be shot. Sporadic EOKA ambushes, not very proficiently mounted, were encountered from time to time, fortunately without casualties, one being against the Argylls' football team. Then another large-scale cordon operation was mounted code-named 'Goldfish' involving three Argylls companies. A number of suspects were rounded up, there were shooting incidents, and weapons, ammunition and explosives were discovered in a number of villages. No hides, however, were found until a week later; one of them was 'cold' and another definitely 'hot'. The Commanding Officer, Lieutenant Colonel Anderson, personally found a third, and later in November another weapon and ammunition cache was discovered.

In December the Argylls were moved to the Larnaca area of Cyprus and settled into Dhekelia camp. It was a quiet area of the island and January and February 1959 passed with little to disturb the garrison life of the Battalion. The new Colonel of the Regiment, Brigadier Freddie Graham, paid his first visit to the Battalion. At the same time a political settlement on the future of Cyprus was reached between the British, Geek and Turkish Governments: Cyprus was to become an independent republic, and sovereign bases at Episkopi, Akrotiri and Dhekelia were to be retained by Britain.

The change from active service to peacetime duties and training was immediate, and during the spring and summer the Battalion worked up to battalion level training for the anticipated move to Germany. Command passed to Lieutenant Colonel Hugh Spens and 1st Black Watch took over the camp on 5 October. The Argylls embarked in the now familiar troopship *Dilwara*, to the music of the pipes and drums of the relieving battalion, and left the island.

CHAPTER 13

THE SIXTIES

BAOR — EDINBURGH

The Argylls reached the pleasant town of Lemgo in wooded hillsides near Detmold in late 1959, and they were destined to remain there for nearly two years. It was a time of a large-scale Army reorganization, and while regimental amalgamations or disbandments were not in question, the depot of The Black Watch was amalgamated with that of the Argylls, at Stirling. An additional measure was the establishment of the brigade system for the infantry, which for some regiments developed into the new 'large regiment' concept. A new Highland Brigade badge, irreverently known as the 'crucified moose', was adopted. In January 1961 a party from the Battalion went to München Gladbach to bid a traditional Scots farewell to 1st Seaforth Highlanders who were on their way to amalgamation with the Cameron Highlanders; the pipes and drums of the Argylls, the Gordons and the Royal Scots Greys formed up on the platform of the railway station to play the Seaforth away.

BAOR soldiering was also undergoing a significant change at the time, and the Argylls were among the first to be introduced to the new range of armoured personnel carriers — although of course such vehicles had been in use during the Second World War. For some years the Royal Armoured Corps, while feeling somewhat demeaned by the task, provided all the drivers, and 'A' Squadron 4th Royal Tank Regiment supported the Argylls. Exercise 'Quick Train' — the call-out alert — was called from time to time, and battalion, brigade, division, corps and army group exercises were the staple of the Battalion's life, together with individual, small-arms, support weapons and specialist training to complete the formal programme.

Those BAOR days are something of a fading memory now. Sport was often of more significance than training in a battalion's life, particularly as there were still numerous national servicemen serving in the ranks. Boxing and football had long been the Argylls' most serious sports. The adjutant's diary, maintained by Captain Patrick Palmer, shows that the Argylls beat the Gordon Highlanders 6 bouts to 5 and against the Royal Scots Greys 8 bouts to 3. In February the Battalion took the BAOR football cup from the Leicestershire Regiment by 2 goals to 1, the presentation being made by General Sir James Cassels, CinC BAOR.

In May the Pipes and Drums played at the British Trade Fair in Moscow, not a million miles from those places named on the Colours as battle honours, and it was in that same year that new Colours were presented to 7th and 8th Battalions at Stirling. Then the adjutant's diary reports on 31 December 1961:

'The traditional lunch was served by the officers and SNCOs to the soldiers. The Atholl Brose was piped up to the Sergeants' Mess and distributed to the protesting sergeants by the two junior subalterns. The recipe is from Islay and is known only to the Officers' Mess steward. A howling mob led by Pte Menzies and some pipers roamed the camp and arrived at the main gate at the same time as the RMP vehicle, which rapidly went into high reverse. Pipers piped until dawn and the rest is silence.'

Such was the fabric of BAOR soldiering.

Edinburgh in 1962, as now, meant a very different kind of soldiering. It is deemed necessary to employ one extra battalion in the British Army to carry out the public duties in Scotland for which Redford Barracks battalion is furnished.

The Castle Guard and at times Holyrood Guards had to be found. Guards of honour at Waverley Station and for the Monarch in residence at the Palace of Holyrood House were needed for the annual Royal season. The regimental mascot Cruachan, a Shetland pony, was frequently seen on parade. The military band and Pipes and Drums were in constant demand for the garden parties and banquets; so were endless fatigue parties for a hundred and one tasks in and around the capital, and in support of the Edinburgh Tattoo.

One of the honours for the resident battalion is to mount guard at Balmoral Castle, based at the small barracks at Ballater nearby. Every man is hand picked for 'reliability' on guard and fitness for beating the moors for the royal grouse. The annual Ghillies Ball is an event the soldiers find gratifying, attended as it is by the Regiment's own Colonel-in-Chief.

In 1962 the Royal season was prolonged into October by the state visit to Edinburgh of that most popular of foreign sovereigns, King Olav of Norway. This was the first and only time that there has ever been such an occasion outside London or Windsor. On a domestic note, the Battalion returned from leave on 3 January 1963, '...less 26 absentees who may have genuine excuses, such as being snowed up in Argyllshire. The whole Barracks is under about 6 inches of snow', snow that was to last into March all over the United Kingdom. In February the Argylls beat the Loyals in the UK boxing championships by 8 bouts to 3. There was also a military training programme to be fulfilled, often a low priority for the Edinburgh battalion. As time went on, training for the Battalion's overseas tour had to be taken more seriously. The Argylls were to be posted with the families to Singapore.

BORNEO

Britain's responsibilities in the Far East were in a state of considerable flux at this time. The Federation of Malaysia had been established, including the two former colonies of North Borneo and Sarawak which shared an island with the Sultanate of Brunei and Indonesian Southern Borneo. In late 1962 there had been a revolt in Brunei by nationalists, determined that the country should not be absorbed into Malaysia, which had to be quelled by British troops. But President Sukharno of Indonesia was by this time determined to seize the whole of the island, including Brunei with its vast oilfields. In early 1963 guerrillas began to infiltrate the province of Sarawak, which lay between Indonesian Borneo and Brunei in the north. What followed was deemed not a war but 'confrontation'.

The Argylls' return to Singapore in 1964 was a poignant reminder of the Regiment's past, but there was work to be done to settle in the families and train for jungle warfare. Deployment of the Battalion to Borneo was achieved by air and sea, the company areas of responsibility being the '4th Division of Sarawak', in the Belait and Tutong districts. (The 'Divisions' of Sarawak were numbered west to east, one to five.) The Battalion operation order stated:

'*Situation. Enemy Forces.* While the Indonesian policy of confrontation continues and the internal threat remains, there is always danger of acts of sabotage, armed insurrection or public disorder taking place in Brunei and Sarawak. Trained saboteurs are capable of attacking the Shell installations at Seria [Brunei]. Such raids can be carried out by raiding parties from the sea or by parachutists. They are more likely to be carried out by Clandestine Communist Organization (CCO) forces who have daily access to the area and the opportunity to plan and reconnoitre in detail. *Mission.* To render immediate military assistance to the Police and Government in the Seria area. Tasks to destroy enemy incursions into the area; to dominate by active patrolling the jungle and to gain information on any activities of CCOs and infiltrators; to gain the confidence of the local inhabitants.'

The initiative was always with the enemy in such warfare and operating from platoon bases, the Argylls had to be instantly ready to react with force or stealth in follow-up operations, depending on an interpretation of the enemy's intention — often very difficult to discover or guess.

On 4 May 'A' Company reported a contact by a five-man patrol led by Corporal Watson in the area of Pa Lungan:

'A figure clad in OG uniform with a peaked cap and 58 type pouches,' reads the report, 'and carrying a small carbine rose from the undergrowth. The patrol commander fired ... six rounds and the man stumbled forward but continued running and was lost in the jungle ... The patrol found blood trails for about 20 yards.'

Local trackers were brought up subsequently and found the tracks of six men. They concluded that these must have been the leading elements of a fighting patrol of up to company strength which had been met head on.

Lieutenant Colonel Glen Kelway Bamber, the CO, was to spend much of his time visiting the company areas and platoon positions, since at times the Jocks felt very isolated. Air support, artillery support and rapid reaction reserves were available on the end of the radio. But apart from the contact described, the Battalion area along the border with Indonesia was relatively quiet for some weeks, while patrols by 'D' Company in river craft proved more interesting than fruitful in terms of contact with the enemy. Major John MacMillan (subsequently GOC Scotland and son of General 'Babe') was later to say about service in Borneo:

'No one can generalise about a tour in Borneo because the situation changes so often. Patrols may take on a pattern for a week or two, but then enemy activity, financial or political restrictions, or a lucky break may change the emphasis. In general terms, however, one patrol is very like another.'

He compared the idyllic view of the countryside from the air, and the 'stinking squelch of the treacherous mud, the razor-backed ridges of the hills and the tangled growth of the jungle' where the Jocks lived and worked.

A week after the handover of the Battalion to Lieutenant Colonel Malcolm Wallace, some mortar bombs were fired at a platoon position by an Indonesian patrol late at night. In the morning a follow-up patrol went out on the orders of Major Sandy

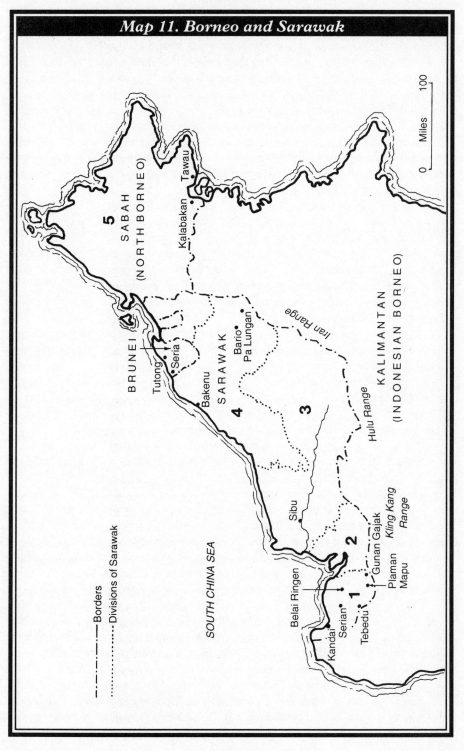

Map 11. Borneo and Sarawak

Boswell, with Sergeant Brian Baty (who won the Military Medal and was soon to be commissioned) and his 'Combat Tracker Team' together with half a platoon under Sergeant Frank Sutherland. (These specialist teams comprised two NCOs, signallers, riflemen, two Iban trackers and two dog handlers — twelve men and two dogs all told.) Another tracker team under Sergeant Gow with Sergeant Robson and eight men from the Pipes and Drums in support set up an ambush. No 1 platoon commanded by Lieutenant Simon Sloane was flown to an ambush position as well. During the morning Sergeant Baty's team contacted the enemy near Pa Butal, and two Indonesians were killed and a large amount of kit, weapons and ammunition was captured. It is thought that the infiltrators believed they had crossed the border and were safe to relax. A short while later four more insurgents, escapees from Sergeant Gow's ambush, were killed.

In mid-September the Argylls returned to Singapore. Individual and collective training continued and the domestic life of the Battalion was resumed. Courses in dog handling and language training were both given prominence.

But in February 1965 the Argylls were back on operations, with Bn HQ in Balai Ringen Camp, co-located with 'A' Company, the reserve. Other company bases were at Gunan Gajak and Plamen Mapu from twenty to forty kilometres distant. It was a period of some uncertainty, as the enemy's intentions were particularly obscure. On 18 February 1965, for instance, the commander's diary reports:

'Thirteen refugees arrived after a two days' walk from Indonesia, representing the entire population of village, because of enemy looting and threats of conscription.' They had been 'frequently visited by enemy patrols of strength 20/30.'

A further 73 refugees arrived shortly after.

On 1 March Major John MacMillan, OC 'D' Company, reported that 30 enemy had been in the area close by, their tracks being 24-48 hours old. A follow-up operation was mounted. And the war diary is full of entries such as:

'Report of barefoot tracks of ten men in area Grid– leading to border. Ten single shots heard from border area at Grid– and fresh cut tracks lead SW towards border. Camp 12 hours old for 20 men found at Grid–.'

Troops were moved frequently by Whirlwind helicopters and the task of dominating the jungle was faithfully carried out. In May the Argylls lost Private William Hill, a son of the Regiment, in a fire fight with the enemy. Then on 5 June Lieutenant David Thomson and his platoon laid a successful ambush in the Kandai Border area as part of Operation 'Claret', an authorized cross-border operation. Eleven insurgents were killed with only one slight casualty in the platoon and Thomson was awarded the Military Cross for this action. Later in the month the Argylls returned to Singapore.

The third and final operational tour in Borneo began in November 1965. Company positions initially were at Serian, Pang Amo and Plaman Mapu, and at first all was quiet. Then on 12 December 'possible cooking smoke' was spotted and 'engaged with 15 rounds of mortar from D Company's mortars'. On Christmas Day an RAF Belvedere flew along the forward positions distributing free cigarettes, a small consolation for the Jocks separated from their families and more normal festivities.

During this period there was a programme in which some of the local Chinese were re-settled for their own protection. On 13 January the intelligence report states that:

'A large group of Chinese IBT [Indonesian Border Terrorists] who have been undergoing training in the Hong Kong area, are being deployed in small groups along the Sekayan river. It is believed that the intention of these small groups is to infiltrate into Sarawak, followed by acts of aggression and terrorist raids against the native population.'

Operation 'Ratcatcher' was the code-name given to a redeployment of two companies to meet the increased threat to Serian, but enemy activity was confined to the SAS area alongside the Argylls. On 15 February a border scout 'reported tracks of 30 men 5 kilometres north of Tebedu' and 'A' Company set off in pursuit, joined by elements of 'D' Company. Crossing into 2/7 Gurkha Rifles' area, the composite force of Argylls came under command of the Gurkhas. Contact with the enemy was made by other Gurkha companies and for the next two days the Argylls set up a 'net' in the hope of catching retreating enemy. The diarist admitted that they '...are still finding gaps in the border ... the task of cutting off 10 kms of jungle is proving very difficult'. In early March, however, 'D' Company killed at least six enemy in an ambush.

In April the Battalion handed over the operational area and returned to Singapore. The remaining time in Singapore was uneventful and in November 1966 the Battalion returned to the UK, their new posting being Seaton Barracks, Plymouth. In December the Battalion was put on 'provisional warning' to move to Aden in June for a nine-month unaccompanied tour. Lieutenant Colonel Colin Mitchell took over command in January 1967.

A large exercise was held on Stanford training area in Norfolk and a counter-insurgency test exercise took place on Dartmoor in March. Internal security training was conducted in the barracks and 'up country' at Okehampton. In May, when the Argylls were informed that they were to be deployed in the Crater district of Aden, the Battalion carried out a street patrols and cordon exercise — 'Crater Crisis'. Lieutenant General Sir Geoffrey Baker, having watched the training at Plymouth, wrote to the CO:

'I should like to congratulate you most warmly on the thorough "imagination" of the training you're carrying out. Everything I saw warmed my old heart — and I have just written to the CGS to tell him so. What a delightful and proficient lot of officers you have. Compared with some units, you are in a different league.'

This was praise indeed from one of Britain's finest post-war field commanders, and a man of the highest intellect.

ADEN

The withdrawal from Aden was a sad chapter in the history of Britain's transference of power from colonial administration to local government. In fact by the time the Argylls reached the colony in June 1967, all the signs of retreat were there. Terrorists operated freely in the towns as well as up-country, and British soldiers were by and large only protecting themselves, their families and expatriates. British rule was due to end in 1968, but even though the fledgling Aden Federal Government by now had no chance of taking over power properly, the date was brought forward to November 1967. To add to the confusion there was virtual civil war between the two 'liberation' factions, the National Liberation Front (NLF) and the Front for the Liberation of South Yemen (FLOSY).

On 20 June, before the main party of the Battalion had arrived to take over Crater, there was an insurrection in the town by the Aden Armed Police. For some time British troops had mainly visited Crater by daylight. At the same time the Aden Federal National Guard mutinied against the British in the Khormaksar district, killing a number of Royal Corps of Transport soldiers. In Crater a patrol of the Royal Northumberland Fusiliers was cut off: later they were found, done to death in a particularly brutal fashion. Two Land Rovers taking Major Moncur and escorts of the Royal Northumberland Fusiliers and Major Bryan Malcolm of the Argylls, accompanied by Privates 'Porcus' Hunter and Moores of the Argylls' recce platoon were ambushed as they attempted to investigate the situation; all but one, a Fusilier, were killed. Attempts to penetrate the mountain passes into Crater by armoured troop carriers failed and the Queen's Dragoon Guards in Saladin armoured cars were denied permission to fire their 76mm guns to cover the infantry.

The use of heavy weapons was considered by HQ Middle East Land Forces as the only guarantee of success in re-entering Crater and that would have been too provocative. (Tanks had been withdrawn from Aden six months earlier, and they had never been used in internal security duties in the colony.) The Argylls assumed responsibility for the sealed off Crater area on 25 June.

Despite advice that re-entry would be a bloodbath for both the British and the Adenis, the Argylls' CO, Lieutenant Colonel Colin Mitchell, sought and received permission, first to send deep penetration patrols into the district, and in due course to mount an operation to re-occupy the whole of Crater. In the meantime companies in turn established themselves in mountain-top picquets to observe enemy activities in Crater.

Over the months Colonel Mitchell had trained the Battalion to a very high level of efficiency; discipline and high morale are twin factors and the Argylls had both. Now that the Highland Brigade had been absorbed into the Scottish Division, the Regiment had re-adopted their old regimental cap badge. Furthermore Mitchell, knowing the high political risk of an operation such as he was planning, ensured that the British press were present while Crater was reoccupied. It proved to be an amazing bravura performance.

At 1900 hours on 3 July, 'B' Company in the lead under Major Patrick Palmer, supported by 'A' Squadron of the Queen's Dragoon Guards crossed the start-line and advanced along Marine Drive into Crater. Pipe Major Robson received the order to sound the regimental charge 'Monymusk' and then 'B' Company's march, the 'Glendaruel Highlanders'. Mitchell's tactical HQ was close behind. Machine-guns opened up from the Sultan's palace and were silenced by the QDGs' return fire. Everyone had been carefully instructed only to return fire on orders. Within the hour 'B' Company's objectives, the old Legislative Council building and the Chartered Bank, had been seized.

The Treasury building was given up by the armed police after Major Nigel Crowe, speaking Arabic, had urged them to surrender and avoid bloodshed. 'A' Company under Major Ian Robertson passed in rear and occupied Sira Island.

'It was now obvious', admits Colonel Mitchell in his account of the operation, 'that we were over-reaching the limits of exploitation agreed ... so I spoke to the acting Brigade Commander on the wireless and said that as the initiative was so completely ours ... permission [was requested] to let us go on and exploit up to the civil police station. This was the rewarding moment for any commander, when you know your own chaps will cut through opposition like a knife through butter. You can feel it in the air and breathe in the aggressive confidence. We were in luck.'

The advance continued and most of Crater was reoccupied during the morning. Contact was made with the Armed Police in the afternoon in their barracks, which was by now cut off from both sides by the Battalion. For political reasons the Armed Police mutiny against British rule was forgotten and those who had fired on and killed British soldiers never prosecuted. From then on the security of Crater would be a matter for the Battalion.

The success of the operation, however, was greeted by world-wide publicity and very little of it hostile; Colonel Mitchell felt that he had the full support of the High Commissioner, but the action undoubtedly embarrassed some government ministers and therefore some military commanders in London and Aden itself, embarrassment which re-surfaced later.

Having re-entered a 'no-go' area, the Argylls quickly re-established firm control. Enemy snipers and 'grenadiers' frequently sought opportunities to retaliate against patrols and static picquets. Instructions were given by the CO to return fire without waiting for orders, to which he added:

'If you have no ammunition you are to go in with bayonet. It is better the whole battalion dies in Crater to rescue one Jock than any one of us comes out alive.'

Such promises did much to reassure the soldiers, who were often isolated in small patrols or picquets for a considerable time. 'The battalion', said one of his officers, 'would do anything for Colin Mitchell.' Thus was 'Argyll law' established and maintained. 'Life in Crater is virtually returning to normal,' stated the commander's diary, but later the terrorists became bolder and the incidents more frequent. This was seen by the Battalion as a direct consequence of the order from HQ MELF to 'throttle back and adopt a less aggressive posture'. By the end of the first four weeks of occupation the Battalion had lost two men killed, Corporal Scott of the Pipes and Drums and Lance Corporal Orr of 'D' Company; six Jocks had been wounded. The Battalion had accounted for eighteen 'genuine' terrorists killed.

It was naturally a very trying time for the Battalion. First they had to accept the Armed Police's extremely suspect loyalty. At the same time there was a power struggle going on between the two rival terrorist groups; snipers and grenade throwers were at work and an elusive mortar bomber attacked at random, a tactic which caused much unease. Continued press coverage at once encouraged the Battalion in its work, but proved to be a double-edged weapon.

The government had long decided on abandoning Aden, but militarily disengagement was a dangerous game. An elaborate plan was drawn up. On the night of 25/26 November with great secrecy, the Argylls withdrew from Crater, passing through 1st Battalion The Parachute Regiment and 45 Royal Marine Commando. These three units then flew out, covered by 42 Commando, who were helicoptered last of all to HMS *Albion*. The news was circulated worldwide within hours on the morning of 26 November. It was a military success but politically it was a retreat.

The Regiment's record in Aden was a proud one. The Argylls had done what they were ordered to in their own way: five had been killed and twenty-four wounded in the process. The *Thin Red Line*'s editorial in September 1968 accurately summed up the mood of the nation:

'To Colin Mitchell the whole regiment and indeed *most* of the country would want to thank him for the action in Crater and for revitalising the image of the Army which has become so drab.'

Crater was symbolic, and there is a major place for symbolic action where an Army is conducting real military operations.

It is appropriate at this point to record the post-war history of the volunteer battalions of the Regiment. Both 7th and 8th Argylls had been temporarily disbanded in 1946, only to be re-formed a year later. In 1967 they joined together as 3rd Battalion TAVR III, on the formation of the 'Territorial Army and Volunteer Reserve', but only remained in being for one year. 'E' Company of 7th Battalion, however, then joined with companies of other regiments to form the 51st Highland Volunteers, a new TAVR I battalion. In due course they absorbed members of 3rd Argylls, when with other TAVR III battalions, it was disbanded. In 1981 the three companies — from Stirling, Dumbarton and Grangemouth —formed a complete Argyll battalion, 3rd Battalion 51st Highland Volunteers, to which was added a Cumbernauld Company. In the 'Options for Change' reorganization of the Territorial Amy (1993-5) the Battalion continues in being and adopts the '7th/8th Battalion' title.

The artillery roled battalions faced different reorganizations and eventual oblivion. The 54th Light Anti-Aircraft Regiment RA (A and SH) was renumbered 554th and continued in service until 1955 when its members transferred to 8th Argylls and 402 Light Regiment RA (A and SH) TA. This regiment had been formed in 1947 from the old 5th and 6th Battalions which had served as 91st and 93rd Anti-Tank Regiments respectively. Known as 277 Field Regiment RA (A and SH) TA, it was disbanded in 1967.

DISBANDMENT AND RE-FORMATION

On their return from Aden the role of a UK-based battalion seemed an anticlimax indeed. There had been enormous press interest in the Battalion's activities in Aden, and it continued unabated during the early months of 1968. This was at first welcome because a major recruiting drive was under way in Glasgow and the west of Scotland. But press coverage while tickling the Jocks, proved to be something of a burden to some in the Regiment and a bore to others. The commanding officer's story is told in forthright terms in his autobiography *Having Been a Soldier*, written after retirement. As well as being exciting, it is a seminal book for anyone wishing to study the phenomenology of the 'regimental system', where the personality-intensive factors are predominant and military 'methods' are unequivocal.

The Battalion trained hard for their new role in Strategic Command, and in July 1968 took part in a practice deployment by air to Cyprus. Then, on 11 July the diary reported the:

'..confirmation of what we have all known to be imminent. Denis Healy [Secretary of State for Defence] announced today in Parliament that the Argylls are to be one of the six major units that are to disappear in the defence cuts. The Battalion's reaction was as might be expected, disappointment, resentment and surprise ... The Jocks ... had perhaps built up the feeling that ... this could not happen to us.'

In addressing the Battalion Lieutenant Colonel Mitchell stated that, '...while there's life there's hope and a lot can happen in the four years', the period given as the maximum length of time allowed for continuation. 'Mad Mitch' was given a standing ovation by the Jocks. (The nickname had been given to him by the press.)

In due course there was a meeting at Stirling Castle with the former and present Colonels of the Regiment, the CO and CO designate and other eminent men in the Regiment's family, but the Argylls' reputation had seized the public's imagination particularly in Scotland and there was a spontaneous campaign —which the Regiment could scarcely have stopped had they wanted to — to 'Save the Argylls'. A million signatures were gathered in support of the Regiment. Others, however, considered the campaign undignified, comparing the quiet departure of such regiments as the Cameronians and York and Lancaster Regiment as proof of their different style.

George Younger MP, later Secretary of State for Defence, was the prime mover in Parliament for the campaign. But in the House of Commons adverse references were made against the Argylls within the safety of parliamentary privilege. A former Minister, Barbara Castle, had alleged heavy-handedness in Cyprus, and Tam Dalyell, an MP descendant of the famous old soldier General Tom Dalyell who raised the Royal Scots Greys in 1681, had spoken against the Regiment's tactics in Aden.

There is one potent argument in use at times of Army reorganization which states that a low position in the table of seniority is the fairest way of selecting regiments for disbandment or amalgamation. Another argument, based on practicalities, states that because the 'regimental system' so lacks any sort of consistency as hardly to be a system at all, regimental recruiting and retention figures taken over time are the best means of deciding which regiments ought to be retained. Comparisons of 'efficiency' between regiments, certainly in the late 1960s, were highly subjective, even though the intuition of senior officers was often near the mark. The Argylls certainly scored heavily in the last two of these criteria and the *Thin Red Line* journal of the time goes to great lengths to prove conclusively the strength of the Regiment, a strength which none could deny. All this activity appeared to be of no avail.

The Argylls had at least two years to serve. The Battalion spent the autumn of 1968 practising air-mobility and a second deployment was made to Cyprus. This time the Argylls exercised on the island under their new CO, Lieutenant Colonel Sandy Boswell. In March 1969 the Battalion moved from Plymouth to Berlin.

In many ways the pattern of life in Berlin had remained unchanged since the tour fifteen years earlier. But the west part of the city had grown and prospered, marred by the Berlin Wall which had been erected in 1961. A new generation of soldiers, however, made up the Battalion. Limited training was conducted in the city, and major exercises at Soltau, Vogelsang and Sennelager in West Germany. Endless guards, border patrols, alert standby duty, two seasons of formal drill — Queen's Birthday, Allied Forces and battalion parades — all in the full glare of publicity, comprised life in Berlin. The annual inspection graded the Battalion 'excellent', showing there was no slackening of pace and morale.

In June 1970 the Battalion moved to Fort George, for what was believed to be its last station before disbandment. Nevertheless, recruiting tours were sent throughout the Regiment's area with good results. Then came a welcome surprise. The Regiment was not to disband. The Army cuts had been announced by a Labour government just at the time that the crisis in Ulster had begun; in August 1970 a new Conservative Secretary of State offered the alternative, which was a reduction to company strength — 126 men. The compromise was accepted in the thinly disguised hope that it could be restored in due course to a full battalion.

The Colonel-in-Chief visited the Argylls in October informally and spent '...an unforgettable day for all of us in the battalion and we hope for Her Majesty'. The Queen met a large number of the soldiers as she toured the Fort and had tea with the wives. Before leaving, Her Majesty was 'piped' past the Battalion in what was to be her farewell visit before its reduction. In December and January drafts began to leave to be 'attached' to other Scottish regiments and Balaklava Company under Major Ian Purves Hume assembled as the remaining regular Company of the Battalion.

On 20 January the '1st Battalion the Argyll and Sutherland Highlanders (Princess Louise's) Balaklava Company' was formed at a parade at Stirling Castle where HM the Queen inspected the Company and took the salute. The Company then moved to Barnard Castle where it began individual and collective training on the Yorkshire training areas, followed by a week at the Parachute Regiment's battle school in Wales. A support platoon was formed and equipped with 120mm Wombat anti-tank guns and 81mm mortars. The Company was as viable an independent sub-unit as it could be, given its limited manpower and equipment. Cruachan, the regimental pony mascot, was retained on strength and the Pipes and Drums continued in being.

In May Balaklava Company moved by air to Gibraltar for a six-month tour. There was heightened tension between the Spanish and Gibraltarians at the time, and the border had been closed. Guard duties were interspersed with small-arms shooting, IS training, formal guards and parades for visitors, sports, visits to HM ships, adventure training in Morocco and relaxation in a Mediterranean station. Then on 13 October the OC received news from the MOD, '...which announced that we were to be restored to battalion strength ... due to the Northern Ireland situation and satisfactory recruiting position. It was such a surprise to us ... by lunchtime the celebrations were all under way', noted the diary. Celebrations were also held in numerous other places, notably in Scotland!

The tour ended in November and the Company were quite pleased to leave Gibraltar which had proved to be boring at times, particularly as the Spanish authorities were refusing permission for the British troops to visit Spain.

CHAPTER 14

TWENTY YEARS ON

NORTHERN IRELAND: BANDIT COUNTRY AND BELFAST

The last chapter of the history of the first two hundred years of the Regiment's existence is a curious one. In a post-industrial, post-modern and even according to some a post-military age, the position of something so traditional as the British regimental system is rather uncertain. With the benefit of hindsight, after the withdrawal from Empire the British Army has arguably been living on borrowed time. BAOR has been comprised of a similar number of troops as had been deployed worldwide in support of local troops to defend the Empire in peacetime during the hundred years before the Second World War. The recent Gulf War had a surrealistic character about it, which baffled experts and laymen alike. The British regimental system, however, is an enduring phenomenon, as exemplified by the regimental strength of the Argyll and Sutherland Highlanders.

In January 1972 1st Battalion re-formed at Ritchie Camp Kirknewton, and there was a brief ceremony when the Colours were handed back by Balaklava Company to the Colonel of the Regiment, Major General Freddie Graham, who in turn passed them to Lieutenant Colonel Patrick Palmer, the new Battalion Commander. The diary points out that, '...Major Ian Purves Hume kept his promise to Lt Col Sandy Boswell by handing over the command of the Argylls to a lieutenant colonel and not another major'. Within a week Battalion strength had grown to 273 all ranks, with 'returning' drafts following — those attached to other Scottish battalions for the past year. Over the next weeks and months the Argylls worked up towards their first Northern Ireland emergency tour, Operation 'Banner', with a programme of shooting, signals, patrolling and intelligence training, and acquainting themselves with a large array of modern internal security devices. It should be pointed out that most Argylls had already served two or more Operation 'Banner' tours with the Royal Scots, Royal Highland Fusiliers and other battalions.

Northern Ireland to this day is the result of a compromise border, and two opposing sub-cultures: a minority draw real inspiration from violence as a way of life. Their cause has little to do with genuine religious belief, national prosperity, welfare, or constitutionalism. Sadly there is evidence to suggest such a phenomenon could grow and dominate life in many an advanced nation in the 21st century.

Northern Ireland was now entering its fifth year of trouble. Originally sent to protect the Catholic minority, then in support of the Royal Ulster Constabulary against the Provisional Irish Republican Army, by this time the British Army was trying to keep terrorists from both communities apart and contain the violence, while various political solutions were sought. Unfortunately the Army itself became a focus of hatred for many

Catholics, symbolizing British 'oppression'. To the other community it became a symbol of the Union, a not very welcome image either. The internment of suspected and known terrorists, without the full process of the law, had been ordered in August 1971, while the abolition of the Stormont parliament and direct rule from Westminster followed in March 1972.

Members of the Regiment's advance party came under fire shortly after they arrived, while touring the Catholic Ballymurphy area of Belfast on 5 July while the Battalion followed by sea from Campbeltown, arriving on 28 July. The Battalion's area of responsibility was in the 'bandit country' of South Down and South Armagh, based in various towns and at border police stations. 'A' Company was initially in Dungannon attached to another battalion. The first major shooting incident was on 30 July, when a Thompson machine-gun was fired at Corporal Sinclair's patrol in Newry.

So this period was the height of the troubles. By the end of the Argylls' first fortnight there had been no less than nine shooting incidents, nine bombs and eight arson attacks; ten weapons, 400 plus rounds of ammunition and ten pounds of explosives had been recovered. There were thirty miles of border to patrol and guard, and thirty border crossings to watch, although most of them had been officially 'closed'. Operation 'Motorman' took place on 31 July which was the Army's Province-wide operation, including the re-entry into no-go areas in Londonderry and the rounding up of numerous suspects. In this operation the Argylls in conjunction with a squadron of the Royal Scots Dragoon Guards:

'...mounted a lift operation. Nine wanted men were picked up and one rifle, three shotguns and an assortment of ammunition was found. 'D' Company entered the Derrybeg housing estate to the accompaniment of banging dustbin lids, whistles, and a barrage of bottles and stones. At one stage a rubber bullet was fired into the riotous crowd, but resistance faded and some people actually told 'D' Company that they were glad to see them, and were looking forward to their first "peaceful night's sleep in months".'

Throughout the next two days a 'pig' armoured carrier of the Argylls was shot at and a car bomb exploded in Newry, as Support Company and the RUC were clearing the area. Fortunately there were no casualties.

During the four months of their tour there were hundreds of incidents in the Argylls' area. Cross-border shooting; a near-hit explosion of a culvert device against a foot patrol; angry crowds — 'one man assaulted a Jock, but with minimum force was speedily restrained and handed over to the RUC'; vehicle check-point arrests; finds of ammunition and weapons; bombs placed in a hotel, a customs office and a magistrate's house; bank raids; sectarian attacks on individuals, claymore mine attacks and shootings at mobile patrols.

The Argylls' first casualty was Lance Corporal Boag who fortunately survived a machine-gun attack. The most serious incident was when the Argylls were victims of a most appalling crime on 10 September. A patrol was motoring along a narrow road between Dungannon and Benburb in County Tyrone, when a command wire bomb, estimated to contain 500 pounds of explosives, was set off as their Saracen armoured personnel carrier was passing over it. The Saracen was thrown in the air and landed upside down twenty metres away. Privates Douglas Richmond and Duncan McPhee were killed outright, Lance Corporal William McIntyre died of his injuries a day later and three others were taken to hospital 'very seriously ill'.

Later, 2nd Lieutenant Stewart Gardiner was shot and fatally wounded while investigating a bomb, and firing continued for a while. More culvert bombs were discovered, and there were further bomb attacks against public buildings, some of them fortunately discovered before they were detonated. Typical extracts from the Battalion log read: 'B Coy had a contact at 1238 hrs near Drummackarall, where both a foot and helicopter patrol came under automatic fire. There were no casualties and about 200 rounds were returned. The gunmen, or some of them, were seen to escape South in a car.' And on 31 October: 'A VCP of 5 Platoon stopped a car containing three young men. The car smelt strongly of Co-op mix [explosives] and also had two masks in it. The occupants were handed over to the RUC for questioning'. Then on 3 November: 'In the first burst of firing Pte Hewins was hit in the thigh. During a lull in the battle the RMO landed [by helicopter] but was immediately pinned down [by fire]. Eventually Hewins was moved to a spot where a Sioux helicopter could land ... The terrorist gunfire came from several positions and they fired about 400 LMG and 80 Armalite rounds. A total of eight men were detained after the contact.'

Incidents such as these continued until the end of the tour and there were more fatalities. Private David Harper was killed when hit by a train on a railway bridge. In the last week before leaving the Province Captain Bill Watson and Colour Sergeant James Struthers were killed by a booby-trap to which they had been lured; Private John McGarry was killed accidentally; and on the very last day two RPG 7 rockets and some armour-piercing rounds were fired at the RUC station at Crossmaglen occupied by a platoon of Argylls; fortunately there were only minor injuries. So ended the Argylls' first emergency tour. Since the IRA operated so frequently from across the border, the Battalion had been involved in operations that could be called counter-insurgency; 'internal security' was an understatement.

In November 1972, Brigadier Boswell (Later Lieutenant General Sir Alexander Boswell) took over the colonelcy of the regiment from Major General Freddie Graham, after his remarkable fourteen years in the appointment.

Back in Edinburgh the Argylls settled into normal duties and training. But they became *Spearhead* battalion in March 1973 — one company at 24 hours' notice and the Battalion at 72 hours' notice to move anywhere in the world. There was little surprise when they were immediately warned to return to Northern Ireland. The event which precipitated their return was a referendum in the Province, and the companies spent three weeks on attachment to various battalions mainly in Belfast. Support Company claimed a record for '...having been under command of four battalions in one day'. Fortunately there were few incidents affecting the Battalion, but they were highly active in their duties.

In Edinburgh the Argylls resumed their training as an air-portable battalion, and continued the programme required of the public duties battalion described in an earlier chapter. During the Queen's visit to Edinburgh in June Her Majesty presented new Colours to the Battalion at a parade in Queen's Park beside the Palace of Holyrood House. In the speech Her Majesty commented that:

'...it can be seen that all your traditions have been safely preserved and strengthened ... you are the inheritors of a proud tradition, and I am sure the good name of the Argylls will be safe in your hands.'

The day ended with dinner in the Officers' Mess. Her Majesty, accompanied by Prince Philip and Princess Anne, stayed two hours longer than expected, which was an indication of Royal approval. 'What a day!' reported the Adjutant's diary.

Two months later at the Edinburgh Tattoo's last performance, where the public duties' battalion always had to provide arena parties, the Jocks:

'...permitted themselves two practical jokes on the esplanade. One concerned an attempt by a sergeant to kiss Flora MacDonald in public. The other was a rather energetic send off for Bonnie Prince Charlie. Both incidents were in perfectly good taste and amused the fee-paying public, but not the General's box.'

Such is the stuff of regimental legend.

Intensive training for a further tour in Northern Ireland started in September 1973, including a visit to Lydd ranges and the IS training 'village'. On 11 November the Battalion moved to Belfast where they took over the Ardoyne and Shankhill areas, abbreviated wittily to match the Regiment's short title 'A and SH'. As were all troops in Belfast at this time, they were under command of the Colonel of the Regiment and the Commander of 39 Brigade, Brigadier Sandy Boswell.

Although they had had a brief taste of Belfast city life earlier in the year, the experience was rather different from serving in 'bandit country' in South Armagh, where most of their experience had been gained. The Battalion diary and intsums catalogue a long list of armed robbery, intimidations, shootings against the security forces, 'kneecapping' by terrorists against their own people, the burning down of clubs and public houses, bombs concealed in vehicles, bombs thrown, bomb hoaxes, illegal military-style funerals, Orange Lodge marches, illegal road-blocks, reprisal killings and abusive women. As well as the Catholic Provisionals and Official IRA, the Protestant Ulster Defence Association and Ulster Volunteer Force were also active; purposely or unwittingly they added to the confusion, and occasionally even fired on the soldiers.

The Battalion scored a number of successes in this 'Op Banner' tour. Intelligence was good and several substantial finds of weapons were recorded. The log reveals such incidents as:

'A Mr J.M. was found shot but was not seriously wounded in the leg. He was being punished for some reason, but was not keen to tell why.'

'A patrol spotted a milk float parked in the Crumlin Road with a beer keg behind the cab. ATO was tasked and defused two bombs totalling 250 lbs of explosive.'

'A Company arrested a wanted IRA man in the Highfield Club. The operation was planned with good information received by the intelligence section.'

'Support Company tried to arrest a man wanted by the RUC. About 20 taxis blocked the road, but the situation was rapidly restored and. . . the arrested man removed to the RUC station.'

On Christmas Day 1973, following a shooting in the Ardoyne area, 'A' Company arrested two girls. At the RUC station it was discovered that they each had a concealed weapon under their clothing. Then on 28 December an ugly crowd assembled after a shooting. Support Company were fired on and, returning fire, scored a hit. Shooting from the Protestant Shankhill and Catholic Ardoyne areas continued throughout the night. 'D' Company found a gunman paralysed by drink sitting in a nearby playing-field. The wild shooting in the area that night probably indicated that he was not the only gunman whose aim had been affected by alcohol. Come Hogmanay, there was 'regrettably no dram' for the Argylls.

In February 1974 significant weapon and ammunition stores were found by the Battalion, but in one search 'D' Company had to fire 'baton rounds to keep the locals under control'. The IRA were by now resorting to 'pillar box' bombs which injured members of the public quite indiscriminately when they exploded. The names of the probable perpetrators were known, but never found to be at home when the security forces called. On 26 February the Battalion handed over to 3rd Battalion The Parachute Regiment and the Queen's Own Highlanders piped the Argylls away. The Battalion had been spared from death and injury this time, and the weapons recovered were a record so far for any battalion on an emergency tour.

Three more months of public duties in Edinburgh awaited the Argylls on their return, and part of the summer was spent on exercise in Cyprus. The island was relatively peaceful, the training areas good and 'adventurous training' — parachuting, off-shore cruising, sub-aqua swimming and rock-climbing — gave the Battalion a happy break. On their return to Edinburgh, conversion training began for their new role as mechanized infantry, prior to the move to Osnabrück in November.

1974–1979

Osnabrück had seen some bitter fighting during the Second World War; it lies just north of the Teutoberg Hills, which with their forests had proved a natural defence line guarding the northern part of Germany. But Osnabrück in 1974 was a prosperous and thriving city, with a large British garrison forming part of 2nd Division's area. The Argylls had much work to do in perfecting the techniques of armoured warfare in 12 Mechanized Brigade. The Battalion was wholly responsible for providing its own drivers for the armoured personnel carriers, a change from Lemgo days, and the platoon and company battle drills involved using the APCs to give machine-gun fire support to the dismounted infantry, adding considerably to their fire power. During the Battalion's time in the garrison the Brigade was re-designated a Task Force, a formation thought to give more flexibility in command and control, but after a couple of years brigades were restored to the order of battle.

As the summer of 1975 approached, preparations were made for a further spell in Northern Ireland, and in July the whole Battalion moved to Sennelager training area, where a great deal of time was spent in 'Tin City', a complex specially built to resemble built-up areas in Northern Ireland. 'B' Company was actually deployed to Belfast and the Maze prison as reinforcement in case of trouble on 12 July, a day of remembrance, celebration and marches for the Protestant community, but the Company returned after three days. The full Northern Ireland tour began at the end of the year.

Little had changed in Belfast during the twenty-one months the Argylls had been away. The Europa Hotel was bombed as they arrived, and the first few weeks were notable for dozens of hoax bombs. Corporal Barr and his patrol of Support Company received much publicity for rescuing four children found unconscious in a flat, their mother already dead from leaking gas. This demonstrated the value of a genuine 'hearts and minds' approach towards the long-suffering people of the Province. The Argylls guarded the Crumlin Road gaol for a while and there were several finds of weapons nearby. Constant patrolling, planned searches and rapid cordons and searches in response to numerous bomb scares kept the Battalion fully occupied throughout December.

In January 1976 the terrorists began attacking shops with explosive devices and the hoax-bombs continued to be regularly reported. Every one had to be treated seriously. Then a smear campaign was started by the republican press. It centred on the alleged 'Nightmare of Mum-to-be', a women said to have been 'lifted' by 'B' Company and taken to Hastings Street 'Torture Chamber'. 'She had refused to open her bag of chips when asked to do so by the patrol,' went the story. An imaginative interpretation of the facts clearly reveals both viewpoints, and 'innocence' lacks a precise definition in such a situation as Northern Ireland.

Random shots were fired from time to time by gunmen, and the Falls Road was blocked for a while by demonstrating taxi drivers. At the end of the month a foot patrol was attacked in the Shankhill Road area by a hostile crowd and a shot was fired by the patrol in self-defence. There were unfortunately two civilian casualties, one of whom died. Retaliatory shots were later fired at an RUC and RMP joint patrol.

Then in February there were demonstrations in support of an IRA hunger striker who had died in Wakefield prison. Shots were fired, blast bombs and grenades were thrown, and over a period of three days crowds of youths assembled and hurled missiles and abuse at the patrolling Argylls. The security forces' base in the Springfield Road came under attack several times, and on one occasion the situation looked serious enough for the troops to fire 38 baton rounds — hardened rubber missiles aimed below the knee — effectively inducing a crowd of 150 to disperse. Arrests were made during the next few days, intelligence being plentiful and particular rioters being easily identified. On 16 February a funeral procession numbering some 200, many dressed in para-military uniforms, passed through the Battalion's area. On this occasion there was no violence, but often such processions were conducted deliberately to provoke trouble. A few days later the body of a Roman Catholic man was found in an alley beside the Mayo Street — Shankhill Road junction. His throat had been cut, severing his jugular vein, a shocking reminder of the cheapness of life among the worst section of society in the Province.

The last month of the tour passed with more murders, shootings, hoaxes, arson, weapons finds and arrests. The Battalion returned to Osnabrück in early April 1976, having again sustained no casualties. Busy activities were resumed and there was a change of routine when the Argylls visited the British Army Training Unit Suffield training area in Canada. Lieutenant Colonel Alastair Scott Elliot had 'B' Company and supporting arms under operational command, including two squadrons of The Royal Tank Regiment. Work-up training was conducted at Soltau and a testing month was spent in October-November in realistic mechanized battlegroup training at BATUS, with field firing by both infantry and supporting armour, the sort of training which could not be conducted in Germany. In BAOR the full range of sport continued, the diversity perhaps making up for the reduced amount of time available compared with previous BAOR service — a sad result of the continuous over-stretching of the Army for the past twenty years. Football of course was pre-eminent and the Battalion team carried off the Divisional Cup, while boxing and cross-country running fixtures in the Westphalia League provided other sporting interest.

The first few months of 1977 passed quietly. In April Combat Team (Argyll companies with supporting arms) training took place at Soltau, which was visited by Prime Minister the Rt Hon James Callaghan. A silver statuette of Cruachan was presented to the Colonel-in-Chief to mark the Jubilee celebrations, and the Argylls were in administrative support of 4th Armoured Division who found the parade troops for the Silver Jubilee Parade on 7 July. The Battalion Colour Party was on parade, as were the Military Band and Pipes and Drums for the largest parade staged by the British Army for many years.

Lieutenant Colonel Ian Purves Hume took over command. A new Northern Ireland tour was soon announced and Battalion HQ reacted with orders for increased fitness training and battalion cross-country running at 0745 hours on Monday mornings. 'Tin City' was revisited to polish up on IS training. The move took place over 27-8 October and the pipers of the Gordon Highlanders met the Argylls on arrival: the Gordons had recently suffered seventeen casualties in the Turf Lodge area of Belfast. The Argylls' tactical area stretched from Turf Lodge to the Lower Falls Road, embracing Ballymurphy, Whiterock, Beechmont, Clonard and Distillery.

The Provisional IRA were active at this time but, compared with previous tours, at fairly low level; hijacking of cars and vans and hoax bombs with a few random shooting incidents was their score for the few weeks in October-November. Incidents from the Battalion record read:

'Support Company stopped another car at a vehicle check point; one of the occupants looked ill, and on being asked if anything was wrong, said that he had been hijacked. All occupants were arrested...'

'Sgt Murray and his patrol saw a man on the Falls road filling up his car with a jerrican. When they approached he ran off ... despite five follow up searches, he could not be found. Being a gentleman, he left a girl sitting in the car with two incendiary devices under the seat. She was arrested.'

'In the early hours of the morning 16 November six ... bomb carriers and planters were arrested as part of a city-wide lift operation. Some have talked enough to incriminate...'

'During the evening three youths were knee-capped in the Turf Lodge, a case of disciplining minor criminals'.

This was the way the IRA meted out often deserved justice, but scarcely according to the normal rules of fitting the punishment to the crime. To add to the excitement there was a nationwide firemen's strike and 60 members of The Black Watch with two 'Green Goddess' fire engines were attached to the Argylls. This strike merely served to encourage incendiary attacks, and after two devices had started a fire, a third unexploded device was discovered next to a fire hydrant. The area was cordoned off, under the eye the brigade commander, Brigadier John MacMillan, son of the former Colonel of the Regiment Sir Gordon MacMillan. Brigadier John had himself served with the Argylls until the reduction of the Battalion, then commanded 1st Gordons and subsequently was to become GOC Scotland.

Whereas on previous tours there had almost always been a direct response to the activities and successes of the security forces, it was noticeable that the terrorists and their supporters were more reluctant to react during this period. That said, on 10 December a grenade was thrown over the wall of the Tactical HQ in the Springfield Road, where a short while before there had been a considerable number of troops in the yard. It was thought that a batch of Russian grenades had recently reached the Province, and more grenade incidents occurred, but only minor injuries were suffered. A few days later there was a major 'lift operation' mainly in the Argylls' area, resulting in fifteen arrests of Provisional IRA members.

In the second half of the tour there were a number of weapon finds; more arrests; the visit of 'Miss A and SH ... she is a very shapely model and was brought over by the *Daily Record* ... many thanks to them'; band displays, and on 31 December two escorted pipers played carefully selected tunes '...around the more evil parts — the majority of people who came onto the streets enjoyed it, while some started dancing'. This hearts and minds exercise was perhaps a reminder to the locals that the peoples of Scotland and Ireland are related. On 4 January 1978 six youths in a car broke through a VCP and:

'...attempted to run down Sgt McGuire of A Company and a member of his patrol. He fired three shots and scored six hits on the occupants. None were seriously injured and there was no ill feeling among the locals.'

Incidents continued on most days and on 29 January, near to the anniversary of Bloody Sunday (when in 1972 The Parachute Regiment had shot dead thirteen suspected terrorists), there was a lot of trouble with burning vehicles, and a patrol of 'D' Company had a narrow escape from a 21-pound bomb which they inadvertently detonated. Shootings and arms searches marked the last few weeks of the Battalion's tour, before they returned to Osnabrück at the end of February 1978.

The Argylls spent a further six months in Osnabrück where their new divisional commander was Major General Boswell; in October the Battalion moved to Bourlon Barracks at Catterick. Life in North Yorkshire was no less busy than in BAOR. The winter of 1978/9 is remembered for a period of industrial disputes, the 'winter of discontent', and the Army was frequently on standby to maintain essential public services during strikes. Her Majesty the Queen visited the Battalion in November, and in March 1979 the Argylls provided the Queen's Guard at Buckingham and St James's Palaces. Over the Christmas period two companies from the Battalion went to Northern Ireland to escort tankers during a strike. The CO's notes in the *Thin Red Line* emphasize the difficulties of the year when there had been no '...opportunity to remain and operate as a complete entity'. But that again reflected the overstretch of commitments placed on today's Army.

HONG KONG

The Battalion was not given much forewarning of the move to Hong Kong in July 1979. It was a 'Spearhead' alert battalion duty and was necessitated by an influx of many thousands of illegal immigrants, known as IIs, crossing the border into the colony from China. Due either to a weakening of the Chinese Army's ability to watch the border on their side, or a political decision to reduce their presence and embarrass the Hong Kong government, it was necessary to police the border on the Hong Kong side with many more soldiers and an increased state of vigilance. The colony has a vast population crammed into a tiny area, and could not then — nor can it now — cope with the scale of the numbers seeking to live there in preference to China. The Battalion was deployed to the New Territories on the mainland very soon after arrival; the weather was unbearably hot.

'Most of the movement', reports the *Thin Red Line*, 'was by night or when the weather conditions were at their worst ... There was a real contrast between the excitement when a party of IIs were spotted and the later anti-climax when you realized what pathetic and demoralized human specimens you had captured.'

In the rugged terrain where the patrols operated OPs, both overt and hidden, were manned and ambushes laid to intercept the IIs. As there was so much night activity and it was difficult to catch up with sleep in the heat of the day, it was extremely difficult to adjust quickly to the routine. Because the Argylls were on an emergency tour, there was little opportunity to experience normal garrison or civilian life in Hong Kong — at that time a favourite overseas posting for the British Army.

As the weather improved and the companies rotated, the task became more interesting. At least the platoons had the knowledge that if days passed without catching IIs, deterrence was working. In early August the colony was struck by Typhoon 'Hope', with wind speeds of up to 150 miles per hour and rising water levels of 30 feet within fifteen minutes. The Argylls immediately responded by assisting the authorities in rescuing the inhabitants of nearby villages. During the two months' tour most members of the Battalion managed to snatch short periods of 'rest and recuperation' on Hong Kong island.

THE EIGHTIES

The last six months in Catterick were followed by the Battalion's move to Northern Ireland in March 1980. This was the Argylls' first tour in the Province as a resident battalion, complete with the families: the station was Ballykelly, an old RAF camp which, though in great contrast to former billets in Ulster and allegedly modern, comfortable and with every amenity at hand, was still very rudimentary. The life and routine too was quite different. 'A resident tour', states the *Thin Red Line* editorial 'does require a more gentlemanly pace.' So they thought.

At first the four companies rotated on a monthly basis, one based at Strabane, County Armagh, one as brigade reserve, one on guards and escorts and the remaining company on training and leave. Strabane tactical area of responsibility was 40 x 26 kilometres in area, with 30 kilometres of border, much of which was on the river line. The duties were similar to those carried out during the Battalion's first tour in 1972, consisting of mounted, foot and helicopter-borne patrols, with the aim of deterring terrorist action, clearing routes, finding culvert devices and possible mortar base-plate sites; setting up snap vehicle check points and manning static ones; watching for illegal border crossings; establishing area security against 'lurking soft targets' and area sweeps; escorting convoys of military vehicles; and frequent searches for arms and ammunition. One change from previous tours was the increased number and effectiveness of the Ulster Defence Regiment's operations, many of which came under command of the Argylls. Intelligence-gathering too was of enormous importance on a daily basis, but 'genuine suspicion' had to be balanced so as not to provoke the local people by 'harassment'. During the two years there was a reduction of the emergency tour or 'roulement' battalions deployed at any one time, and the Ballykelly battalion was, according to the post-tour report, '...used to plug temporary gaps in the southern part of the Province, and as a source of reserve troops in times of crisis or shortfall'.

Thus the routine became non-routine fairly early on. Although the Strabane commitment was soon reduced, commitments were increased elsewhere, including deployments at Dungannon, Armagh city and Auchnacloy (almost on the border), and the Argylls worked even more closely with the Royal Ulster Constabulary and UDR. Deployment to Londonderry city was called for on one occasion in 1980, during a period of heightened tension concerning the campaign of hunger strikes in various prisons.

Fortunately the first few months were relatively free from significant incidents. 'An Ulster tour', the battalion diary states, 'is no longer the excitement it once was. The most part of ... a soldier's time is now spent either on guard or reserve, and the reserve is rarely used'. Although the GOC, Lieutenant General Sir Richard Lawson, complimented the Battalion with the words 'You are Magic', the CO, Lieutenant Colonel Hugh Clark, was actively engaged in combating complacency and the 'letting slip of standards'.

Incidents of course occurred from time to time, as the diary reports:

'Minor aggro took place in Strabane in the early hours of this morning [9 August 1980]. In two minor incidents crowds of 15 and 30 people stoned the RUC stations at Strabane and an RUC patrol. Compared to the early days of the campaign this is nothing. A shop in Plumbridge was fire bombed during the night and a lurk patrol heard what was thought to be automatic fire.'

Three days later:

'The Glorious Twelfth. Not only a busy day for sportsmen but in Londonderry another day of marches. C Company were deployed to the City in support of the 1st Battalion Staffordshire Regiment and D Company were on their guard in Strabane. B Company were called to 30 minutes notice to move ... but were not deployed. Minor aggro did occur in Derry, but C Company did not get involved. The QM chaired a messing meeting in the Junior Ranks Cookhouse ...'

But on 17 August:

'At 1905 hrs this evening, two VCPs of the anti-tank platoon of C Company were on patrol near the border in South Fermanagh when they came under fire from four gunmen in the Republic. Approximately 150-200 rounds of automatic were directed at the patrols which were commanded by Cpl Bell. No casualties were sustained and fire was returned by the patrol and by two other patrols which were dug in in support. Some 750 rounds were returned at the enemy who escaped. It casts a question mark over the standard of our marksmanship.'

On 25 October, Balaklava Day, the Battalion football team scored a notable victory over 1st Battalion Scots Guards by 3 goals to 1. Normal life carried on.

Four occurrences marred the year. The first was the indictment of four members of the Regiment in a murder case which had occurred during the tour of 1972. This brought unfortunate publicity, but was an indication of the problems of using troops in the internal security role, when the level of frustration often reaches boiling point. In an incident at a VCP a woman was accidentally shot dead, which again brought adverse publicity, but fortunately no retaliation. Then there was a fire in the Officers' Mess which destroyed a number of pictures and silver, including the fine centre-piece of the 93rd Highlanders, a memento of the Regiment's service in India. Finally, on 11 November, Corporal Owen McQuade was shot dead while driving a 'families detail' to a hospital in Londonderry.

Towards the end of the year and into 1981 there was heightened tension in the Province, caused by the hunger strike of IRA prisoners in the Maze prison. There was also a prison officers' strike which involved the Argylls in extra guard duties. Then in January 1981 Corporal Milligan's quick reaction force patrol raced to the scene of the attempted murder by loyalists of Mrs Bernadette McAliskey, née Devlin, the prominent civil rights publicist and former Westminster MP, thus proving that keeping the Queen's peace is an impartial activity.

The reduction of the direct participation of the Army in order to allow for greater participation by the Royal Ulster Constabulary was achieved during 1981, and it had the effect of making the Argylls' operational duties more routine. If the Battalion's contribution had been '...undramatic, unsung and possibly only appreciated by those with whom we have worked most closely, then this must be indicative of success,' reads Lieutenant Colonel Clark's post-tour report.

From April 1982 Cyprus was the new home of the Battalion, based at Akrotiri, 'a sportsman's paradise'. Although the threat of unrest among the Greek and Turkish inhabitants was not high, the Battalion's tasks were to a certain extent similar to those in Northern Ireland. One company rotated through Ayios Nikolaos in the Eastern Sovereign Base Area, while the rest of the Battalion operated in the Western Base Area at Episkopi. The Battalion carried out mainly static guards in the former, and provided mobile reaction platoons in the latter. When in camp companies were concerned with normal peacetime duties and training, which gave them much needed opportunities to improve military skills and procedures, training that had gone by the board in Northern Ireland. The first battalion exercise for more than two years was held in July; a Queen's Birthday Parade was held and then there was a seemingly endless programme of sport — soccer, tug of war, athletics, running, cricket, swimming and every imaginable water sport, as well as skiing in the Troodos mountains. The Regiment also fielded a polo team for the first time in a very long while. Elsewhere a war in the Falkland Islands was fought and won, but the Argylls were not invited to take part. The new CO, Lieutenant Colonel David Thomson, MC, took command and a new Colonel of the Regiment, Major General Patrick Palmer replaced General Boswell when the latter assumed the appointment of Colonel Commandant of the Scottish Division. In March 1983 the first full battalion exercise named 'Boar's Head' was mounted, involving all phases of war and lasting six days.

In mid 1983 there was a 'terrorist scare' and the Battalion was put on a high state of alert for Operation 'Sediment', the guarding of the Sovereign Base areas. This chiefly involved patrolling, VCPs and static guards on 'vulnerable points' in the various garrisons, including the married quarters' areas. Later in the year another battalion exercise took place over a large area of Cyprus. At the end of the year the Battalion's contribution to the life of the Island and general efficiency was recognized by a coveted award, the 'Tickle Prize', duly presented by the GOC. As the two-year tour in Cyprus ended there were many happy memories of life on the island among the families and the Jocks.

In January 1984 the Argylls returned to Edinburgh for two years as resident public duties' battalion. As the CO, Lieutenant Colonel David Thomson, noted, they were '...very much on show' and there were those, ' who will not be slow to criticise any shortfall in our performance'. With the overstretch of commitments for a present-day battalion, great efforts had to be exerted to ensure that a balance of public duties, military training and family life was maintained. Additionally, defence of the 'home base' was being taken much more seriously than hitherto, and the picture was being painted in glaring colours of *Spetznaz* infiltrators in their thousands, followed by massive airstrikes, disruption of shipping and an invasion by tens of thousands of ground troops. Exercise 'Brave Defender', the largest home defence exercise since the Second World War, took place in 1985. The Battalion was given a 'tactical area of responsibility' in Strathclyde, and working with civilian organizations, notably the police, fire and ambulance services, became part of this role. The promotion of good civil-military relations and co-operation was a feature of the 1980s, and is part of modern-day soldiering in 'military home defence', a role re-discovered.

For the Jocks there was the usual round of garrison duties, ceremonial and support functions. A particularly memorable regimental event took place in July when the Colonel-in-Chief visited the Battalion. Lieutenant Colonel Anthony Neilson took over command in early 1985, and in mid year the Battalion exercised in Saskatchewan, Canada with field firing and tactical training up to battalion level, with mortar and artillery support, training which cannot normally be conducted in the UK. Edinburgh Castle, Holyrood House and Balmoral guards, ceremonial for the General Assembly of the Church of Scotland and support for the Edinburgh Tattoo — that most brilliant of military theatrical performances, staged by floodlight on the Edinburgh Castle Esplanade to the accompaniment of massed pipes, drums and bands and fireworks — were the activities in which the Argylls projected their image of a cheerful and efficient military organization, comprising six hundred real human beings.

Service at Colchester from 1986 to 1988, although still in United Kingdom, was altogether different from Edinburgh. The new role was to act as a reinforcement of BAOR in 19 Brigade of 2nd Infantry Division. Northern Ireland training, however, began almost at once because the Battalion was warned off for yet another emergency tour. This accorded with the policy of keeping as few regular battalions in the Province, but calling for troops at short notice from mainland Britain when trouble was expected. For the two months from April to June 1986, the Battalion was split up with companies under command of other battalions at Magherafelt, Omagh, St Angelo and Clogher. In the event the tour passed relatively peacefully and with no casualties among the Argylls.

One of the consequences of an unaccompanied tour in the Falkland Islands, long after the campaign, was that realistic field exercises could be mounted with a change of scenery and fewer restrictions than in either the UK or West Germany. The Battalion spent four months in the Falklands, which included an exercise to South Georgia; all parts of the two main islands were visited, guarded and exercised over. The *Thin Red Line* journal scarcely conceals periods of boredom for the officers and men, which was the inevitable result of being stationed in a truly isolated part of the world, all but uninhabited, and without even the excitement of an Emperor to disinter, as an earlier battalion of Argylls had experienced on St Helena in 1840.

LOOKING TO THE FUTURE

Back in Colchester the Battalion could concentrate once more on their BAOR reinforcing role. There was training on the newly issued SA80 rifle, and Fox armoured cars for the recce platoon, interspersed by an exercise in Belize. The Battalion had to find again the Queen's Guard at Buckingham and St James's Palaces, as well as Windsor Castle. There was another large-scale exercise in Canada in mid 1989, and conversion training began before the move to Minden, where the Argylls were to become a 'mechanized battalion'.

The final page of the history of the Regiment thus far, reflects the heightened consciousness of the present state of Britain's Army and its place in the world. In the first year of the Argylls' tour the extraordinary revolutions in Eastern Europe occurred. While it was apparent that the role, size and composition of BAOR could hardly remain unchanged, the traditional BAOR training continued during the first part of 1990. Even while the Berlin Wall was coming down, increased security of barracks and married quarters' areas had to be stepped up — an ironical situation indeed, but necessitated by a new bombing and shooting campaign by the Provisional IRA both in the UK and on the Continent.

The Gulf War in 1991 included a number of individuals from the Regiment in the deployment to Saudi Arabia, in specialist appointments. They witnessed a war, at least in part, that had been dreamt about for forty-five years as taking place in Europe, while the course of the war was a major surprise to military and civilians alike. The symbolic state visit of the Colonel-in-Chief to Washington shortly afterwards, in May 1991, was made the more memorable, it is hoped, by the inclusion in the Queen's party of four regimental pipers, and a new pipe tune composed by Sergeant Jim Motherwell was played at the dinner given by Her Majesty for President Bush. The tune is aptly called 'Desert Storm', the code-name of the Allied offensive in the Gulf War.

Meanwhile the Battalion was ordered for Northern Ireland duty at short notice during the war, taking responsibility for areas of west and north Belfast. Many terrorist incidents were recorded, of which 38 were classified as serious, most of them being shootings or grenade incidents. The Commander Land Forces at the time was Major General David Thomson, soon to take over the Colonelcy of the Regiment. The *Thin Red Line* states: 'As always, nearly everyone in the battalion enjoyed the tour in Belfast'.

The Argyll and Sutherland Highlanders, it appears, are to be spared the 'Options for Change' Defence cuts, and perhaps nobody had the courage to fight the Argylls again. 'New Management Strategy', the Army's management plan, should present no more of a problem for the Battalion than their winning the Combat '90 TV military skills competition. Northern Ireland tours there will be for the foreseeable future; there will also be a need of a contribution to the defence of Western Europe; and the requirement will continue to prepare for unexpected commitments anywhere in the world with Britain's allies and friends. The Argylls can surely look forward to at least two more centuries of service.

BIBLIOGRAPHY

Regimental records comprising *Adjutants' Diaries*, battalion *Reports, Intelligence Reports* and the journals *The Argyllshire Highlanders' Regimental News* and *The Thin Red Line*.

Anderson, Brigadier R. C. B., *History of the Argyll and Sutherland Highlanders, 1st Battalion, 1909–1939*, Constable, Edinburgh, 1954.

— *History of the Argyll and Sutherland Highlanders, 1st Battalion, 1939–1954*, Constable Edinburgh, 1956.

Ascoli, D. N., *A Companion to the British Army, 1660–1983*, Harrap, London, 1983.

Barker, Lieutenant Colonel F. R. P., *History of the Argyll and Sutherland Highlanders, 9th Battalion, 54 Light AA Regiment, 1939–1945*, Nelson, London, 1950.

Blake, George, *Mountain and Flood, The History of the 52nd Lowland Division, 1939–1946*, Jackson & Son, Glasgow, 1950.

Brewsher, Major F. W., *The History of the 51st (Highland) Division, 1914–1918*, William Blackwood, Edinburgh, 1921.

Burgoyne, R. H., *Historical Records of the 93rd Sutherland Highlanders*, Richard Bentley, London, 1883.

Cameron, Captain I. C., *History of the Argyll and Sutherland Highlanders, 7th Battalion, From El Alamein to Germany*, Thomas Nelson, London, 1946

Cavendish, Brigadier A. E. J., *Am Reisimeid Chataich; The 93rd Sutherland Highlanders, 1799–1927*, published privately, 1928.

Dunn Pattison, R. A., *The History of the 91st Argyllshire Highlanders*, William Blackwood & Sons, Edinburgh, 1910.

Edwardes, Michael, *The Battles of the Indian Mutiny*, Pan Books, London, 1963.

Ewing, J., *History of the 9th (Scottish) Division, 1914–1919*, John Murray, London, 1921.

Flower, Desmond, *History of the Agryll and Sutherland Highlanders, 5th Battalion, 1939–1945*, Thomas Nelson, London, 1950.

Frederick, J. B. M., *Lineage Book of the British Army*, Mounted Corps and Infantry, Hope Farm Press, New York, 1969.

Goff, G. L., *Historical Records of the 91st Argyllshire Highlanders*, Richard Bentley, London, 1981.

Graham, Lieutenant Colonel, F. C. C., *History of the Argyll and Sutherland Highlanders. 1st Battalion 1939–45*, Thomas Nelson, London, 1949.

Grierson, Lieutenant General Sir James Moncrieffe, *Records of the Scottish Volunteer Force, 1859–1908*, William Blackwood, Edinburgh, 1909.

Groves, Lieutenant Colonel Percy, *History of the 91st Princess Louise's Argyllshire Highlanders*, W. & E. K. Johnston, Edinburgh, 1894.

— *History of the 93rd Sutherland Highlanders*, W.W. and E. K. Johnston, Edinburgh, 1895.

Malcolm, Lieutenant Colonel G. I., of Poltalloch, *The Argyllshire Highlanders, 1860–1960*, Holbeid Press, Glasgow, 1960.

— *The Argylls in Korea*, Thomas Nelson, London, 1952.

Malcolm, Lieutenent Colonel A. D., *History of the Argyll and Sutherland Highlanders, 1939–1947, 8th Battalion*, Thomas Nelson, London, 1949.

Martin, Lieutenant General H. G., *The Fifteenth Scottish Division, 1939–1945*, William Blackwood, Edinburgh, 1948.

McElwee, Major W. L., *History of the Argyll and Sutherland Highlanders, 2nd Batalion (Re-constituted), 1944–1945*, Thomas Nelson, London, 1949.

Mitchell, Lieutenant Colonel Colin, *Having Been a Soldier*, Hamish Hamilton, London, 1969.

Monroe, Surgeon General William, *Reminiscences of Military Service with the 93rd Highlanders*, Hurst & Blackett, London, 1883.

Morrison, A. D., *7th Battalion The Argyll and Sutherland Highlanders, the Great War, 1914–1919*, The Regiment, Stirling.

Pratt, Paul (ed.), *History of the Argyll and Sutherland Highlanders, 6th Battalion, 93rd Anti-Tank Regiment, R. A.*

(A&SH), Thomas Nelson, London, 1949.

Salmond, J. B., *The History of the 51st Highland Division, 1939–1945*, William Blackwood, Edinburgh, 1923.

Selby, John, *The Thin Red Line of Balaclava*, Victorian and Modern History Book Club, Newton Abbott, 1972.

Sotheby, Lieutenant Colonel H. G., *The 10th Battalion, Argyll and Sutherland Highlanders, 1914–1919*, John Murray, London, 1931.

Stewart, Brigadier I. Mac A., *History of the Argyll and Sutherland Highlanders, 2nd Battalion, (The Thin Red Line), Malaya Campaign, 1941–42*, Thomas Nelson, London, 1947.

Stewart, Lieutenant Colonel J., and John Buchan, *The 15th (Scottish) Division, 1914–1919*, William Blackwood, Edinburgh, 1926.

Sutherland, Douglas, *The Argyll and Sutherland Highlanders*, Leo Cooper, London, 1969.

Thompson, R. R., *The Fifty-Second (Lowland) Division, 1914–1918*, MacLehose Jackson, Glasgow, 1923.

Whitton, F. E., *History of the 40th Division*, Gale & Polden, Aldershot, 1926.

INDEX